The Complete Book on

BALANCING

In Contract Bridge

MIKE LAWRENCE

Published by
Devyn Press, Inc.
Louisville, Kentucky

FIRST PRINTING 1980
SECOND PRINTING 1982
THIRD PRINTING 1988
FOURTH PRINTING 1989
FIFTH PRINTING 1990
SIXTH PRINTING 1993
SEVENTH PRINTING 1996
EIGHTH PRINTING 2000
NINTH PRINTING 2006

Printed in the United States of America.

Published by
Devyn Press, Inc.
3600 Chamberlain Lane, Suite 230
Louisville, KY 40241
1-800-274-2221

Library of Congress No. 84-223527
ISBN 0-939460-13-0

INTRODUCTION

If you never play serious (tournament) bridge, put this book down politely but firmly. If you're a serious bidder and have a serious partner or two, *Balancing* is worth its weight in gold to you; but if you play rubber bridge or if you play tournament bridge only for recreation, this book will do you no good. In fact, it may harm you by discouraging you from reading one of the many entertaining and instructive books on the play of the cards that would improve your results.

If you have read the first paragraph and are still with me, it's fair to assume that you play tournament bridge and that you're at least moderately serious about the game. Very good. Clutch *Balancing* in your left hand, rummage around for money or a credit card with your right hand, and proceed to the cash register without wasting any time.

It's not unreasonable for you to ask why. I'll keep it short so that you can get on with the book with a minimum of delay.

To begin with, Mike Lawrence, winner of two world championships and a few dozen North American championships, is also one of the great bridge teachers of our day. He teaches the methods that make him a winner.

His style of writing is not pedantic, not even literary. He writes the way he talks. You can read this book as though you were listening to Mike Lawrence telling you how to bid as his partner in any kind of tournment, from a club duplicate right up to a world championship. If you were listening to Mike talk and were about to play as his partner you'd be paying him several hundred dollars per session. It's cheaper to read the book. Also better, since you can review any point that puzzles you until you're sure you have it right.

It won't do you much good to buy *Balancing* and put it unread on your shelf. The ACBL won't let you put your bookshelf in to bid a hand for you.

If you want to get value for your money, skim through this book to get an idea of the ground it covers; and then go over it slowly, a few pages at a time. Get your favorite partner to buy a copy and read it at the same time. Compare notes every few days. At the end of a month or so, you'll both know what you're doing when the opponents open the bidding and then stop at a very low level without opposition.

How much will this help your game? The situation will arise about once or twice per session. You'll probably score an average of four or five match points more per board in such situations if you and your partner use Mike Lawrence's methods than if you just try to muddle through.

If you're interested in picking up about half a board per session, this book is just what your bridge doctor ordered.

If it sounds like a lot of work, you have a good ear. It is. But tournament players are a brainy bunch, and if you want to beat them consistently you must do your homework.

A few words of encouragement: The work is enjoyable. If you're a serious bridge player, you'll enjoy learning Mike Lawrence's ideas. Even if you didn't learn a thing about *balancing*, Mike's comments would give you a clear idea of the structure of partnership bidding.

Time to look for the cash register. After all, you want to win that tournament next month, don't you?

—Alfred Sheinwold

Books by Mike Lawrence

HOW TO READ YOUR OPPONENTS' CARDS
Prentice Hall — 1973

WINNING BACKGAMMON
Pinnacle — 1975

JUDGMENT AT BRIDGE
Max Hardy — 1976

THE COMPLETE BOOK ON OVERCALLS IN CONTRACT BRIDGE
Max Hardy — 1980

TRUE BRIDGE HUMOR
Max Hardy — 1980

THE COMPLETE BOOK ON BALANCING IN CONTRACT BRIDGE
Max Hardy — 1981

PLAY A SWISS TEAM OF FOUR WITH MIKE LAWRENCE
Max Hardy — 1982

DYNAMIC DEFENSE
Devyn Press — 1982

MAJOR SUIT RAISES
Texas Bridge Supplies — 1982

THE COMPLETE BOOK ON HAND EVALUATION IN CONTRACT BRIDGE
Max Hardy — 1983

PLAY BRIDGE WITH MIKE LAWRENCE
Devyn Press — 1984

FALSE CARDS
Devyn Press — 1986

CARD COMBINATIONS
Devyn Press – 1986

SCRABBLE
Bantam Press — 1987

MIKE LAWRENCE'S WORKBOOK ON THE TWO OVER ONE SYSTEM
Max Hardy — 1987

PASSED HAND BIDDING
Lawrence & Leong – 1989

BIDDING QUIZZES, THE UNCONTESTED AUCTION
Lawrence & Leong — 1990

THE COMPLETE GUIDE TO CONTESTED AUCTIONS
Lawrence & Leong — 1992

TOPICS ON BRIDGE
Lawrence — 1990

MORE TOPICS ON BRIDGE
Lawrence — 1992

ıct Bridge

reserved.

Library of Congress No. 84-223527
ISBN # 0-939460-13-0

BALANCING
Foreword

Not too long ago, I got together with a friend of mine for a sectional Swiss-Team-of-Four. Not having played together recently, we met for the usual half hour or so of system discussion prior to game time.

"Notrumps, 15 to 17?"

"Sure. Jacoby, Texas OK or two-way Stayman?"

"Prefer Jacoby and Texas. Do you like inverted minors? etc., etc., etc."

Very familiar discussion. Always the same or so it seems.

We sit down for the first round.

One notrump by him.

Two hearts by me.

Alert! That is a transfer to two spades.

Two spades by him.

Four clubs by me.

Alert! That is a stiff club with good spades and a slam try.

Four notrump by him.

Five spades by me.

Alert! That shows two aces and some other feature he fancies.

Really. All this system stuff is paying off. Six spades bid and made. Just like we had been playing together for years instead of minutes.

Next hand.

One club by RHO.

One spade by me.

Two diamonds by LHO.

Three hearts by partner.

Alert by me. Partner has a weak hand with good hearts.

We take a good save at four hearts doubled. Glad we discussed this.

I begin to marvel at how closely our understandings seem to coincide. Sure we had a system discussion, but it is clear that much of our thinking was along similar lines even in areas that were not discussed or which were glossed over. Two hearts that beat as one?

We compare. The match is a clear victory, the slam not being bid at the other table, and on the ensuing hand where we saved, hearts were never mentioned. Other results were favorable so we won handily.

We sit down for the second match.

LHO opens with one club and that is passed around to me. I try one notrump with a scattered 13 count and partner raises to two notrump. It occurs to me that I'm not sure whether I have a good hand or a bad hand by my partner's lights, but by mine it's good so on to three notrump.

Not so hot. Partner has a decent ten count and I go two down against normal defense. One notrump was high enough. I wonder who bid too much. But before I can find out, I hear RHO bid one club which is passed to partner who bids two clubs.

"What's that?" asks RHO.

"Well," I answer "we play Michaels for the majors if it is a cue bid immediately after the opening bidder but . . ."

"Never mind" said RHO, sensing my insecurity. "I pass."

So now I had to work it out. Perhaps it was still Michaels. But perhaps it was a game force. Or was it asking for a club stopper? Suffice to say I got it wrong again.

So with two bad results under our belt, I was about to say something but LHO rudely opened two spades which of course was passed around to me. What else? This time I had a nice 16 count with spades stopped so I tried two notrump.

"What's that?" asked LHO with a bit of a sneer.

"Unusual," said partner confidently.

I will spare you the details.

We go back to compare.

"We are terrible," say I.

"Not to worry," said they.

"We are really terrible," says partner. "We balanced on every hand and got them all backwards. We had no idea what we were doing."

"Not to worry," said they. "Our opponents did too and they didn't either."

Well, two "not to worries" are better than a "we are terrible" and we did win. But it was no fault of ours. True, we had no idea what we were doing, but neither did our opponents and it turned out that we won because we played our bad contracts better than they played their bad contracts. But it was a hollow victory.

Later in the day during the dinner break partner and I had a chance to discuss what had happened during that round and to compare ideas. It was amazing how far apart we were. It seems that the common foundation which we had enjoyed in our constructive and competitive auctions was just not there in our balancing auctions.

Wondering if our problems were peculiar to our partnership, I asked our teammates how they would have handled the various balancing situations we had faced, and they had no agreements either.

Amazing.

Why should this be?

Surely balancing is an important aspect of bridge and it deserves at least as much discussion as what you should lead from three small, or what you should bid in response to Blackwood when holding two aces and a void. But for some reason people just don't spend that time. My first thought was that people didn't discuss it because it is not as exciting as strong notrumps or overcalls. It is not a dynamic topic.

But then it occured to me that perhaps the reason for no discussion is that the ACBL convention card has no room on it for re-opening conventions and, perforce, people never think of it when they get together for discussion with partner, this usually just prior to game time. People are slaves to habit, and that habit usually starts with either

"15 to 17?" or

"12 to 14?"

So regardless of the reasons for its relegation to obscurity, it is a fact that less has been said about balancing than any other important area, and I hope to correct part of that here.

TABLE OF CONTENTS

PART I.
BALANCING

Chapter One.
After One of a Suit, Pass, Pass

There are literally hundreds of possible re-opening sequences, and I don't intend to cover more than a few of them. But by starting with the simpler sequences and definitions, it will be possible to present ideas which can be used to develop solutions to the more difficult problems.

Let's start with the basic sequence:
One of a suit Pass Pass ?

Your options are many, including
1. double
2. one notrump
3. one of a suit
4. two of a lower ranking suit
5. a jump to two of a higher ranking suit
6. a jump to three of lower ranking suit
7. a jump to three of a higher ranking suit
8. a cue bid
9. a jump to two notrump
10. pass

There are even more obscure actions such as jump cue bids or a jump to three notrump or even jumps to the four level. But these are too rare to worry about. Knowing the basic sequences will take care of 99% of the hands and the others will fall into place by process of elimination.

1. *Double.* There is just about no hand which would have doubled an opening bid on your right which would not also double the same bid if in the re-opening seat. The question is how much less you can have to still qualify for a double.

No one vul

1♣-Pass-Pass-?

♠ Q 10 8 7   A clear double. Certainly less than you would need
♡ K 9 5 4   for an immediate double.
◇ A J 3
♣ 4 2

No one vul

1♣-Pass-Pass-?

♠ A 8 7 6   Double again. As your shape gets better and better,
♡ 10 5 4 2   the values you need get less and less. This hand is far
◇ K Q 8 6   from a minimum.
♣ 3

Both vul

1♣-Pass-Pass-?

♠ 10 6 5 4　　　　　　Even vulnerable, this is a fine double. You should feel
♥ K J 10 7　　　　　　no qualms about this.
◊ K 9 8 5
♣ 3

Vul vs not

1♣-Pass-Pass-?

♠ 8 7 6 5　　　　　　You should want to double with this hand. Your
♥ K 10 9 3　　　　　　shape is ideal and your few values are working. The
◊ Q J 8 2　　　　　　dangers are that partner might bid too much expecting
♣ 3　　　　　　　　　more, but in practice that doesn't happen if partner uses
　　　　　　　　　　　a moderate amount of caution in his actions.

Do the opponents have a game they have overlooked? Most unlikely. One of
the axioms of balancing is that when you are short in opener's suit, and they pass
it out, they won't have a game in that suit. If they do have a game, it will be in
another suit, and here you have no particular worry about any other suit.

Will partner double them hoping you have more? Perhaps, but if partner gives
you a little leeway, even this should not occur. In practice, you will rarely have a
hand this weak in the pass-out seat. I can not remember the last time I had a hand
with good distribution which I passed out.

Vul vs not

1♣-Pass-Pass-?

♠ J 8 7 6　　　　　　Pass. Actually, there was a hand and this was it. Note
♥ Q 9 6 4　　　　　　the huge flaw in the form of the club king. Not only is it
◊ Q 4 3 2　　　　　　worthless (probably) but it decreases the chance that
♣ K　　　　　　　　　partner will have useful values.

No one vul

1◊-Pass-Pass-?

♠ Q 8 7 6　　　　　　Double. Decent shape and adequate values. Two
♥ K 5 4　　　　　　　clubs would be a clear error. Note that RHO could have
◊ 3　　　　　　　　　a few points and if so might have dragged up a bid if
♣ A 10 8 6 5　　　　　possible. His silence suggests that his length might be in
　　　　　　　　　　　clubs.

Look at these two hands. Partner opens one diamond and RHO passes.

　　　　　♠ J 7 5　　　　　　♠ J 7 5
　　　　　♥ K J 5 4 3　　　　♥ 10 6 5
　　　　　◊ 8 7　　　　　　　◊ 8 7
　　　　　♣ 10 6 5　　　　　　♣ K J 5 4 3

With the first hand, you might venture one heart, but on the second hand you
would pass. This means that if RHO is to present a danger to you, it will be in a
lower ranking suit than the one opened. Remember this principle as it will reap-
pear in the discussion on whether to reopen in a suit.

No one vul

1♠-Pass-Pass-?

♠ 8
♡ 10 7 6 5
◊ K J 9 7
♣ K 5 4 2

With good shape and useful values, you can still double. Be aware though that partner's action will be at the two level. On some marginal hands with less than perfect shape, you need to consider whether partner will have to respond at the one level or at the two level.

No one vul

1♣-Pass-Pass-?

♠ 9 7 5
♡ K 10 6 5
◊ A 5 4 2
♣ J 2

This is certainly marginal but okay. Compare the next hand.

No one vul

1♠-Pass-Pass-?

♠ J 2
♡ 9 7 5
◊ K 10 6 5
♣ A 5 4 2

Here you should probably pass. Your hand is minimal, and partner will have to bid at the two level. Further, your worst suit is hearts and partner will bid those in preference to clubs or diamonds given equal holdings.

In fact, partner with four hearts and *five* clubs might choose to bid hearts. This hand has too many flaws. Pass.

Vul vs vul

1♠-Pass-Pass-?

♠ 8 2
♡ 9 7 6
◊ A J 5 4
♣ A 10 9 3

Double. Your high cards are sufficient to overcome the other flaws.

2. *One notrump.* For the most part, the one notrump re-opening is handled well by most players. None the less, I have seen a number of cases where the range shown by the notrump bidder, and the range expected by his partner were grossly out of whack. Fortunately, this is easy to fix.

What should one notrump show? If you asked ten good players, you might find less agreement than you expected, and if you asked ten inexperienced players, the discrepancy could be even greater. The ranges I'm going to recommend are a consensus of most of my partners and you can adjust them to suit your fancy.

If you think me inconsistent in saying there is little agreement and at the same time saying most people handle one notrump re-openings well, let me explain. My thought is that most partnerships have a reasonable idea of what partner has, but I think they use a poor range of points. If you use one notrump to show 16 to 18, that will be fine when it comes up, but you will have problems on the far more common 12 and 13 point hands. The ranges I intend to show are both safe and effective and they will be useful far more often than some of the other ranges.

So. What should the range be?

I would say your lower range is something like a good 11.

Now comes the tricky part. Your upper range is about 14 points if you are re-opening after one club or one diamond, but it is about 16 after one heart or one

3

spade.

The reason for this is that if you don't bid one notrump over, say, one spade with your 15 or 16, but double instead, partner will probably bid two of some suit. Now, to catch up on your values, you would have to bid two notrump, and if partner had a poor hand, you would be too high for no particular reason. Far better to bid one notrump on 15 or 16 and be a bit conservative. Miss a game? Don't worry. You will save a lot on those hands where one notrump is your limit. Note also that when LHO has opened one heart or one spade, he rates to have a five card or longer suit and this may afford the defense an effective start. One club or one diamond carries no such guarantees.

1♠-Pass-Pass-?

♠ K 8	A minimum one notrump. Double would be poor
♡ 10 6 5	because you would feel awkward about passing one
◊ K J 8 7	spade, and rebidding one notrump after doubling shows
♣ A J 5 4	more.

Both vul

1♠-Pass-Pass-?

♠ K 7 6	Double, followed by one notrump. This does not
♡ A Q 2	show as much as if you doubled an opening bid on your
◊ K J 4	right and then bid one notrump.
♣ Q J 8 3	

No one vul

1◊-Pass-Pass-?

♠ 4 2	Values are there for one notrump, but it might well be
♡ K J 7	best to pass. They are in your best suit. Nothing wrong
◊ Q J 9 8 7	with bidding but you should consider the alternative. If
♣ A J 3	the opponents were vulnerable, then pass would be
	clear cut.

No one vul

1♡-Pass-Pass-?

♠ J 3	One notrump. You would far prefer to have the nine
♡ Q 6 5 4	or ten of hearts, but this is an acceptable minimum.
◊ A Q 10	
♣ K 5 4 2	

Both vul

1♡-Pass-Pass-?

♠ K 4	Tough. Double would show better spades, and pass is
♡ 10 6 2	conservative. I would try a notrump but would be ner-
◊ A J 5 4	vous. Note that bidding one notrump with no stopper
♣ A Q 6 3	requires maximum high card points to justify this
	action. Also, your holding in their suit will never be less

than three cards. If one notrump gets passed out, it should be okay even if they run the heart suit. If you get doubled you should probably have second thoughts and run. Redouble should be takeout by you showing the minors. Something like what you have here.

4

No one vul

1 ♡ -Pass-Pass-?

♠ K 7 6   One notrump. A good hand, but not worth doubling.
♡ Q J 6 3   Partner may well bid two clubs or diamonds and you
◊ A 5 4   will either pass and maybe miss a game, or you may try
♣ K Q 7   two notrump and go down. Best the conservative one
                         notrump now.

1 ♠ -Pass-Pass-?

♠ K Q 9   Still one notrump. Just as above. On this hand, dou-
♡ 7 6 5   ble by you is guaranteed to get two of something from
◊ A K 8 6   partner, and you don't have the values to continue. One
♣ A 4 2   heart and one spade by the opponents are room con-
                         suming and it is harder to re-open accurately than after
one club or one diamond. You should strive to re-open the bidding as often as
possible, but it is not necessary to be pushy about it once you have decided to reopen.

3. *One of a suit.* The decision to re-open with one of a suit is based on many
interrelating factors. These are:

1. How good must your suit be? Must it be five cards or is four sufficient?
2. What strength do you require? Do you need seven points, ten points, or
   more? What is the upper range?
3. What is your holding in LHO's suit? Do you have wasted values? Do you
   have shortness or length?
4. Do you have more than one suit to bid? Should you balance in your longest
   suit?
5. Are there any suits unaccounted for? Are you weak in an unbid major?
   Especially, what do you have in spades if that is an unbid suit?

Let's look at these items separately.
How good must your suit be?

No one vul

1 ♠ -Pass-Pass-?

♠ 8 7 6 5 4   One spade is clear. Given adequate strength of hand
♡ A 8   this suit makes it. Other things being equal, any five
◊ K 10 4   card suit is acceptable for re-opening at the one level.
♣ K 5 4

No one vul

1 ◊ -Pass-Pass-?

♠ A 2   Four card suits present different problems. If the suit
♡ Q J 10 7   you intend to re-open in is four cards long, it implies
◊ 8 6 5 4   your hand is more balanced than if you have a five bag-
♣ A 9 7   ger and that suggests double or one notrump could be
                         chosen as alternatives. Here you should reject the alter-
                         natives and select one heart.

♠ J 8 7　　　　　　　Probably one spade. Poor suit, but such a good hand
♥ 3　　　　　　　　that you want to bid. You could pass one diamond hop-
♦ A K 4 2　　　　　ing to beat it a few, but experience shows that close deci-
♣ A 6 4 2　　　　　sions be resolved in favor of bidding.

All of this seems to suggest that many four card suits
are worth while for re-opening purposes. Of course, if you don't want to re-open
on this hand, then you are entitled to disagree with the premise that J 10 8 7 is
worth a bid.

I do think one spade here is clear cut, but to justify it here would require discussing how the auction will proceed. That is another chapter.

What strength do you require to re-open with one of a suit?

No one vul

1♣-Pass-Pass-?

♠ K J 8 7 5　　　　With a goodish five card suit, most aggressive players
♥ 3　　　　　　　　would bid one spade on this hand. Conceivably, they
♦ Q 5 4 2　　　　　would do it with the same suit and poorer distribution,
♣ 10 6 5　　　　　e.g.

♠ K J 8 7 5
♥ 7 2
♦ Q 9 7
♣ 7 4 2

This would be a matchpoint minimum. At IMPs, you could pass. Note that the
less you have, the better your suit will be.

No one vul

1♦-Pass-Pass-?

♠ 8 7 6 5 4　　　　One spade here would be risky. Even though you
♥ Q 10 7　　　　　have more high card points than in the previous hand,
♦ K 3 2　　　　　　your suit is poor and your high cards of questionable
♣ K 4　　　　　　　value. That diamond king is suspect. Also, in the likely
　　　　　　　　　　event the opponents play the hand, you do not really
　　　　　　　　　　want a spade lead.

Not vul vs. vul

1♣-Pass-Pass-?

♠ A Q J 8　　　　　One spade is fine. A minimum hand, but good shape
♥ 7　　　　　　　　and a very good suit.
♦ 10 6 5 4
♣ 8 6 3 2

Vul vs. not

1♣-Pass-Pass-?

♠ A Q 9 8 7　　　　Somewhere along the line, you will get a hand which
♥ A 2　　　　　　　is good enough to double first prior to bidding your
♦ A Q 5 4　　　　　suit. The strength of your hand will perforce depend on
♣ 7 6　　　　　　　the system of responses to your re-opening one-level
　　　　　　　　　　bids. For instance, if partner would respond to one

spade with as few as five or six points, you could wait for about 19 or so before doubling and bidding your suit. On the other hand, if partner won't respond to one spade without ten points, then in order not to miss good game contracts, you will have to double with as few as 16 points. I'll get into this problem in the section on responding to a re-opening bid and present this hand in anticipation of that. For the time being, are you sure that you and your partner are in agreement as to what to do with this hand?

What is your holding in LHO's suit?

This point is critical in that your contract may be won or lost within this suit. Secondary honors such as the queen and jack may well be worthless, and the king may do no more than offer safety from immediate attack. Even if the opponents can't get their tricks immediately, you may have to lose them later if no discards are available or if RHO can lead the suit before the discards can be taken. Your holding in LHO's suit will be one of the factors you consider when debating what to do on close decisions.

Should you always re-open in your longest suit?

This will depend on the strength of your hand and whether you intend to show both suits. If you feel that your only objective is to get your opponents a bit higher, you might simply bid your strongest suit intending to quit the auction immediately. This is usually the case when you have a weak hand with a good four card suit higher ranking than opener's and a weak lower ranking five bagger.

Not vul vs. vul

1 ◊ -Pass-Pass-?

♠ Q 8 7 4 2
♡ A Q 10 7
◊ A 8
♣ 3 2

One spade. Good enough that you might take another bid if the opportunity affords itself. Double runs the risk that partner will bid clubs.

Vul vs. vul

1 ◊ -Pass-Pass-?

♠ A K 10 7
♡ 4 2
◊ 7 3
♣ Q 8 7 6 3

One spade. On hands where you have enough for one call only, it is usually most effective to bid your best suit, regardless of the relative lengths. Not only are you getting your best suit in, but you are far less likely to run into trouble than by bidding two clubs which is a trick higher.

Not vul vs. vul

1 ♣ -Pass-Pass-?

♠ K Q J 9
♡ 8 7 6 5 4
◊ 3
♣ Q 4 2

Even though you could bid either suit at the one level, one spade is best. This will be your only contribution unless partner forces the issue. Your purpose in bidding on hands like these is an effort to get the opponents higher, and one of the side benefits is that of getting partner off to a good lead.

7

Not vul vs. vul

1 ◊ -Pass-Pass-?

♠ Q 8 4 2
♡ 3
◊ A K 5
♣ 7 6 5 4 2

This is the kind of hand with which you can try a matchpoint adventure. One spade or two clubs could work, but you'd better be right. One spade is probably better than two clubs for a number of reasons. It's one trick lower, you would prefer a spade lead (marginally) and there is the greater danger of clubs in RHO's hand rather than spades. Remember that RHO might bid a heart or a spade on marginal hands where two clubs on the same values would be ridiculous.

Both vul

1 ♡ -Pass-Pass-?

♠ A Q 8 7
♡ 8 6 5
◊ 2
♣ A K 9 7 4

Double would be atrocious, so your choices are between one spade and two clubs. Here you can expect to take a second bid if the auction permits. You should start with two clubs intending to bid spades later. If you bid one spade, it will be awkward to introduce clubs later as that would run the risk of getting a preference back to spades. Only if two clubs gets passed out might you do poorly, and then only if spades was the better spot. More on new suits at the two level in a later section.

What suits are missing?

One of the most embarrassing things you can do is re-open and watch the opponents who are content to play at the one level suddenly bid and make a game.

Fortunately, this doesn't happen very often. But when it does happen, it is usually true that their game was in an unbid major. Very seldom does their side have a game in the suit opened, because they would have been able to evaluate that fact; i.e. responder would evaluate his hand accordingly and take some action. But sometimes when you re-open, opener can show a new major, allowing responder to re-evaluate his hand enormously and attempt to reach a game.

Responder might have this hand:

♠ J 10 4 2
♡ 7
◊ 10 6 5 4 2
♣ Q 3 2

Hearing partner open one club, he would pass. But if LHO bid one heart and opener now bid one spade, responder would compete to at least three spades. Opener, with any kind of maximum, could continue to a successful game when without a balance, they were about to play in one club.

Here is a complete hand to show this sort of occurrence:

North
- ♠ J 10 4 2
- ♡ 7
- ◊ 10 6 5 4 2
- ♣ Q 3 2

West
- ♠ Q 9 3
- ♡ K J 5 2
- ◊ A Q 7
- ♣ 8 7 6

East
- ♠ 6 5
- ♡ A Q 9 6 4
- ◊ K J 8 3
- ♣ 9 5

South
- ♠ A K 8 7
- ♡ 10 8 3
- ◊ 9
- ♣ A K J 10 4

North	East	South	West
—	—	1♣	Pass
Pass	1♡	1♠	2♡
3♠	Pass	4♠	Pass
Pass	Pass		

This will probably make exactly four, and West might even double!

What went wrong here? East has all of the things so far discussed as necessary for re-opening. He has a good suit. He has shortness in opener's suit. He has adequate values. The one thing he doesn't have is one of the unbid majors, in this case spades.

Now it would be somewhat timid for East to pass in fourth chair, but the danger is recognizable and should be considered when he re-opens.

For the most part, the danger suits will be majors. Only infrequently will your opponents find life in an unbid minor. True, they may be able to compete in an unbid minor, but they will seldom have a game. This is for the reason that game in a minor requires extra values and the opponents would have had to overlook an enormous amount of values.

I wasn't going to include this hand because I thought it might scare some people away from balancing, but I couldn't stand it. I held:

- ♠ K 8 7
- ♡ 2
- ◊ A K J 9 7 6
- ♣ K J 2

One spade was passed around to me and I tried three diamonds. By our agreements, this shows a good hand. It went double, pass, four hearts, pass by me, six hearts on my left. Dummy put down:

- ♠ A Q 10 x x
- ♡ A K x x
- ◊ — — —
- ♣ A Q x x

Declarer had a stiff spade and six hearts to the jack. They made seven. While I was cogitating over why I hadn't left one spade alone, East began complaining to West that he should have bid seven. Oh well.

In a serious vein, I have no doubts that three diamonds was correct and what

9

happened was singularly unlucky. Not only did the opponents miss a game, but they missed a slam. And then they bid it the second time around! This is really the parlay of a lifetime.

The following is a short quiz which will make reference to all of the preceding points.

No one vul

1♣-Pass-Pass-?

♠ K 7 2
♡ J 5 4
◇ A K J 8 7
♣ 4 2

One diamond is likely to be best. You have a good suit and more than adequate values. The alternative is double, and that runs the unnecessary risk of playing a four-three major suit contract. If partner bids hearts or spades after one diamond, you will be assured of a five card suit. Note that there is nothing wrong with a four-three fit, it is just that if you have reasonable alternatives, you should consider them.

No one vul

1♣-Pass-Pass-?

♠ 8 2
♡ Q 3
◇ A J 9 8 5
♣ K J 10 7

This hand is easily worth a diamond bid, but those two major suit doubletons should give you second thoughts. Almost surely the opponents have at least one major suit fit, and perhaps two. Your partner is marked with moderate values and chose not to bid. He probably doesn't have a five card major and only if he is four-four in the majors will the opponents not have an eight card fit. A risky alternative is one notrump and I would consider that dangerous but enterprising.

No one vul

1♣-Pass-Pass-?

♠ 3
♡ A J 4
◇ K Q 9 7 5
♣ A 4 3 2

Even though spades constitute a clear threat, your hand is good enough to bid one diamond. Your good defensive potential plus the possible four or more spades in partner's hand gives you license to bid with this some- what dangerous distribution. A point in your favor is that your hand is so good that partner won't have too much. This means that he could easily have five spades but not have had the values to bid them. Compare this with the situation where partner is marked with good values but has passed. This points more strongly to weakness in the higher ranking suits or he would have bid with his values.

Vul vs. not

1◇-Pass-Pass-?

♠ K Q 10 8 7
♡ 9 6 5 4
◇ 3 2
♣ Q 5

One spade. With weak hands where you may well be outbid, be content to get your best suit mentioned. Dou- ble would be poor as partner could bid clubs and you have too few values to make up for your lack of clubs. The opponents are probably going to play this one. Get partner off to the best lead.

Vul vs. not

1 ◊ -Pass-Pass-?

♠ K Q 10 8
♡ A 10 5 4
◊ 4 3 2
♣ K 7

Double and pass if partner bids two clubs. Your hand is good enough and only if partner has to bid clubs on a four bagger will this work out poorly. One spade would be a serious error. You expect this may be your hand so you should try to maximize your chances of getting to the best spot.

Vul vs. not

1 ♡ -Pass-Pass-?

♠ K J 9 7
♡ A 5 4
◊ J 6 4 3 2
♣ 7

One spade. In keeping with re-opening in your best .suit and at the one level.

No one vul

1 ♡ -Pass-Pass-?

♠ J 7 6 5
♡ A 10 5
◊ K Q J 3 2
♣ 5

Two diamonds. Some people would advocate double followed by two diamonds if partner bids two clubs. But what happens if partner bids three or even four clubs if the auction should get competitive?

Vul vs. vul

1 ◊ -Pass-Pass-?

♠ K Q 7
♡ Q J 4 2
◊ 4 3 2
♣ A J 3

Double. Anything else would be a serious error. With adequate support for all suits both one heart and one notrump would suggest a low opinion of partner's dummy play.

4. *Reopening with two of a lower ranking suit.*

Strangely enough, this situation does not come up all that often. I would guess that I choose to reopen with one of a suit about four times as often as I decided to reopen with two of a suit. The reasons for this may not be too clear, but they are useful to know.

The first reason is the obvious one. A two level bid guarantees a five card suit, and it should be a pretty good one at that. This means that all those hands with four card suits and mediocre five card suits which were worth a one level call are not worth two level calls.

The second reason is that you do need extra values in the form of high cards in addition to suit quality already discussed, so some minimum hands worth one level bids will have to be passed if your only option is a two level reopening.

The third reason is a little obscure but it may be the most important. When you are considering reopening in a suit at the two level, it usually means you are not interested in suits higher ranking than opener's. Note that if opener's bid was one spade, there is no higher ranking suit. But if the suit was hearts or diamonds, and you are reopening in a lower suit, it means there is the danger of those higher ranking suits. Incidentally, even if LHO has opened with one spade, you have to worry about the heart suit if you are contemplating bidding clubs or diamonds. The only two level reopening where you can ignore the "missing suits" is

One spade-Pass-Pass-Two hearts

If opener wants to bid three clubs or three diamonds, that's life, but he won't often have the hand to justify it.

And lastly, RHO may have length in suits lower ranking than opener's. Remember, with marginal hands, he might have responded in a higher ranking suit but couldn't do so in a lower ranking one.

To determine what a two level reopening looks like, it is useful to look at the factors discussed when reopening at the one level. These are:

How good must your suit be?

At the two level, you have to have some extra sources of tricks and that is almost always going to come primarily from the trump suit. The more you have in high cards, the more you can fudge in terms of your suit, but I would rate Q J 9 x x as the minimum and any six card suit will do in a pinch.

How many points do you need?

For a two level reopening bid, you need a reasonably decent hand. I would say ten useful high card points would be enough, other things being equal.

I expect to get some static on this point. Another well-known author has suggested you reopen on something like this:

No one vul

1 ♠ -Pass-Pass-?

♠ 9
♡ 8 7 2
◊ 10 4 2
♣ A J 10 8 7 6

Two clubs was recommended on the theory that partner had at least 15 points. The trouble with this is that two clubs is unlikely to end the auction. If partner has as much as you expect him to have, he will be bidding something, three notrump for example, and that's unlikely to succeed opposite this hand. Really it's hard to envision a plus score. Either partner has a good hand and he bids and we go down, or partner has a mediocre hand and the opponents get together in another suit and find a better contract, perhaps even a game.

In fairness, this author uses a reopening double to show opening bid strength and feels a bid should show less. But even so, this much less is hard to accept.

One other personal aside. Many people "trap" by passing good hands when their RHO reopens the bidding. The idea is to double them later if possible. My experience is that this doesn't work against most good opposition and it does make it difficult to bid when the hand belongs to your side. The hands that fall into this category most often are something like this.

After one heart by RHO

♠ K 2
♡ K Q 10 7 4
◊ A 8 3
♣ K J 3

Many players will pass hoping to double the opponents in some final contract. But what usually happens is the auction goes

| 1 ♡ | Pass | 1 ♠ | Pass |
| 2 ♣ | Pass | Pass | Pass |

. . . and the opponents make or go down one when it was your hand for three of a minor or perhaps even three notrump.

Or, it might go:

| 1 ♡ | Pass | 1NT | Pass |
| Pass | ? | | |

You could double this, hoping for the killing you had waited for, but now what happens is that they run to two of a minor and you find you can't hurt them there.

I think it is better to bid one notrump and try to achieve something instead of waiting for a miracle.

In some cases, you have good hands which just don't have a convenient bid and on these you can pass and hope for the best, but you are doing it because there is no good way for you to get into the auction immediately.

After one heart on your right, you would be forced to pass all of these good hands:

♠ J 2
♡ K J 9 7 5
◊ A K Q 2
♣ 7 6

Not enough for one notrump.

♠ 8 6 5 4
♡ A K Q 10
◊ A 6 5 4
♣ 7

Wrong shape for double. No suit to overcall.

♠ 3
♡ A Q 10 9 8 7 5
◊ A K 8
♣ K 2

Just nothing you can do.

♠ Q J 8 7 5
♡ A Q 10 9 8
◊ K 2
♣ 7

One spade. Don't pass when you have something useful to bid.

♠ 3
♡ A K J 10 7
◊ A J 10 8 4
♣ 7 6

Two diamonds as above.

What is your holding in the opener's suit?

As in all cases where you are considering reopening, your holding in opener's suit will be one of the determining factors. Potential losers in this suit are far more often lost than potential losers in other suits. Let's say LHO has opened one spade and you have one of these two hands:

♠ 4 3 2   ♠ 4 3
♡ A 3   ♡ A 3 2
◊ A K Q J 10 9 8 7   ◊ A K Q J 10 9 8 7
♣ — — —   ♣ — — —

Even though both hands have four losers, you would certainly rather have the second hand.

♠ 4 3 2   ♠ 7
♡ 7   ♡ 4 3 2
◊ A K Q J 10   ◊ A K Q J 10
♣ A K Q J   ♣ A K Q J

Likewise, you would rather have the second hand after LHO opened one spade. The reasons for this are that you anticipate the defense attacking the spade suit and you have no real expectation that partner will be able to stop that attack. Partner may have some help in spades, or he may have some help in hearts. After a spade bid you would expect that help to be more likely in hearts than in opener's bid suit, spades.

Should you reopen in your long suit if you hold a two-suiter?

This depends on the quality of your hand and suits. With less than the "ten" points required, you will have to bid something at the one level or pass, particularly if your two level suit is not good enough.

Lastly, you must again be concerned about the missing suits. If you are short in an unbid major, that should sway you on marginal decisions.

Some reopening hands:

No one vul

1♠-Pass-Pass-?

♠ K 5 4
♡ 3
♢ Q 9 8 4
♣ A K 10 8 7

Certainly worth two clubs, although as always, you should be worried about the missing major suit. Here, to compensate for the heart suit, you have good defensive potential. Note that on this sequence, your partner can easily have five or even six hearts along with a good hand and not have been able to overcall. Overcalls at the two level are far more disciplined than overcalls at the one level. This means that while you must be concerned about the heart suit, your worst fears need not always come true. Your partner can easily have them locked up.

Compare with the earlier hand:

1♠-Pass-Pass-?

♠ 8 2
♡ Q 3
♢ A J 9 8 5
♣ K J 10 7

On this hand, your fears are known to be real. I would say the danger of reopening to be four or five times as great as on the hand just discussed.

Vul vs. vul

1♠-Pass-Pass-?

♠ 8 6
♡ J 8 7 6 5 4
♢ A 7 6
♣ A 2

Two hearts. Two defensive tricks and an extra heart to make up for the poor suit and minimum values. Double would be very poor. You could do this if either ace were a king, but that would be about as weak as you would want.

Vul vs. not

1♡-Pass-Pass?

♠ Q
♡ Q 10 7
♢ Q J 8
♣ K J 7 6 5 4

This is a dangerous hand, to say the least. You have a stiff spade, an unbid major. You have wasted cards in hearts and spades. You have poor spots in clubs. Offensively, the only plus is the sixth club. You could bid two clubs at matchpoints but that runs substantial risks. If opener wants to compete, you have no defense against anything short of a grand slam. Your heart holding is extra bad. One of the goals of balancing is to push the opponents higher, and if they do go higher in hearts the suit will be breaking well for declarer. You would far prefer a singleton heart to a singleton spade. If opener rebids his suit, or any suit for that matter, you would like to have him face at least one bad split. Whatever contract opener plays it will be easier for him if you have Q 10 7 of hearts than if you have a stiff.

Hard as it may seem, I would suggest a pass of one heart with the hand being discussed.

14

Had the opening bid been one spade instead of one heart, it would be very reasonable to bid two clubs. Your hand would be minimum, but it would be acceptable.

No one vul

1♠-Pass-Pass-?

♠ 4 2
♡ 8 6 5
◇ A Q
♣ A K J 8 7 6

Still two clubs. Eventually, you will get a hand so good that you will want to do more than merely reopen. This will cause you to choose some of the stronger reopening actions available to you which will be discussed soon.

Not vul vs. vul

1♡-Pass-Pass-?

♠ 8 6 5 4
♡ 4 2
◇ K Q J 9 7
♣ K 3

Two diamonds. You should feel that it's the opponents' hand and you would like to push them up a bit. Two diamonds will do that safely and it will get partner off to a good lead. On weakish hands your main intent is not to buy the contract. It is only to nudge the opponents higher. Hopefully where they can be set. For your side to make something in spades would require that partner have four decent spades and a fair hand. With such a holding he might have bid over one heart.

No one vul

1♡-Pass-Pass-?

♠ K Q 8 7
♡ 4 2
◇ A 2
♣ 10 7 6 5 4

One spade. With weak hands, you bid your best suit and quit.

Vul vs. vul

1♡-Pass-Pass-?

♠ Q 8 6 2
♡ A 3
◇ K 3
♣ Q 10 8 4 2

Here you don't have a best suit. You don't have values for one notrump and pass is not out of the question. If you want to reopen, it is between one spade and two clubs. I would go with one spade on the theory that it is a safer suit than clubs, (higher ranking vs. lower ranking than opener's suit) and it can be bid a level lower.

5. *The reopening jump to the two level.*

Finally getting out of the normal spectrum of reopening bids, we get to the first of the special cases. By special I don't mean they are more difficult or complicated, they are merely among the less common reopening actions.

What does it mean when it goes one club, pass, pass, to partner's two spades? Is it weak, strong, in-between? Is it a six card suit? Longer? Can you pass?

The most common misconception is that it is a weak bid similar to the weak jump overcall.

This idea is easily dispensed with.

First: The purpose of the weak jump overcall is to make it difficult for opener and responder to maintain a smooth exchange of information. But when responder passes opener's bid, that is one of the most informative of all possible actions. Preempting now as reopener has little to gain because opener pretty well knows the extent of his side's potential.

Second: When you assign a meaning to a bid, you want to assign a meaning such that it will come up often enough to be useful. Here is an extreme example. When the bidding goes   1♠-Pass-Pass-?

. . . You could play that two hearts shows four good spades and six diamonds with at least twenty points. If you were using this convention and you had

♠ K Q 8 7
♡ 3
◇ A K Q 10 7 6
♣ A 2

. . . and you heard the auction go   1♠-Pass-Pass-?

you would be prepared for this hand. You would probably be the only person in the room so prepared. But you would have to wait a long, long time to get much mileage out of this convention. And, in the meantime, you would have troubles on other hands where a more useful treatment of two hearts could be used.

The point of this is that you want to use a treatment which has some expectation of occurrence. Now when the bidding goes   1♣-Pass-Pass-?

what are the chances of your holding a weak hand with a six card suit? Remember that partner couldn't bid, which implies weakness (this is not a guarantee of course) and RHO didn't bid, which does guarantee weakness. Furthermore, your long suit suggests a little distribution around the table giving the other players extra reason to bid. This means that in practice, you are not likely to have the hand for the weak jump reopening often enough to bother with. Even in the event you get the hand, it is not likely to be effective given the fact that opener knows the kind of hand he is facing. He won't be doing any more bidding unless his hand calls for it or unless he's nuts. And that is not worth playing for.

So what should a jump show if it's not weak?

There are a number of possibilities ranging from an invitational bid to a strong bid to various conventional meanings such as two-suiters, etc. The most common usage is to play a jump as showing about 15 points plus or minus with a decent six card suit. Or perhaps a seven bagger with a point or two less. I won't get into any theory here about what is right because it is clearly a reasonable interpretation which has withstood the test of time and it fits nicely into the scheme of things yet to be discussed.

Here are some examples:

No one vul

1♣-Pass-Pass-?

♠ Q J 9 8 7 4   Two spades. A routine example.
♡ A 2
◇ A K 3
♣ 10 7

Vul vs. vul

1◇-Pass-Pass-?

♠ K Q 3   Two hearts. Good suit, slightly more than a minimum
♡ A K Q 8 7 4   opening bid.
◇ 4 2
♣ 7 2

16

Not vul vs. vul

1 ◊ -Pass-Pass-?

♠ J 10 9 7 4 2   Two spades is about right. You would like slightly
♡ 3   better spades but any other approach could prove more
◊ A 2   troublesome.
♣ A K J 7

Vul vs. vul

1 ◊ -Pass-Pass-?

♠ Q J 10 8 7 5 4   I would try two spades as the most descriptive call
♡ A 2   available. The extra spade makes up for a couple of
◊ 3   points. The only real risk is missing four spades when
♣ A 9 7   partner has a moderate hand with a stiff spade.

This convention won't come up a lot, but it will come up far more often than if you treated jumps as weak. And when it does come up, you should get good results. If nothing else, you will have a definition and will be able to avoid misunderstanding.

6. *The reopening jump to three of a lower ranking suit.*

For all of the reasons that weak jumps are wrong at the two level in reopening seat, they are still wrong at the three level. The only question then is what they should be. I suggest you play something like this.

Whereas a jump to the two level shows a goodish six card suit and opening plus strength, a jump to the three level shows a *very* good six or seven card suit with the same strength and is primarily aimed at three notrump.

The reason for this is that most jumps to the two level will be in a major suit, so four of a major is a likely contract. Conversely, most jumps to the three level will be in a minor suit and five of a minor is substantially more difficult to make than four of a major. This is particularly so after an opponent has announced strength. On the other hand, three notrump may well succeed in spite of opener's bid.

Vul vs. vul

1 ♡ -Pass-Pass-?

♠ Q 2   Three clubs. This shows a good six plus suit with
♡ 3 2   more than a minimum opening bid.
◊ A J 6
♣ A K J 9 8 3

No one vul

1 ♠ -Pass-Pass-?

♠ 8 7   Three diamonds. Definitely aiming for three notrump
♡ K 4   rather than five diamonds.
◊ A K Q 10 8 6 5
♣ 7 3

No one vul

1 ♠ -Pass-Pass-?

♠ 7 2   Three hearts. This is the one case where you are
♡ Q J 9 8 7 6 2   jumping in a major suit at the three level. Your emphasis
◊ A Q   is no longer on three notrump so your suit need not be
♣ A 2   as good.

17

Vul vs. not

1♣-Pass-Pass-?

♠ 8 7
♡ A J
◊ A K J
♣ Q 10 8 5 4 3

With the club suit this poor, two clubs is enough. To make three notrump, partner needs two spade stoppers plus a club honor, or one spade stopper and two club honors. In those cases where three notrump can make, your partner will often be bidding. You will not miss many games by bidding two clubs on hands like this.

No one vul

1♣-Pass-Pass-?

♠ A 2
♡ A 2
◊ A Q 3
♣ K 9 8 7 6 5

Hard hand. Probably double followed by three clubs. More on this later.

7. *The jump to the three level in a higher ranking suit.*

You can get a lot of opinions on this one. The one thing that's clear is that it won't come up very often. The important thing is that you have an agreement, and what it is doesn't matter too much as long as it is reasonably safe and sane. For whatever it's worth, I offer this. Play the jump as a good preempt with which you expect to make your contract opposite a random ten count.

No one vul

1♣-Pass-Pass-?

♠ K J 10 8 7 6 4
♡ 3
◊ A J 5
♣ 4 2

A normal sound preempt. The main thing is, it is not a pile of trash.

No one vul

1◊-Pass-Pass-?

♠ Q 8 6 5 4 3 2
♡ K 4 2
◊ K 3
♣ Q

One spade is enough. Poor suit. Garbage.

Not vul vs. vul

1♣-Pass-Pass-?

♠ A Q 2
♡ J 10 9 8 7 4 3
◊ K 4
♣ 7

Three hearts. Your suit is not exactly wonderful, but it is solid.

Both vul

1◊-Pass-Pass-?

♠ K J 4
♡ Q J 10 8 6 4 2
◊ A 10
♣ 5

Three hearts. This is actually on the light side. But the suit is good and the values all sound.

Both vul

1 ◊ -Pass-Pass-?

♠ A K Q J 8 7 4   Three spades. If your side were not vulnerable, part-
♡ 10 2   ner would not expect as much. You would choose two
◊ 7 3   spades instead. Under no circumstances should you bid
♣ 9 5   four spades. Too many losers. Partner needs three tricks
to cover your losers and he will know if he has them.
With the definitions we've discussed, you will be able to describe hands like these
and can avoid getting to silly games. Over your three spades, partner may be able
to choose three notrump when that is right.

Something like this

♠ 8 3
♡ A J 9
◊ K Q 10 8 5
♣ Q J 8

. . . will produce three notrump routinely, but will fail in four spades whenever
the defense leads or shifts to hearts. Much better to take a cold three notrump,
and that's not possible if you have already skipped past it to four spades, or if
your side has its understandings confused.

8. *The reopening cue bid.*

This is another of those unusual sequences that never seem to come up. And
when it does no one knows what's happening. You have a fleeting discussion, and
maybe if it comes up again sometime during the same year, you'll get it right. But
that's only if you're playing with the same partner. If you are playing with a different partner, then good luck.

Frankly, I have not discussed this sequence in the last five years and during that
time, it hasn't come up. Which is why I haven't discussed it, I suppose.

So I asked my friends what a cue bid should mean. And sure enough, they had
no understandings either. It was either this or that or perhaps something else. The
one thing we did agree on was that it showed a strong hand. And the reason that
you cue bid instead of doubling was that you did not want partner to make a penalty pass. This means you hold a very strong offensive hand, probably a one-
suiter, although possibly a two-suiter.

Here are some hands that suit this idea:

No one vul

1 ♣ -Pass-Pass-?

♠ K Q 10 9 8 7 6   Two clubs. Slam might be on in spades or diamonds.
♡ A K   As there is no number of spades you can bid which.is
◊ A Q 10 7   forcing, you start with a cue bid. What you don't do is
♣ — — —   double, because it runs the risk that partner will pass for
                 penalties. You'll beat them of course, but if partner has
three or four spades and a stiff diamond or the spade jack and diamond king, or
just the diamond king with length, then you would be trading a sure slam for a
smaller penalty. The other thing you don't do is leap to four spades. You could
easily find yourself playing a laydown grand slam in game only.

Both vul

1♡-Pass-Pass-?

♠ Q 2	Two hearts. You hope to hear partner bid notrump.
♡ 2	Once again, you don't want to double and hear partner
◊ A Q 3	pass for business. Note that both of these hands have
♣ A K Q J 10 8 7	been characterized by good points, one outstanding
	suit, and have been offensively rather than defensively
	oriented.

How far is your cue bid forcing? I suggest you play it forcing until you reach three notrump or four of a suit. This means the cue bid is a game force except that you can stop in four of a minor. Here the auction might be something along these lines.

1♡-Pass-Pass-2♡
Pass-2♣-Pass-3♣—still forcing
Pass-3◊-Pass-4♣
Pass-Pass-Pass

Partner, holding

♠ K 8 7 6
♡ 8 6 5 2
◊ 10 5 4 3
♣ 2

. . . can pass. He isn't passing because of the stiff club. He is passing because he has a bad hand. With the spade and diamond kings, he would go on to game.

Both vul

1♡-Pass-Pass-?

♠ A K J 10	Double. Do not cue bid. If partner makes a penalty
♡ 3	pass, you'll kill them. And given the length partner has
◊ K Q 10 9	in hearts, he is not going to have length in other suits
♣ A K Q J	also, so your offensive potential won't be as great.

Vul vs. not

1♣-Pass-Pass-?

♠ A Q 10 8 7 6	This is a cue bid. A rare case where you have a huge
♡ A	two-suiter in the reopening seat. The reason it is more
◊ A K Q J 7 6	unusual than a huge one-suiter is that everyone else has
♣ — — —	more shape. Somebody usually has something to say
	and it will rarely get to you in the balancing chair.

9. *The reopening jump to two notrump.*

This isn't a very common action either, and just knowing what it means is likely to be enough. The one thing it shouldn't be is the unusual notrump. If you are in fourth seat with ten minor suit cards, regardless of the major suit opened, you should be wondering where all the major suit cards are. Partner may well have opener's suit stopped, but the other major is somewhere and more likely than not, the opponents have a fit in it.

In my life, I have only once wished I was using the unusual notrump in the reopening seat. And when the hand was over, I was glad I hadn't been able to.

There remains to decide what two notrump should show, and my suggestion is the natural one. Use it to show about 19 or 20 points. This is simple, efficient, and it works. There may be other uses, but they will require systemic understandings and what you don't want is to have complex treatments in situations that are as rare as this one.

No one vul

1♠-Pass-Pass-?

♠ Q 8 7   Two notrump. Double followed by two notrump is
♡ A 2   possible, but you don't want partner to bid and rebid
◇ A K J 10 7   hearts or possibly hearts and then clubs. Nor do you
♣ A J 7   want to double and then have to bid three diamonds
over two hearts by partner. Not only does two notrump
describe your hand, but now you won't feel so bad if partner persists in hearts.

No one vul

1♠-Pass-Pass-?

♠ K 2   Two notrump. Again, you do not want to double and
♡ A Q   hear spades and hearts from partner.
◇ Q J 10 8 7
♣ A K 10 6

Vul vs. not

1♡-Pass-Pass-?

♠ A Q 2   Double. Two notrump, unlike one notrump, does
♡ 10 6 4   guarantee a stopper. After partner's response, you can
◇ A K 10 7   cue bid if you still want to try for game.
♣ A K 4

Difficult Hands.

Every now and then you get a hand which might produce game opposite a random seven or eight count. But the shape doesn't quite fit any of the requirements for special jumps and the strength is not enough for a cue bid. I've made a few references to this situation in some of the earlier discussions.

Basically, the problem is with hands of 16 or more points which do not fall into the reopening bid structures so far covered.

Here are some typical problem hands.

1♠-Pass-Pass-?

♠ A Q 10 7 5	♠ A 2	♠ J 2
♡ 3	♡ A K Q 10 8 7	♡ A 5 4
◇ A K 4 2	◇ A J	◇ K Q 10 9
♣ A J 3	♣ 4 3 2	♣ A K J 4

On the first hand, you are too good to bid one spade.

On the second hand, you are too good to bid two hearts, and not good enough to cue bid.

On the third hand, you are too good for one notrump and not good enough for two notrump.

The usual solution is to double and then take some additional action to describe the whatever extras you may have. There are some dangers however and you will have to cater to them.

First, the auction may go in such a way that you may have to show your suit at an excessively high level. There may be competition which will make it awkward for you.

Second, partner may get in your way, bidding suits you don't want to hear, again forcing you too high.

Reviewing the earlier three hands:

No one vul

1♣-Pass-Pass-?

♠ A Q 10 7 5   Double. Over one heart, bid one spade. Over one
♡ 3   notrump bid three spades. And over one diamond,
◊ A K 4 2   jump to two spades. Note that there is nothing partner
♣ A J 3   can do to get in your way. You are prepared for any-
                  thing he can do.

♠ A 2   Double, followed by a jump in hearts. Partner can
♡ A K Q 10 8 7   pass, but with any kind of excuse will continue.
◊ A J
♣ 4 3 2

♠ J 2   Double, followed by one notrump. This is a maxi-
♡ A 5 4   mum for this sequence.
◊ K Q 10 9
♣ A K J 4

The range you will need for one of these extra strength showing auctions will vary according to your rebid. If you double and rebid at the one level, it shows a good opening bid. If you rebid at the two level, you show a king or so more.

No one vul

1♣-Pass-Pass-?

♠ A Q 10 7   Double first and then rebid
♡ K Q J 9 5   1. One heart over one diamond
◊ Q 8 7   2. Raise one spade to two
♣ 4   3. Two hearts over one notrump
                  Note that whatever partner chooses, you will have
enough to justify any of your possible bids. When partner bids one notrump, he is promising some values, so your two heart bid doesn't require as much. Compare the next hand.

No one vul

1♣-Pass-Pass-?

♠ K 2   Bid one heart. If you double, partner will frequently
♡ K Q J 9 5   bid one spade. Now a two heart call would be an over-
◊ A Q 4   bid. Even though this hand is the equal of the prior
♣ 9 6 4   hand, you can anticipate that partner's bid will make it
                  awkward for you. Better to make a slight underbid and
keep firm control of the auction than to allow things to get out of hand.

No one vul

1◊-Pass-Pass-?

♠ 3 2   Bid two clubs. True, you have a good hand, but not
♡ A Q 7   that good. Double first will get you some number of
◊ 8 6 4   spades from partner and you won't be able to cope.
♣ A K Q 8 6

Both vul

1 ◊ -Pass-Pass-?

♠ A K Q 8 6
♡ 3 2
◊ 8 6 4
♣ A Q 6

Almost the same hand. Double is right because you can get your spades in at whatever level the auction permits. Anticipate the auction.

Both vul

1 ♡ -Pass-Pass-?

♠ A J 2
♡ 7 2
◊ Q 8 6
♣ A K J 8 7

Double, with the intention of bidding two clubs after one spade by partner. If partner bids two diamonds after double, you should pass as you are not strong enough to double and then bid three clubs.

Vul vs. not

1 ♠ -Pass-Pass-?

♠ 4 2
♡ A 6 2
◊ K J 7
♣ A K Q 10 6

Double, followed by three clubs if partner bids two hearts or two diamonds. This is not really that good a hand and on a bad day you could go down quite a few in three clubs. But if partner has some scattered values, game can exist so you have to give it a try. The important thing is to realize that this is not much more than a minimum for this sequence.

Chapter Two.
Reopening after one notrump.

When one notrump has been passed around to you, you can reopen by
1. Bidding a suit.
2. Using one of many artificial devices, i.e. Landy, Astro, etc.
3. Double for penalties.

I don't intend to get involved with conventional treatments. Whatever suits you is probably OK. The main decision is *whether* to reopen. The method is up to you.

I suggest you be very active whenever your distribution is worthwhile.

No one vul

1NT*-Pass-Pass-?

♠ K Q J 8 6 4
♡ 5 3
◊ 4 3
♣ 10 6 5

* 15-17 HCP
Two spades, without question. Even if Vul, you should act. This hand is far from a minimum.

No one vul

1NT*-Pass-Pass-?

♠ 3
♡ K 10 9 8 4 2
◊ 10 6 5 4
♣ 3 2

*15-17 HCP
Two hearts. The only real danger is that partner will get excited. But as long as he keeps in mind that opener has 15-17, there should be no trouble. Only if partner has a huge hand plus a *good* fit should he be bidding.

For example:

1NT-Pass-Pass-2 ♡
Pass-?

♠ K Q 8
♡ 10 2
◊ A 6 5 4
♣ K J 3

Partner should pass.

♠ K Q 8 2
♡ 3
◊ K Q J 9
♣ K Q 4 2

Pass again.

♠ A 4 3 2
♡ J 10 7 6
◊ K 2
♣ K 4 3

Three hearts. When you take any action over partner's reopening bid, you need a fit in addition to the high cards he already expects you to have.

♠ K Q 2
♡ J 7
◊ K 10 9 8
♣ A Q 9 4

Two notrump only. This shows a hand which fell just short of doubling the one notrump opening. There is almost no hand worth a jump to three notrump because any hand that good should have acted sooner.

Both vul
1NT-Pass-Pass-?

♠ Q 10 8 6 4
♡ J 10 4 3 2
◊ 7 6
♣ 3

If you have a convention to show the majors, then you should use it. The point here is that when your shape says bid, then you don't need much in the way of high cards.

No one vul
1NT-Pass-Pass-?

♠ 8 2
♡ A 10 6 5 4
◊ 3
♣ K J 6 5 4

Again, if you have a convention, you should get in there.

No one vul
1NT-Pass-Pass-?

♠ 10 6 5 4 2
♡ A Q 10 6 5
◊ 10 2
♣ 3

Again, the shape says bid. If you can show both suits, do so. If you can't, then you should still feel like bidding something and I would try two hearts. If doubled it might be wise to trot out to two spades.

No one vul
1NT-Pass-Pass-?

♠ Q 10 8 6 5
♡ K 5 4
◊ K J 5
♣ K 2

When you haven't much in the way of distribution, you will have to find partner with a fit, as well as points. Bidding two spades will work if partner has a few spades but not otherwise. Even if he has ten or so points, they won't be worth much if he has a stiff spade.

It would be better to pass one notrump.

When you have a six card suit, or a two-suiter which you can show systemically, then you can assume a playable trump suit exists, and can act on many marginal hands.

On hands where you feel like bidding, but have no clearly worthwhile suit or distributions suitable to a convention, then you are probably balanced or semi-balanced. When this is the case, it is usually best to go quietly unless you have substantial high card values. The reason for this is that the only available bid for these hands is double. Partner, unless he has a weakish hand with a long suit, usually passes for want of a better action. This means that one notrump doubled is the contract and that most of your values are "onside" for declarer. You will need good hands to double because your side's points will carry less weight than under normal circumstances. This is the only case where you need a decent hand to reopen with a double, as compared to most suit-oriented auctions.

Unfortunately, in many reopening situations there are ethical considerations. Did partner flinch over the one notrump opening? Did he ask questions? Did he appear bored with the proceedings? Sad to say, there are many players, and some of them surprisingly good, who both

1. Demonstrate appropriate interest in their hand, depending on the values held, with the full expectation that partner will act accordingly.

2. They, and their partners, do act on the information.

Not everyone does this with malice, but the ones that do, do it very well.

Assuming that none of this behavior applies to anyone reading this, it is necessary to determine what double shows. In practice, it turns out you need about the same values as the opening bidder when they have opened a strong notrump, i.e. not less than 15 useful points. And when they have opened a weak notrump you need a little more than this announced minimum. I.e., if they show 12-14, you need a very good 13 or more. If they show 13-15, you need a very good 14 or more.

No one vul

1NT*-Pass-Pass-?

♠ K J 7   *15-17 HCP
♡ K J 4   A very minimal double. On the minus side is that all
◊ Q 10 7 6   your points are soft and may prove worthless. On the
♣ A J 3   plus side, whatever partner leads, you will like it. If partner has a five card suit, it should be easily established.

Vul vs. not

1NT*-Pass-Pass-?

♠ A Q 6 2   *15-17 HCP
♡ A K 6 3   This is worth a double, but you run the risk that part-
◊ K 5 4 2   ner will lead a club. A better action would be (on this
♣ 7   hand) Landy or Ripstra. I am not recommending any convention per se, but am pointing out that it is better to play than it is to defend. If partner were to have something like

♠ 10 7 4 3
♡ 10 5
◊ Q 6
♣ Q J 5 4 2

. . . then two spades would be a lock for +110 to +170 while one notrump doubled would result in anything from +100 to −380. Of course, if partner has something like

♠ 10 7   ♠ 10 2
♡ J 4 2   or worse,   ♡ 8 5
◊ J 9 6   ◊ Q J 8 3
♣ K J 8 4 2   ♣ Q J 8 6 5 4

. . . then one notrump doubled would be better than two hearts. Getting back to the hand in question, even though you have only four card suits to offer, it is better to try to play in one of them if your system permits it. Dummy play is always easier than defense.

If you don't have a convention to handle the combinations of suits you have, it is better to double than to guess which of your suits to bid. The advantage of a convention is that if offers a choice.

No one vul

1NT*-Pass-Pass-?

♠ A Q 10 7   *15-17 HCP
♡ A K 8 6   Double. Even if you have a convention to show the
◊ Q 10 2   majors, your hand is balanced. Partner may well lead a
♣ 4 3   club, but;

1. You have one to return, if you think that best.
2. Partner may lead something else.

One last comment here. I have already said that if your shape is useful, you should strive to reopen. With conventional understandings you can pursue this to some outrageous extremes.

No one vul

1NT-Pass-Pass-?

♠ A J 9 7
♡ K Q 10 6
◊ 10 9 6 5
♣ 3

Not unreasonable at all to bid two clubs for the majors. Your four card suits are strong and your shape excellent. Partner can choose from two suits and may well have four of one of them. Even if he has three only it may work out well. At IMPS, or if vulnerable, you could pass, but the idea of bidding with this hand would still be sound.

No one vul

1NT*-Pass-Pass-?

♠ A Q 8 3
♡ 7 6 5 4 2
◊ J 10 7
♣ 3

*15-17 HCP

Again, two clubs for the majors, if possible. Note that if partner has equal length in the majors, he will bid hearts. This means that on questionable hands, you must be well prepared for hearts, as partner will be more inclined to bid them. Compare the following.

1NT*-Pass-Pass-?

♠ A Q 8 3 2
♡ 7 6 5 4
◊ J 10 7
♣ 3

*15-17 HCP

If you bid two clubs, partner with J x x of both hearts and spades, will choose hearts. This just means that on close decisions, you should pass if you are likely to miss your best suit.

If it seems like I've been touting two clubs for the majors, it's only that it is an easy convention to use by way of example. Most of what I've discussed can be applied to other conventions as well. If you use other conventions and are happy with them, don't change. If you don't use a convention, then two clubs for the majors is a good one to start with. I suggest you try it. But conventions have drawbacks and if you don't wish to bother, it won't often make a difference.

How far can you go with all this?

Vul vs. not

1NT*-Pass-Pass-?

♠ 3
♡ Q 10 9 8 6 5
◊ J 10 6 5
♣ 4 2

*15-17 HCP

At matchpoints, two hearts would hardly be unreasonable. The only real dangers are that partner may get excited, or you may find partner with a totally unsuitable hand. Bidding is certainly worth these risks, however. At IMPs I would pass when vulnerable, but would bid otherwise.

No one vul

1NT*-Pass-Pass-?

♠ A J 10 3
♡ Q J 9 7
◊ 4 2
♣ 10 6 5

*15-17 HCP

Two clubs for the majors, if available, would be a good but aggressive matchpoint tactic. Vulnerable, or at IMPs, bidding would be a bit much, but the idea is sound.

Most of the examples so far have dealt with reopening after a strong notrump. This is because most players do use some strongish notrump range, i.e. 15-17, 16-18, or even an occasional 14-16. Precision players have ranges of 13-15 as do some "standard" players.

Against a 13-15 notrump, you should be slightly less inclined to reopen than after a strong notrump. The reason for this is that the partner of the weak notrumper almost always runs when he holds a bad hand. Experience has shown that it is better to escape with weak hands rather than to pass and let the opponents start doubling.

This means that when it goes 1NT (13-15), pass, pass, to you, RHO probably has a few values. You therefore need a little bit extra in addition to good distribution to justify reopening.

One other reason for passing includes the consideration that they may be in a poorish contract. Most of the other pairs playing a strong notrump will have been able to bid out their hands. Perhaps they have a major suit fit which has been missed.

If you want to add a conventional understanding, you can play that double of a weak notrump is for takeout, showing the majors. Now, two clubs will be natural. This is done on the theory that the opponents have some values, RHO would have bid with a yarborough, and therefore double for penalty is unlikely to occur.

An interesting chicken-egg syndrome occurs here. If your opponents know that a reopening double by you is for takeout (after 13-15 NT) then they might decide not to run. If you then knew that they wouldn't run prematurely, you might decide to play the reopening double for penalty. They, in turn, would redecide to run as per usual on bad hands, and you would consequently resurrect the takeout double. This could go on forever. Fortunately, it never seems to happen this way.

Chapter Three.
Reopening after both opponents have bid.

There are hundreds of different possible sequences where you might consider reopening, and it would be very difficult to consider them all as we did after a one level bid was passed out. All of these cases can be vaguely broken down however into two categories and a number of generalities made for each.

These cases are:
1. The opponents have a fit.
2. The opponents have no fit.

Case One. The Opponents Have a Fit.

Auctions like these show positive fits.

1♡	2♡	1♣	1♡	1♣	1◊
Pass		2♡	Pass	1♠	2♠

1♣	1♡
1NT	2♣

Auctions like the following do not show true fits and should be treated carefully.

1♡	1♠	1♣	1♡	1♡	1NT
2♣	2♡	1♠	2♣	2♣	2♡
Pass		2♡	Pass	Pass	

This last sequence tends to show a fit, but as it shows extra values, you should be cautious.

1♡	2♣
2◊	2♡
Pass	

On those sequences where your opponents have shown a fit and limited values, your attitude toward reopening should range from strongly inclined to obsessive. It is almost inexcusable to allow your opponents to play at the two level when they *want* to do so.

I can't really remember the last time I was allowed to play in two clubs or diamonds when we began with

1♣-Pass-2♣-Pass   or   1◊-Pass-2◊-Pass
Pass-?   Pass-?

These auctions are always the start of reopening sequences where everyone suddenly finds something to say.

These are typical auctions:

Pass-1♣-Pass-2♣
Pass-Pass-2♡-Pass   or
Pass-3♣-Pass-Pass
3♡-Pass-Pass-Pass

1◊-Pass-2◊-Pass
Pass-Dbl-Pass-2♡
Pass-Pass-3◊-Pass
Pass-3♡-Pass-Pass
Pass

29

Sometimes there is even more bidding, and at matchpoints the final contract is frequently doubled.

The sequence

1♡-Pass-2♡-Pass
Pass-?

. . . seldom ends the auction, but on occasion may be passed out. This is because there is only one unbid major, spades. It can be bid at the two level, and this frequently happens. The minors, however, must be bid at the three level, and this is a bit more dangerous.

The last sequence,

1♠-Pass-2♠-Pass
Pass

. . . is the only sequence in this family which is often passed out. This is because
1. You must reopen at the three level.
2. All suits are dangerous.

I've discussed the concept of "dangerous suits" before, and will again, because it is the basis for many competitive decisions.*

Dangerous suits can be generally defined. If responder raises his partner or bids 1NT, then all suits lower ranking than opener's are "dangerous" and all suits higher ranking are "safe."

After one spade by partner, all three of these hands would raise to two spades.

♠ K 8 2	♠ K 8 2	♠ K 8 2
♡ K J 8 7 6	♡ J 5 4	♡ 10 7
◇ J 5 4	◇ K J 8 7 6	◇ J 5 4
♣ 10 7	♣ 10 7	♣ K J 8 7 6

None of these hands has the values to bid the long suit. This means that there is the possibility that the raiser has a very good holding in a suit lower ranking than the one he has raised.

*Refer to my book *The Complete Book on Overcalls in Contract Bridge*, published by Max Hardy.

But if responder could show a higher ranking suit, he would probably do so, particularly if it was a major suit. After one club by partner, these hands would respond one heart or one spade rather than raise clubs:

♠ 9 3	♠ J 9 8 7
♡ K 10 8 6	♡ 7 6
◇ 7 6 3	◇ 10 5 4
♣ A 10 9 7	♣ A Q 9 7

This means that when it goes   1♣-Pass-2♣, 1◇-Pass-2◇, etc., responder will not have a higher ranking suit worth showing.

There are two exceptions, but in practice they are not too important.

After   1♣-Pass-2♣,   you should be slightly concerned about diamonds. Responder might have raised clubs in preference to mentioning diamonds.

♠ J 4 2
♡ 10 7
◇ K J 8 4
♣ A 10 8 7

After   1 ♡ -Pass-2 ♡ , spades are slightly suspect as responder might have raised hearts in preference to bidding one spade. He might have

♠ K 10 8 7 5
♡ K J 3
◇ 4 2
♣ 10 6 5

It would be good bridge to raise one heart rather than to bid a spade. If you bid one spade, you might have to give preference later to two hearts and partner won't know you have actively good hearts rather than a tepid doubleton;

1♡   1♠
2♣   2♡

. . . for example, could show

♠ Q 10 8 7 6
♡ 9 3
◇ A 10 5 4
♣ J 2

The reason I said that the danger of these two exceptions is minor is that most players automatically show their higher ranking suits, ignoring the raise. I think they are making a serious error, but you have to bid according to what actually happens, not what should happen.

No one vul
1♠-Pass-2♠-Pass
Pass-?

♠ K Q 8 7
♡ 5 4
◇ K 6 5 4
♣ 10 6 5

An automatic two spades. Your three clubs is not a bad holding because the opponents have raised. This suggests shortness in partner's hand and increases the chances that partner will hold spades. Double would be a serious error as it might induce partner to bid hearts at too high a level.

Both vul
1♠-Pass-2♠-Pass
Pass-?

♠ 10 7 6 5
♡ Q 10 8 4
◇ A 10 8 5
♣ 8

Double. When you have the right shape, you should probably reopen and then look at your hand. Note that all suits are available for partner at the two level. Even though you are vulnerable, you could do this with less. Passing out two clubs on this sequence would require a really bad hand.

No one vul
1♣-Pass-2♣-Pass
Pass-?

♠ K J 4
♡ Q 8 6 5
◇ K 6 5 4
♣ 10 2

Double again. With decent shape you have to get in there on any excuse. This is still not a minimum.

Vul vs. not
1♣-Pass-2♣-Pass
Pass-?

♠ K Q 2
♡ A 10 5
◇ Q 5 4
♣ 9 8 6 5

Even though holding four clubs, it is right to double. Partner is likely to have singleton club so unless he is 4-4-4-1, he will have a five card suit. Your values are all working and this will be a suitable dummy.

No one vul
1♣-Pass-2♣-Pass
Pass-?

♠ 10 7 6
♡ K J 4
◇ Q 6 5
♣ K J 6 5

Enough is enough. Here, much of your strength is wasted in clubs. With this distribution, you need your values where they will be useful to partner. Pass!

No one vul
1♣-Pass-2♣-Pass
Pass-?

♠ 10 7 6
♡ K 8 4
◇ A Q 10 6
♣ 8 6 4

Double again. Working values. When your shape is minimal, it is still usually right to double when you have the magic holding of three or four small in their suit.

No one vul
1♣-Pass-2♣-Pass
Pass-?

♠ 4 2
♡ Q J 8 7
◇ 7 6 5
♣ A 5 4 2

Two hearts. You almost surely have a fit. Note that when you reopen in a suit, you may well have length in their suit. Otherwise you might have reopened with double. One very important concept here is that you don't have to worry about missing suits as you did when reopening after a passed out one bid. If responder had four spades, he would have bid them rather than raise clubs. Therefore you can count on your partner to hold four of them. (Three maximum for responder. Four maximum in opener's hand, else he would have bid them. Two in your hand, and consequently four or more for partner.)

No one vul
1 ◊ -Pass-2 ◊ -Pass
Pass-?

♠ 8   Two hearts. Whenever you can reopen in a "safe"
♡ 10 8 7 6 5   suit, you need very little encouragement to do so.
◊ Q 4 2   Again, not to worry about where the spades are. Your
♣ A J 6 5   partner has five or more. This fact incidentally suggests
                    they aren't very good or he would have bid them. He is
marked for about 11 to 13 points, and would have bid with a good suit. This
means his values will be in hearts or clubs, which suits you fine.

Vul vs. not
1 ◊ -Pass-2 ◊ -Pass
Pass-?

♠ Q 9 2   Double. Three clubs would be terrible. This suit is
♡ Q 10 6   very "dangerous" so you shouldn't rush to bid it, espe-
◊ 4 2   cially at the three level. With adequate major suit hold-
♣ A Q 10 9 3   ings and better than a minimum, double is clearly right.
                    Note that on many hands where you reopen, you do
not really expect or even hope to buy the contract. All you want is to jack the
opponents up just one trick higher where your chances of defeating them are
improved.

No one vul
1 ◊ -Pass-2 ◊ -Pass
Pass-?

♠ K 2   This hand, in spite of its high cards is not clearly
♡ A 4 2   worth reopening. The "dangerous" suit concept means
◊ K 8 7   just that. The fact that you have a good hand doesn't do
♣ Q J 8 6 3   that much for your reopening potential because it just
                    means your partner has that much less. When the auc-
tion goes
1 ◊ -Pass-2 ◊ -Pass
Pass-?

. . . to you, you can be sure that their side has from 20 to 23 points and that your
side has from 17 to 20 points. That's a fact. When you have five points, partner
has at least 12. When you have 12, partner has at least five. It's a basic fact that
your side has a range of points. The only thing that you can tell when you person-
ally have a lot of points in the reopening seat is that your side may have the upper
range of the total possible points for your side, and you can tell whether the
points you have are working or wasted. The hand in question here has 13 points,
but the king of diamonds, even though worth a trick, is not as good a card as if it
were elsewhere. If partner has a stiff diamond, then you would have one diamond
loser with or without the king. This hand is about as good as you will ever have
in reopening seat, else you would bid earlier, but even so, the dangerous suit rule,
plus the diamond wastage, suggests a pass. At IMPs, it would be automatic.

Vul vs. vul
1 ◊ -Pass-2 ◊ -Pass
Pass-?

♠ Q 6 5
♡ K 5 4
◊ 3
♣ Q J 10 9 8 6

Even though clubs are dangerous, you can withstand most bad splits. All you need are a few useful high cards, and those are more or less guaranteed. As unsafe as three clubs was on the previous hand with 13 points, three clubs here on 8 points is automatic, certainly at matchpoints and probably at IMPs.

Vul vs. not
1 ◊ -Pass-2 ◊ -Pass
Pass-?

♠ 10
♡ Q 10 8 4
◊ 10 7 5
♣ A K J 9 7

Two hearts. This hand is very important. It demonstrates clearly the differences in safety when reopening in higher ranking suits as opposed to lower ranking suits. Given additionally that clubs must be bid a level higher, you should feel that two hearts is at least 20 times as preferable as three clubs.

No one vul
1 ♡ -Pass-2 ♡ -Pass
Pass-?

♠ Q 10 8 4
♡ 9 8 7
◊ K 2
♣ A 6 5 4

Two spades. On this sequence spades are slightly suspect, but the three little hearts are a definite plus. You should feel no qualms about this one.

Both vul
1 ♡ -Pass-2 ♡ -Pass
Pass-?

♠ 3
♡ 9 7 6 5
◊ K J 8 7
♣ A 10 5 4

Two notrump—unusual. This is extremely safe. Partner almost surely has a stiff heart, so he will have a four card or longer minor about 95% of the time. With his expected strength, this hand will produce a plus result almost every time. Note that even though both clubs and diamonds are dangerous, you are offering a choice of two suits, and one of them will be right.

Both vul
1 ◊ -Pass-2 ◊ -Pass
Pass-?

♠ 3
♡ K J 8 7
◊ 9 7 6 5
♣ A 10 5 4

This hand is identical to the previous hand. Theoretically, you could bid two notrump unusual for the lower ranking suits, but that would be silly. Hearts will be the right suit for your side nine times out of ten, so it is unnecessary to force your side to the three level just find the right suit. Why play three hearts when two is enough? Only when clubs is correct is it right to bid two notrump.

Both vul
1♡-Pass-2♡-Pass
Pass-?

♠ K 6 2
♡ 10 7
♢ J 10 7
♣ A Q 5 4 2

Double. When you have a stiff or doubleton in the opponents' suit, you reopen somehow.

No one vul
1♡-Pass-2♡-Pass
Pass-?

♠ 10 6 4
♡ K Q
♢ J 9 8 7
♣ K 6 5 4

As bad as this is, wasted hearts and all, it is right to double. Vulnerable, pass would be best, but not vulnerable, it is a reasonable action.

No one vul
1♡-Pass-2♡-Pass
Pass-?

♠ K Q 8 7
♡ 9 8 4
♢ J 10 7
♣ K J 5

Two spades. Your hearts suggest shortness in partner's hand so partner rates to have a few spades. It is better here to bid two spades than double, because a four-three spade fit will play better than a four-three minor suit contract.

Partner, with

♠ J 6 5
♡ Q 2
♢ Q 6 5 4
♣ A Q 6 4

. . . might bid an inspired two spades after you double, but he might reasonably bid three clubs. In fact, if he can count on you to bid spades on a good four card suit, then he won't have to make a brilliant guess and will always bid his minor suit on hands like this.

Vul vs. not
1♡-Pass-2♡-Pass
Pass-?

♠ K Q 6 4
♡ 3
♢ Q 10 6 5
♣ K 5 4 2

Double. No need to guess with two spades. You almost certainly have a fit unless partner is specifically 3-4-3-3, but you have no reason to believe your fit is in spades.

No one vul
1♡-Pass-2♡-Pass
Pass-?

♠ J 9 7
♡ Q 6 5
♢ K J 7
♣ A 10 9 3

A crummy matchpoint reopening double. This is done in the hope that the opponents carry on to three hearts. This is a good hand for you to remember when partner reopens with double after a similar sequence. Don't hang him.

No one vul
1♡-Pass-2♡-Pass
Pass-?

♠ 4 2   Another unusual two notrump. Here however, even
♡ 8 3   though holding nine minor suit cards, you don't have as
◊ K 10 7 6   much assurance of a fit as when you were 1-4-4-4 on an
♣ A 9 8 6 5   earlier hand also after 1♡-Pass-2♡. However, at
               matchpoints, you do want to get them higher. Being
able to offer a choice of two suits gives you a far greater degree of safety, even
though both suits are dangerous, than if you were merely reopening in one of
them. A normal matchpoint travesty.

No one vul
1♡-Pass-2♡-Pass
Pass-?

♠ 4 2   Even though you have only four card suits, your
♡ 8 7 6   three card heart holding implies a fit. While this fit may
◊ K Q 10 7   not be wonderful, the third heart is a strong factor in
♣ A J 9 8   judging your chances of finding one. With the good
               quality of your minor suits, this is a safe action situation
at any vulnerability. At IMPs, you might pass if vulnerable, but not otherwise.
Bid two notrump.

No one vul
1♡-Pass-2♡-Pass
Pass-?

♠ Q 2   No need to push a good thing into the ground. Pass. If
♡ Q 8 7   you can't stand it, then two notrump not vulnerable at
◊ Q J 8 7   matchpoints could work, but if it doesn't, don't tell . ⌐
♣ K 10 6 5   you got the idea here.

No one vul
1♡-Pass-2♡-Pass
Pass-?

♠ 10 6 5   Double. With adequate spade support, it would be
♡ 4 2   wrong to commit your side to a minor suit. In addition
◊ K Q 10 7   to the fact that you have spade tolerance you should be
♣ A Q 9 8   aware of how your doubleton heart affects partner's
               hand. When you had three hearts, you could count on
partner's being short, and consequently having more cards in the other suits.
When you have a doubleton heart however, there is no such guarantee. Your
partner may well have three hearts, thus reducing his length in other suits. With
the hand here, the odds on finding partner with a four card minor are less than
half as good as when you held three hearts.
    Now and then, you will run into opponents who play four card majors, and in
balancing situations you will have to be aware of this. These players will quite
correctly raise one heart to two hearts with three trumps. And if this gets passed
around to you, you will have to consider that they may be in a four-three fit. This
means that if you have three of their suit, partner will not always have the shortness you would expect. Partner might also have three. And if you have two, partner may have four.

Now just because they play four card majors does not always mean they have them, and when they bid one heart-pass-two hearts, they may have a five-three fit or a five-four fit just like anyone else. But there is the danger that it is a four-three. This means you must tighten up just a bit against those pairs when reopening. Many players look down on four card major players, but they shouldn't. Perhaps they lose a bit in science but they more than hold their own in the rough and tumble infighting. Reopening against them is one of the more difficult problems presented by their style. Getting back to hands.

No one vul

1♠-Pass-2♠-Pass
Pass-?

♠ 3 2
♡ A J 7 6
◊ K 4 2
♣ Q 10 6 5

A matchpoint double. When the auction starts

1♠-Pass-2♠-Pass
Pass-?

. . . you must be impressed with the earlier mentioned dangers. All suits are dangerous, and they must be bid at the three level. You will still be able to count on partner for certain values, and some of the time you can count on him for good distribution, but you will never be able to count on him to have length in any particular unbid suit. Therefore, reopening doubles can reasonably be made as before, with adjustments for the fact that you are automatically at the three level. But, you will have to be very cautious indeed about trying a suit. This hand has minimal but acceptable shape and values to qualify for a double.

Not vul vs. vul

1♠-Pass-2♠-Pass
Pass-?

♠ 10 6 4
♡ Q J 6 4 2
◊ K 7 6
♣ K 2

A dangerous matchpoint three heart bid. Refer to this auction (page 33)

1◊-Pass-2◊-Pass
Pass-?

On this sequence, clubs are guaranteed to be dangerous. Note the difference after

1♠-Pass-2♠-Pass
Pass-?

Hearts are dangerous in that the raiser may have them. But he doesn't have to have them. He may have clubs or diamonds instead. But the player who raises one diamond to two diamonds denies hearts and spades, and he denies a balanced hand, so what's left is some clubs.

With the hand here, hearts are somewhat suspect, but not for sure. Your holding of three spades suggests a fit so optimism here is okay.

Vul vs. vul

1♠-Pass-2♠-Pass
Pass-?

♠ 4 2
♡ K Q 8 6 5
◊ K 7 6
♣ K 4 2

Scary. A better hand and a better suit than the previous hand, but you are vulnerable and have no particular reason to expect a fit. Double is dangerous because it runs the risk of playing a four-three minor suit fit instead of a five-three heart fit. And three hearts runs the serious risk of finding only one or two hearts. The extra length in spades is really very important in determining your chances of a fit. At IMPs, it would be a terrible reopening action of any sort. At matchpoints, perhaps. But your victories will be small ones and your disasters enormous.

Vul vs. vul

1 ♠ -Pass-2 ♠ -Pass
Pass-?

♠ 3	When your shape is good, anything goes because you
♡ Q 8 6 5	can always count on partner for certain point values.
◇ K 5 4 2	Here he has a good hand and will have at least a four
♣ K 10 6 5	card suit for you except when he is specifically 4-3-3-3

or, and God help you, if he is 5-3-3-2 when the opponents are playing four card majors. Maybe it won't be so bad after all. Partner may elect to pass and perhaps you can beat them. For whatever it's worth, you don't have to worry too much about their spade suit being four cards long. Hearts will be opened with four far more often by four card majorites than spades.

No one vul

1 ♠ -Pass-2 ♠ -Pass
Pass-?

♠ 8 6 2	Double is reasonable. When you have no values
♡ K J 7	wasted in their suit, and adequate support for all suits, it
◇ A 5 4 2	is okay to act. Partner is short in spades thus increasing
♣ K 7 6	the chance that partner has a five card suit.

Vul vs. not

1 ♠ -Pass-2 ♠ -Pass
Pass-?

♠ Q 7	Dangerous to bid here because you have the wasted
♡ 10 5 4	spade queen and you have poor hearts, which is the suit
◇ A J 7 5	partner will bid given a choice.
♣ K J 4 3	When you have cards like the spade queen which are

worthless, you have to feel that you are playing with a 38 point deck rather than the usual forty. The spade queen is not doing you any good but it is a card the opponents don't have. They will still have their 21 or so points and partner will have his eight. If you didn't have the spade queen, you could count on partner for ten, and you could hope for none of them to be wasted. On the actual hand, you know you have that card. Better to pass on this minimum and try to beat them.

Both vul

1 ♠ -Pass-2 ♠ -Pass
Pass-?

♠ Q 3	Double is okay because you have assured values.
♡ K J 7	Even with the spade queen demoted, your other cards
◇ A 6 5 4	are prime and you have a good three card holding in
♣ K 10 6 5	hearts. When you have a good hand like this one, it

does not mean your side has a lot of values. But it does mean that given the auction, your side is apt to have the maximum of the range available to it.

No one vul
1♠-Pass-2♠-Pass
Pass-?

♠ 8 6 5 4   Three clubs is automatic. You have the assurance of a
♡ 3   fit and a good suit, plus partner is marked for a good
◇ 4 2   hand. He is probably just shy of a hand worth a takeout
♣ K J 10 8 7 6   double of two spades. Passing here would be criminal.

No one vul
1♠-Pass-2♠-Pass
Pass-?

♠ 3   Two notrump unusual. The shape is right, so you
♡ J 2   really don't need any high cards to speak of. Partner has
◇ K 10 7 6 5   those, and it only remains for him to produce a three
♣ A 5 4 3 2   card minor. Both minor suits are dangerous here, and
                   your spade holding doesn't suggest partner has either,
but he should have three in one or the other. It is so much safer when you can
offer a choice.

One important aside here. I've been allowed on occasion to play in two hearts
or spades after the example sequence on hands where I had no business playing
there. It was the opponents' hand clear and simple, but for some reason no one
reopened. After the result was in, one of my opponents made a comment along
the lines of "I would have bid, but I was afraid they would bid a game." This is an
example of negative thinking of the worst kind.

Of all the guarantees I can give you, when your opponents bid one of something, pass, two of the same something, pass, pass to you, they can not make a
game. One of the easiest things to do is evaluate your hand after you have found
a fit, and even the least experienced player pretty well understands what a game
contract requires.

What happens is that many people fail to reopen against good players, and that
is the worst of all. I absolutely promise that no capable player has ever failed to
bid after a raise if he has the slightest inkling that he has a game. Only against the
most naive, inexperienced and conservative person who is known as such, should
you not reopen, and then only on questionable hands.

Against good players, if your hand says reopen, then do so! Here's a profes-
sional tip for you. If a good player thinks before passing after partner's raise, he
may well be doing it for your benefit. This is not well thought of, but some, and I
emphasize, *some* do this to scare you out of reopening. Or perhaps they had a
bad hand and were considering bidding three as a preempt. The one thing you
can be sure of is that they can't make a game.

Vul vs. not
1♠-Pass-2♠-Pass
Pass-?

♠ 10 6 4   With good chances of a fit and decent cards, try two
♡ 3   notrump. Note that when you are offering a choice of
◇ K Q 6 4   suits, partner with equal length will chose the lower
♣ K 10 6 5 4   suit. If partner has three each in diamonds and clubs, he
                   will bid clubs. On this hand, you will have arrived in
                   the best suit. See next hand.

Vul vs. not

1♠-Pass-2♠-Pass
Pass-?

♠ 10 6 4	Best to bid three diamonds rather than two notrump.
♡ 3	See previous hand. You don't want to play a four-three
◊ A Q J 8 3	club fit in preference to a five-three diamond fit. The
♣ J 9 6 5	holding of three spades says you probably have a fit,

and a bid of three diamonds is a reasonable try. If you
had two-two in the majors, you would try two notrump because you would not
have as much expectation of a diamond fit. And if your clubs and diamonds were
reversed, you would bid two notrump. All of these distributions should be
reopened at matchpoints, but at IMPs, it gets questionable. I think I would
reopen with two notrump at IMPs when holding

> ♠ 10 6 4
> ♡ 3
> ◊ J 9 6 5
> ♣ A Q J 8 3

. . . because I know I will be in the best suit, but only when not vulnerable.

No one vul

1♠-Pass-2♠-Pass
Pass-?

♠ Q 2	This is typical of reopening disasters. There is so
♡ Q 8 7	much wrong with this hand. Assume you are
◊ A K J 6 5	considering three diamonds. Here are the dangers. First,
♣ J 5 4	you have a doubleton spade. Now that is not bad in

itself, but it is a much better holding when you are
considering a takeout double than when you are consid-
ering bidding a suit. Two spades does not give you any reason to expect a fit in
any specific suit, in this case diamonds. Diamonds is a dangerous suit and bidding
it is a committal action which must be right. If you hear a double, you will go
down, probably badly.

Second, you have the spade queen. This is significant, because your side won't
have so many values that you can afford many of them to be wasted. Third, you
have only a five card suit. It is a good one, but you would like another card in it.
With a spade lead, you may be subject to an early tap, which you won't appreciate. This is one of the advantages of three cards in the opponents' suit. Then
when you bid a suit, you can hope for a fit, and your dummy will be able to take
the tap rather than you.

Fourth, your other cards are soft. The heart queen and club jack are questionable. And last, you are reopening at the three level where good opponents will be
pleased to punish an indiscretion. The objection to double is that you still have
the wasted spade queen, and you have really poor support for two of the suits
partner will bid, including the one he is most likely to bid, hearts.

The next set of sequences to consider is those where the opponents have bid
two or more suits before finding a fit. Auctions such as:

1♣ 1♠	1♡ 1♠	1♣ 1♡
2♠ Pass	1NT 2♡	1♠ 2♠
	Pass	Pass

Against sequences like these, you will wish to reopen as often as possible just as during the sequences already discussed. The usual rule applies. If they want to play it where they are, don't let them.

There are, however, a few new considerations and, perforce, new problems. First, on some of these sequences there will be fewer suits available for your side. On occasion, you will have only one. This seriously cuts down on your flexibility. Second, you must always consider where the opposing strength lies. If opener is on your left, then your values may not be worth as much as if opener is on your right.

There's one constant in all this. When you choose to reopen in a suit, you will be on lead if the opponents compete in the same suit. You don't have to worry particularly about getting partner off to the wrong lead.

Let's see how all this affects your decisions.

No one vul

1♣-Pass-1♡-Pass
2♡-Pass-Pass-?

♠ K 8 7 6
♡ Q 6 2
◇ K Q J 8
♣ 10 7

With four cards in both unbid suits, you should reopen almost without regard to the rest of your hand. True, you have the wasted queen of hearts, but you will find that when the opponents have bid two suits, you frequently have one or more questionable cards. An additional point here is that partner can bid spades at the two level. Double.

Vul vs. not

1◇-Pass-1♡-Pass
2♡-Pass-Pass-?

♠ K J 7
♡ 9 7 6 5
◇ 4 2
♣ A J 10 7

Very reasonable to double. Even though you hold only three spades, the ones you have are good and partner can bid them at the two level. It would be very ostrichlike to pass on the theory that you have four hearts. This hand is so good that you should almost feel that the hand belongs to your side. You have only pure working values and if your partner has any diamond strength, it will be working as well. Don't worry that you are vulnerable.

No one vul

1♣-Pass-1♡-Pass
2♡-Pass-Pass-?

♠ A J 10 7
♡ 6 5 4 2
◇ K J 7
♣ 6 5

As clear as it was to double with the previous hand, it is equally clear to bid two spades here. One thing you must avoid at all costs is doubling with three cards in a lower ranking suit. Partner will bid them at the three level. If at all possible, do something else. Here two spades is a standout. Partner has short hearts and a spade fit. Incidentally, if you feel you might have overcalled with one spade on the previous round, that would have been a sound action.

No one vul

1 ◊ -Pass-1 ♠ -Pass
2 ♠ -Pass-Pass-?

♠ 3   This hand presents a question of theory. If double
♡ J 2   shows clubs and hearts here, perhaps two notrump
◊ K J 9 8 7   should show the minors in spite of the fact that opener
♣ A 10 9 5 4   bid diamonds. If so, it is one of the few cases in which
                      you can employ a takeout bid to show a suit previously
bid by an opponent. Whether or not you should do this is another question. I
would because I don't like allowing my opponents to play at the two level. Especially so here because their spades aren't breaking for them. They will score well
for having been allowed to play at the two level.

Both vul

1 ♣ -Pass-1 ♠ -Pass
2 ♣ -Pass-Pass-?

♠ Q 8   Far too dangerous. Wasted black suit cards plus being
♡ K 10 8 7   at the three level dictates a pass.
◊ Q 10 6 5
♣ K 6 4

No one vul

1 ◊ -Pass-1 ♡ -Pass
2 ♡ -Pass-Pass-?

♠ K 8 7   Still a takeout double. The concept of dangerous suits
♡ 4 2   continues to apply. Your RHO who bid one heart has
◊ 8 7 6   shown a limited hand else he would have continued
♣ A Q 10 8 7   over two hearts. This places his hand in the category
                      that wasn't worth a two over one. If he had four hearts
and five clubs, his response would be one heart rather than two clubs. While his
auction doesn't guarantee clubs, it doesn't deny them either and you should avoid
three level action if something else will do. Remember, it is the suit or suits under
opener's suit which are dangerous when responder shows limited values.

No one vul

1 ◊ -Pass-1 ♡ -Pass
2 ♡ -Pass-Pass-?

♠ K J 8 7   Regardless of your values, you know that your side
♡ ?   has around 19 points. Whatever you have, partner has
◊ ?   the rest. With the spade suit given here, you should
♣ 10 2   always bid two spades unless your hand is truly horri-
                      ble. Even with a lesser spade suit, you should be inclined
to bid them. Remember, when your opponents can play in a voluntarily bid two
level contract on a four-four fit, they are going to get a good result every time,
assuming their bidding and play are remotely sane.

Not vul vs. vul

1 ◊ -Pass-1 ♠ -Pass
2 ♠ -Pass-Pass-?

♠ J 8 7
♡ K Q 10 8 7
◊ 3 2
♣ K Q 5

♠ J 8 7
♡ K Q 5
◊ 3 2
♣ K Q 10 8 7

Reopening at the three level as opposed to reopening with a double is as always a very dangerous action. However, when the opponents have bid two suits, one of those left over for you may not be considered as "dangerous." On this sequence, clubs would be considered dangerous, and hearts safe. I don't mean to say that three hearts is a safe bid, but it is safer than three clubs would be on the second of these two hands.

Another important point of this hand is that the opponents' auction does not guarantee an eight card fit. It is entirely reasonable for opener to raise on three. There is the distinct possibility your partner also has three spades. Not a good combination. Had their auction been 1 ♠ -Pass-2 ♠, then this would be a far less serious danger.

If you are vulnerable, you should not reopen with hands such as these. If you feel you must, do so with confidence. Reopening sequences are delicate things and if you squirm around before eking out a bid, you will be telling the world you don't have it.

Vul vs. vul

1 ♣ -Pass-1 ♠ -Pass
2 ♠ -Pass-Pass-?

♠ A 9 6 4
♡ 4 2
◊ Q J 9 8 7 6
♣ 3

You won't reopen vulnerable at the three level very often. When you do, it will be based on knowledge of a fit rather than that you have a bunch of points with some random suit. This hand is typical of what you will have for a three level action.

Vul vs. vul

1 ♣ -Pass-1 ♠ -Pass
2 ♠ -Pass-Pass-?

♠ 3
♡ 4 2
◊ Q J 9 8 7 6
♣ A 9 6 4

You could try three diamonds here, but you should feel that the value of this hand is at least two tricks worse than the previous hand. This hand promises no particular fit, so you may have quite a few trump losers, and you will have to deal with three potential club losers. The prior hand suggested a diamond fit, so you might have only the ace and king of diamonds to lose, and you can expect to get rid of your spade losers by ruffing them.

No one vul

1 ♣ -Pass-1 ♡ -Pass
1NT-Pass-2 ♣ -Pass
Pass-?

♠ Q 10 8 7
♡ K 2
◊ J 10 6 5
♣ A 4 3

This is a curious little auction in that it is the only one where the opponents have a guaranteed fit which did not include an immediate raise. As reopener, you should treat this auction as if it had gone:

1 ♣ -Pass-2 ♣ -Pass
Pass-?

. . . except that hearts is no longer a consideration. Responder has shown exactly the values for a 1♠-Pass-2♠ raise except that along the way he elected to show a four card or longer heart suit. Opener has limited his hand by his one notrump rebid, so you are facing two limited hands.

This hand is clearly worth a takeout double, and under no circumstances should it be interpreted as for penalties. You have the required length in both unbid suits and your values are all working. Do not discount that heart king. LHO has announced a weak hand so there is no reason to feel the heart king is wasted. This hand without the king of hearts would still be worth a double. Note that LHO has bid two suits so is unlikely to have much length in one of the other two. Also, opener did not rebid one spade, which tends to deny a four card holding. The chances here are very good that partner has length in spades.

Not vs. vul

1◇-Pass-1♠-Pass
1NT-Pass-2◇-Pass
Pass-?

♠ 4
♡ A 10 6
◇ 9 5 4
♣ K 10 9 6 4 2

Had the bidding gone

1◇-Pass-2◇-Pass
Pass-?

. . . you would have felt that clubs was a dangerous suit and hearts a safe one. In the hand above though, responder has shown length in two suits, so is unlikely to have a good holding in a third. Therefore, on this sequence it is far safer to try these clubs than after 1◇-Pass-2◇. It may not work, but your chances are worthwhile.

No one vul

1◇-Pass-1♠-Pass
1NT-Pass-2◇-Pass
Pass-?

♠ 4 2
♡ A 10 6 5
◇ 10 5 3
♣ K 10 5 3

You should very much want to reopen on this auction, and this hand qualifies, even at IMPs.

Vul vs. not

1♣-Pass-1♡-Pass
1NT-Pass-2♣-Pass
Pass-?

♠ K J 8 7
♡ A 6 5 2
◇ K 3
♣ 9 7 2

Two spades. When the opponents have a fit, it is always safe to reopen with two spades regardless of how the bidding has gone. This doesn't mean you bid without looking, i.e. you really ought to have some spades for this bid, but it is a rare hand with four spades that shouldn't reopen in some fashion. On some hands with four spades, you should double when holding other unbid suits as well. The important thing is that the presence of those four spades means you should reopen.

44

No one vul
1 ◊ -Pass-1 ♡ -Pass
1NT-Pass-2 ◊ -Pass
Pass-?

♠ 10 6 5 4   This is probably a little bit nervy, but two spades
♡ A 6 5   could well be the winning action. You arrive at this con-
◊ A 9 5   clusion by following the rule to reopen when holding
♣ J 8 2   four spades after the opponents have shown a "fit."
With this quality suit, you would prefer something else;
but, J 8 2 isn't such a good holding that you would want to offer clubs as an alternative. Note also that when you reopen on such a suit, you need all your values
to be working. This is a typical non-vulnerable matchpoint insanity. Do it confidently though and it will either work or be right a large number of times.

No one vul
1 ◊ -Pass-1 ♠ -Pass
1NT-Pass-2 ◊ -Pass
Pass-?

♠ Q 8 2   On this sequence, opener was denied the chance to
♡ J 9 7 5   rebid a four card heart suit. This, plus the crummy heart
◊ K J 4   suit, plus the wastage in spades and diamonds dictates a
♣ A 10 8   pass.
Note that on auctions where the opponents have
found a fit, a four card heart holding of itself does not suggest reopening as
strongly as does possession of a four card spade suit.

No one vul
1 ♣ -Pass-1 ♡ -Pass
1 ♠ -Pass-2 ♣ -Pass
Pass-?

When the opponents have had a three suited auction, you won't want to
reopen on very many hands. Only when spades is the unbid suit will you be able
to bid at the two level. If you are thinking of a three level action it will almost certainly be on a hand where you have strong reason to expect a fit. If the auction
doesn't suggest a fit, then you should forget it. Perhaps you should have overcalled earlier?

No one vul
1 ♣ -Pass-1 ◊ -Pass
1 ♡ -Pass-2 ♡ -Pass
Pass-?

♠ K Q 8 6   Probably acceptable to bid two spades. This is the
♡ 4 2   only sequence where you can bid at the two level after a
◊ 4 3 2   three suited auction and your suit perforce is spades.
♣ K 10 7 6   Most likely, if your suit were any good you would have
bid it earlier, so partner should not expect too much
from you.
It is important for you to note the differences among these three sequences:

1 ♠ -Pass-2 ♠

Your opponents will have an eight card fit whenever they are playing five card
majors, and a fair amount of the time when they are playing four card majors.

45

1♣-Pass-1♠-Pass
2♠-

Your opponents will have at least an eight card fit about 80% of the time. Theorists may disagree with this figure, but it is a practical guess. The important point here is that on sequences such as this, there is a decent chance they have only a seven card fit, which you should consider when estimating partner's holding in their suit.

1♣-Pass-1♡-Pass
1♠-Pass-2♠-Pass
Pass

They will have exactly a four-four fit about 99% of the time. It is very useful to recognize what sort of fit they are likely to have because it will be a key factor on close decisions.

Case Two. Reopening When the Opponents Have No Fit.

These auctions can be broken down into three common types. They are:
1. They have ended in one notrump.
2. They have a pseudo fit where someone has taken a preference.
3. They have no fit, someone having rebid his suit.

1. *The Opponents Have Ended in One Notrump.*

When the opponents have settled in one notrump, it is a little bit dangerous to reopen. They won't have an established fit which is the usual motivation for you to reopen, and you will be forcing your side to the two level when you bid. Auctions ending in one notrump tend to suggest more that your opponents are bidding on high cards, than "fit" auctions such as 1♡-Pass-2♡, so you will have less chance of finding partner with a few extra high cards.

All of this means that you will get doubled more often and more effectively than in other reopening sequences so far discussed. When deciding when to reopen in a suit, you will want to give extra attention to the "safe suit," "dangerous suit" concept.

Lastly, a problem of definition. If you double, should it be for penalty or should it be takeout?

No one vul

1♢-Pass-1NT-Pass
Pass-?

♠ Q J 8 6 5   Conceptually, you could try two spades, as the suit is
♡ Q 4 2   safe. However, when you have any sort of suit worth
♢ 10 7 6   bidding, you may feel that your defensive potential
♣ A 3   should sway you in that direction. Note that you won't
have much of a suit as you would have made a one level overcall the round before. I would say that you would want to pass most balanced hands on this sequence. Should you choose to bid, you do promise a five card suit. Note that responder denies a major suit and rates to have length in clubs.

No one vul

1♣-Pass-1NT-Pass
Pass-?

♠ Q 10 6 4 2
♡ 3
◇ A J 7
♣ 9 6 5 4

When LHO bids one notrump rather than a suit, he tends to have a club fit. Two spades here is safe. You would probably reopen with two spades regardless of the opening bid, but you should be happy to do so after one club, pleased to do so after one diamond, and apprehensive after one heart.

No one vul
1♡-Pass-1NT-Pass
Pass-?

♠ K 7
♡ J 2
◇ Q J 9 8 7
♣ K J 10 7

So risky to reopen in a "dangerous" suit that you should not bother unless it is just too obvious to do so. For this to be the case, you will probably need a six card suit. If you have the suit, you won't have much else or you would have overcalled.

Vul vs. vul
1♡-Pass-1NT-Pass
Pass-?

♠ 3
♡ K 6 5
◇ A J 9 8 6 4
♣ Q 7 5

Here you have the prerequisite suit, good shape, and reasonably working values. And two diamonds is still not all that safe. You should bid it because it will be right more often than not, even at IMPs, but your bad results will be impressive. Any time you catch partner with a stiff diamond, you will be in trouble. And why shouldn't this happen? Partner has at least five spades, or someone would have bid them. And he may have four hearts if LHO has a stiff. There's no reason why partner's last four cards should include two diamonds and two clubs rather than one diamond and three clubs. Given that you have six diamonds and three clubs, the chances of finding partner with only one diamond are significant.

No one vul
1♣-Pass-1♡-Pass
1NT-Pass-Pass-?

♠ J 8 7 6 5
♡ A Q 2
◇ K 4 3
♣ 8 6

Two spades at matchpoints. Once again, you usually won't have too much to reopen with. If you have a suit higher ranking than RHO's, you might already have bid it. Note that RHO can still have four spades. There is nothing about this sequence that guarantees you will find spade support.

Diamonds on this sequence would not be excessively dangerous but there is the chance that RHO might have skipped over that suit in order to respond one heart. There isn't really too much to this except to say that you would like to have some distribution when you elect to reopen. There won't be many hands where you can infer from your cards that partner fits your suit, so all you can expect from partner are certain values.

No one vul
1♦-Pass-1♥-Pass
1NT-Pass-Pass-?

♠ J 10 8 6 5
♥ A 9 6 5 4
♦ 3
♣ Q 2

This hand implies short hearts in partner's hand, so two spades becomes a reasonable shot.

No one vul
1♦-Pass-1♥-Pass
1NT-Pass-Pass-?

♠ J 10 8 6 5
♥ A 9 6 5
♦ 3 2
♣ Q 2

This hand is far removed in value from the previous one. Your partner may hold as many as three hearts. There is therefore less chance of a fit. Adding the small diamond has given you an additional loser to replace the potentially winning long heart. And if partner has an extra heart, it may be at the expense of a spade. One more possible loser. The prior hand was a safe two spades. This one is a risky two spades under any circumstances. Not vulnerable at matchpoints you might try it with the usual caution.

No one vul
1♥-Pass-1♠-Pass
1NT-Pass-Pass-?

♠ 4 2
♥ K 8 7
♦ Q J 8 6 5 4
♣ K 2

Suits lower than opener's remain dangerous. It is expecially so when your opponents are bidding major suits. If either had a fit for the other, they would show it rather than rush to notrump. They might suppress minor suit support to bid notrump, but not major suit support. Your heart king is suspect. Good to pass.

Finally, the question of double. What does it mean when your opponents have settled in one notrump and someone reopens with double?

There are two possibilities here. First, double can be for takeout, showing the unbid suits. And second, it can be penalty oriented showing strength in the suit bid on the doubler's right.

Seems like a simple choice, yet very few partnerships are on firm ground about this, which is unfortunate. Double should have some definition. Random guessing is not the answer.

Should double be for takeout?

Probably not, and for quite a few reasons.

1. The opponents have not found a fit so you have no reason to expect that you have one.
2. If you have the shape for a reopening double, you won't have very good values or you would have acted earlier.
3. You will always be competing at the two level.
4. In addition to the fact that you are competing against a misfit sequence, your combined hands will not play particularly well. Your shortness in RHO's suit will be matched by your partner's length.

1 ♡ -Pass-1NT-Pass
Pass-?

♠ K 4 3 2   Here is a hand with the best of all worlds: excellent
♡ 3   distribution, nothing wasted in hearts, and maximum
♢ A 6 5 4   high cards. In fact, some would have doubled one heart
♣ K 10 8 7   the round before. Yet with all of this going for you, your
                   chances of having something happen are marginal.
    Here is the key. The opponents have denied a heart fit. They almost certainly
do not have eight of them. This means your partner has at least five hearts and
may have more. If he has only five, there's the danger that he is 5-3-3-2 in which
case you will be playing a four-three fit at the two level. Theoretically, a hand
with a five card suit will be 5-3-3-2 only 36% of the time. But when the bidding
goes

1 ♡ -Pass-1NT-Pass
Pass

it is reasonable to assume that opener is balanced, and responder probably so.
This implies that in practice, partner will have the 5-3-3-2 hand far more often
than 36% of the time.
    Even if you find a four-four fit, it won't be easy to play it. When partner tries to
ruff hearts in your hand, he will be overruffed by the one notrump bidder. The
strength of your singleton heart will prove to be an illusion.
    What all this means is that even if you should happen to have a hand with the
ideal shape for a takeout double, the chances of getting a good result are not
nearly as worthwhile as you might have hoped for.
    The alternative is to play that the reopening double is for penalty. You have a
hand with good strength in RHO's suit and an otherwise useful hand as well.

No one vul

1 ♡ -Pass-1NT-Pass
Pass-?

♠ 8 2   Double would be very reasonable if intended as pen-
♡ K J 9 7   alty. If there were no partnership agreement, then dou-
♢ A Q 10 4   ble would run the risk of causing partner to bid spades.
♣ A 6 3   If partner understands that double is primarily for busi-
                   ness, and he still bids spades, you needn't worry because
                   you won't have promised him any.

Both vul

1 ♣ -Pass-1 ♡ -Pass
1NT-Pass-Pass-?

♠ K 3   Double could be worth a bundle to your side. Note
♡ A J 10 8 5   the eight of hearts. If your hearts were A J 10 4 2, you
♢ A 10 5 4   would have far less chance of bringing the suit home
♣ 9 3   defensively.

No one vul

1 ♢ -Pass-1 ♠ -Pass
1NT-Pass-Pass-?

♠ A K 4 2   Pass. Your spade holding is not of the sort you want
♡ K 8 6 5   when you make a penalty double. You want to have sec-
♢ K 4 2   ondary tricks in the suit which will be developed by the
♣ 10 7   lead. Here you have two fast tricks, but no deep poten-

tial. Your diamond king is possibly of no value. Best go quietly.

Vul vs. not

1♦-Pass-1♠-Pass
1NT-Pass-Pass-?

♠ Q J 10 8 3
♡ A 8 4
◇ A J 7
♣ 8 3

A good double. With a spade lead, you rate to develop six tricks. No reason to feel that partner won't be able to contribute something. He ought to have from five to eight points. Perhaps he has a spade honor.

No one vul

1♣-Pass-1♡-Pass
1♠-Pass-1NT-Pass
Pass-?

♠ Q J 9 7
♡ 3 2
◇ A Q 4
♣ K J 9 7

Whether you agree with double or not, it should clearly be for business. Why pass twice and then make a takeout double for one suit? This is typical of what you might have. Strength in both the RHO's suits and a decent hand. Partner may well have hearts stopped. One notrump doubled could go for quite a few tricks even though they have more than half the deck.

My own feeling is that the potential for a large penalty by playing penalty doubles far outweighs the occasional partscore gain you may earn by playing double for takeout. Fortunately, there is a solution for you if you can't decide how you want to play it. You can have it both ways. Play that double is either for takeout or for penalty, and leave it to partner to look at his hand and decide which it is. If he has length in the suit bid on his left, then you must be short so your double is takeout. And conversely, if he has one or two of them, you have length so are making a penalty double.

1♡-Pass-1NT-Pass
Pass-Dbl-Pass-?

♠ J 8 6 2
♡ K 7 6 5 2
◇ K 2
♣ Q 8

Your length in hearts tells you partner has made a takeout double. Bid two spades.

1♡-Pass-1NT-Pass
Pass-Dbl-Pass-?

♠ Q 10 6 5 4
♡ 3 2
◇ K 6 5
♣ J 9 5

Partner should have good hearts, else responder would have raised, so his double is business. Do not bid two spades. Partner has not requested you to bid. Be happy you have a few points and expect to set one notrump doubled.

1♣-Pass-1♡-Pass
1NT-Pass-Pass-Dbl
Pass-?

♠ 4 2
♡ Q 10 8 6 5
◇ A 8 6 5
♣ 7 6

Your heart length says partner is short in hearts. It is a takeout double. Bid two diamonds. You should be pleased to have a good four card suit to bid. You could have had one less diamond and one more club.

1♠-Pass-1♡-Pass
1NT-Pass-Pass-Dbl
Pass-?

♠ J 7 6 5   Again, your short hearts implies partner is making a
♡ 4 2   penalty double. Pass. One nice thing about this hand is
◊ Q 8 7   your good club holding. Partner is hoping you have
♣ K 10 6 5   some club strength and you do. Something like 9 8 5 4 2
would be a disappointment to partner.

Some players may not wish to risk the ambiguity of double and there is a convention for them too. It is called the "two club reopening after dead notrump." All that this pretentious name means is that when the opponents have stopped in one notrump, two clubs is like a takeout double and double is for penalty.

I don't like this for a number of reasons. You lose the ability to reopen with two clubs when you really do have clubs. And you lose the chance to play in one notrump doubled when partner would have decided to convert your takeout double to penalties by passing. And it's easily forgotten.

The one clear thing about reopening after one notrump is that you shouldn't rush to do it. If it is not clear cut, don't bother.

2. *Reopening After the Opponent's Auction Ends With a Preference.*

When the opponents have arrived at two of a suit after a preference has been taken, you will not want to be all that busy about reopening. This is based on the theory that when the opponents have a fit, you should have one as well, and whenever convenient you should try to find it. But when the opponents don't have a fit, it is often best to let them stew in whatever contract they have achieved. Why balance into a marginal contract of your own when theirs was no better?

The problem you face is to determine how good their fit really is. Here are some basic preference auctions and what you might estimate that they mean.

1♡-Pass-1♠-Pass   Very often a doubleton heart. Frequently a doubleton
2♣-Pass-2♡-Pass   club as well. This suggests a misfit for them. Perhaps
Pass   responder has diamonds as well as spades, but insufficient strength to bid them. On this three suit sequence, there is only one remaining unbid suit.

1♡-Pass-1NT-Pass   If the one notrump is not forcing, then the two heart
2♣-Pass-2♡-Pass   bid usually shows two hearts and not more than three
Pass   clubs. A misfit auction.

If the one notrump is forcing, then the two heart bid still shows two hearts, but responder may hold up to four clubs. The reason he didn't pass two clubs was that opener might have had only three of them. (The forcing notrump requires opener to rebid his lowest three card minor if he hasn't a four card suit to show). Once in a while responder will have three hearts, but a somewhat poor hand which didn't want to pass one heart and which didn't want to encourage with two hearts. Some of these system players use this sequence routinely with three hearts and if they do you should be informed by them.

1♠-Pass-1◊-Pass   This last sequence is a preference sequence, but it has
1♡-Pass-2♣-Pass   some unusual qualities. It is the one auction where
Pass   responder increases the level of the bidding to take his preference. He has alternative bids of one spade or one notrump. Had opener rebid one spade himself, then responder would have only

one notrump available at the one level. The reason that this is important is that responder can make one of those one level bids without showing extra strength. This being the case, when responder chooses to prefer to two clubs, he usually has good clubs. Otherwise he would bid one notrump, one spade if available, or even pass.

♠ K 8 2	After
♡ 4 2	1♣-Pass-1◇-Pass
◇ K 10 9 7 6	1♡-Pass-?
♣ J 9 7	responder would bid one notrump.

♠ Q 8 6 2	After
♡ 3	1♣-Pass-1◇-Pass
◇ K J 9 8 7	1♡-Pass-?
♣ J 9 7	responder would bid one spade.

♠ 4 2	After
♡ Q 10 7	1♣-Pass-1◇-Pass
◇ K 9 7 6 5	1♡-Pass-?
♣ J 5 3	responder would do well to pass.

The point of this discussion is that a preference of this sort is actually almost a raise and you can generally treat the auction as though the opponents have found a fit.

1♡-Pass-2♣-Pass	This is a strength showing auction and you won't
2◇-Pass-2♡-Pass	often run into this one as it is seldom passed. Treat it as
Pass-?	showing a fit and proceed very cautiously.

1♡-Pass-1NT-Pass	This sequence is a preference sequence and it guaran-
2♣-Pass-Pass-?	tees a fit. You can treat it as such. Be concerned though that responder usually has a singleton heart which will work against you if you play the hand.

1♡-Pass-1♠-Pass	This sequence shows a preference, but there is a
2♣-Pass-Pass-?	greater chance that responder holds only three clubs. The reason for this is that responder has shown length in

one suit, thus reducing the chances of his holding length in any other specific suit.

No one vul
1♡-Pass-1♠-Pass
2♣-Pass-2♡-Pass
Pass-?

♠ A 6 5	Perhaps you should have bid over one heart; perhaps
♡ 3 2	you should have bid over two clubs. The one thing
◇ K J 9 8 5	which is clear is that you should not bid over two
♣ A 4 2	hearts. It is extremely unsafe to reopen in a "dangerous" suit after a misfit auction. An illegal two diamonds could get doubled, and here you can't even do that.

Note that you have no expectation of a fit, only a few random points.   Also anticipate that the defense will start with a heart through whatever strength your partner may have. The defense will be able to establish a forcing game and you will be subjected to heart leads from opener in a situation where responder will be overruffing behind you.

No one vul

1 ♡ -Pass-1 ♠ -Pass
2 ◇ -Pass-2 ♡ -Pass
Pass-?

♠ 10 6 4 2
♡ 3
◇ K 7
♣ Q J 10 8 6 4

This is the sort of hand you need to reopen with at the three level after a misfit sequence. You need a good suit and decent distribution. Three hearts in your hand would be a terrible holding, and two of them would be bad. Even a singleton isn't so good because your dummy is going to come down with five of them and someone will be sure to comment on this. Probably partner. Those five hearts hopefully will be small ones, so that partner's high cards will be useful, but that isn't too likely. Also, those five hearts will seriously reduce your chances of finding many clubs. On this sequence, there is a good chance of finding a few spades as they might have been raised otherwise. The more I think about it, the less I think of three clubs, even on this hand.

No one vul

1 ◇ -Pass-1 ♡ -Pass
2 ♣ -Pass-2 ◇ -Pass
Pass-?

♠ Q 10 8 7 4
♡ A 6 2
◇ K 7 2
♣ 9 3

Much as I recommend reopening when holding the spade suit, it was difficult to construct a hand where I would want to do it on this sequence. With this hand for example, I would have overcalled one spade earlier, so I wouldn't even have this particular problem. If I had not overcalled, I would be nervous about bidding two spades for a number of reasons. I don't have any reason to expect a fit, and the defense is going to be accurate. Additionally, when the bidding goes this way, opener often has a singleton heart. Having not overcalled, I would reopen, but not enthusiastically. These preference sequences are not contracts that opener will often "want" to play, which is one of the determining factors for you when you consider reopening.

One last caution on this sequence. Responder would bid as he has with four-four in the majors.

Remember, it is extremely important to distinguish between fit auctions and preference auctions. They are not the same.

No one vul

1 ♡ -Pass-1NT-Pass
2 ♣ -Pass-2 ♡ -Pass
Pass-?

♠ K 10 8 7
♡ J 8 2
◇ A 10 5 4
♣ 9 7

Marginally all right to double. You have both unbid suits, but you also have a terrible heart holding. On this preference sequence, your partner will also have three hearts more often than not. I would expect that you do not have a four-four fit and reopening could be hazardous.

Both vul

1 ♡ -Pass-1NT-Pass
2 ♣ -Pass-2 ♡ -Pass
Pass-?

♠ K 7
♡ 8 6 5
◊ A Q 9 6 4 2
♣ Q 2

As with most misfit auctions, you should consider letting them play it. Your heart holding is the worst possible. Your club queen is questionable, and diamonds is a dangerous suit which must be bid at the three level. A good moment to pass.

No one vul

1 ♣ -Pass-1 ◊ -Pass
1 ♡ -Pass-Pass-?

♠ K J 8 7
♡ 10 6 5
◊ K 4
♣ 10 7 6 5

This is a curious situation. The opponents have passed out a one bid, but some of the usual dangers are missing. Notably, the opponents almost surely do not have a game anywhere. There are no hidden suits for them to suddenly discover. This sequence usually shows RHO to have a bad hand which was barely worth a response and opener to have a hand not worth a jump shift. Bid one spade.

Usually there is not much competition after this sequence. Each side may offer one further effort, but as they have limited values they won't be pushing very much.

No one vul

1 ♣ -Pass-1 ◊ -Pass
1 ♣ -Pass-Pass-?

♠ K 10 7
♡ A 2
◊ A J 8 7 5
♣ 10 6 5

One notrump. This shows values similar to when the opening bid is passed out. Here, since three suits have been bid, you will need to have at least two of them stopped. You should have RHO's suit stopped and at least one of opener's.

Note that on this sequence, the unbid suit is hearts. You need five of them to bid them and with values to reopen, you might have overcalled earlier. Against most misfit sequences, or preference sequences, such as this one, you should not reopen aggressively in an unbid suit. Very seldom will you have a hand worth two hearts on this auction.

3. *Reopening When an Opponent Has Rebid His Suit.*

These sequences are usually identified when someone rebids a suit and is passed there by partner. These sequences are typical.

1 ♣ -1 ♡	1 ♣ -1 ♡	1 ♡ -1NT
2 ♣ -Pass	2 ♣ -2 ♡	2 ♡ -Pass
	Pass	

1 ♣ -1 ♡	1 ♣ -1 ♡
1NT-2 ♡	1 ♣ -2 ♡
Pass	Pass

As you can see, there may be as many as three unbid suits to choose from, and as few as one. Also, as you must reopen at the two or three level, there are no natural notrump bids. Just a suit or a takeout double.

No one vul
1 ♡ -Pass-1NT-Pass
2 ♡ -Pass-Pass-?

♠ 8 7 6 5
♡ 4 2
◇ A 10 7
♣ K Q 5 4

Against this sequence, you will want to reopen rather aggressively. With three suits available, almost any excuse for a takeout double will suffice. This is an acceptable double under almost any circumstances. A frequent result of this double is that partner passes for penalties. Opener doesn't always find support and may be playing a six-one fit. Your partner could have four rather good hearts and elect to convert.

Vul vs. vul
1 ♡ -Pass-1NT-Pass
2 ♡ -Pass-Pass-?

♠ K J 8 7 2
♡ 8 6 3
◇ K 8
♣ J 10 7

Two spades. The principle of safe and dangerous suits applies here very strongly. Strive to reopen in a higher ranking suit, but almost never bother to do so in a lower ranking suit.

No one vul
1 ♣ -Pass-1NT-Pass
2 ♣ -Pass-Pass-?

♠ 10 8 7 5 2
♡ 3
◇ K 6 5
♣ A 5 4 2

Two spades. Guaranteed fit and it is much easier to play hands than to defend them. Spades are safe. Absolutely clear to bid.

No one vul
1 ◇ -Pass-1 ♡ -Pass
2 ◇ -Pass-Pass-?

♠ Q 8 7 2
♡ K 2
◇ 7 3
♣ A Q 10 6 5

Double. With only two suits available, there is less chance that partner will be able to fit one of them. Be slightly suspect of RHO's strength. He can have a decent hand with a stiff diamond and have elected to take a conservative view.

No one vul
1 ◇ -Pass-1 ♡ -Pass
2 ◇ -Pass-Pass-?

♠ A 2
♡ Q 10 8 7 6
◇ 9 7
♣ A 6 5 4

This hand presents the chance to make a rather unusual bid. Two hearts. Even though RHO has bid them, LHO's diamond rebid more often than not shows a stiff heart. You will almost always find partner with two and frequently three hearts. Even though you are missing the high hearts, you have good spots and they will be over RHO's holding. With sure tricks on the side, whatever partner has will be useful. I would expect to find partner with something like this:

♠ K 8 7 6 5
♡ 9 4 2
◇ Q 10 7
♣ Q J

You might go down one or you might make an overtrick. I expect that making two hearts would be par.

No one vul

1 ◇ -Pass-1 ♡ -Pass
2 ◇ -Pass-Pass-?

♠ K 6 5
♡ A 6 5 4 3 2
◇ J 7
♣ K 4

Pass. Here you have poor heart spots. Even with six hearts, three losers would not be unlikely. Your side values are not sure winners. Both of your kings could be worthless.

No one vul

1 ♡ -Pass-1 ♠ -Pass
2 ♡ -Pass-Pass-?

♠ J
♡ 10
◇ Q 10 8 7 5
♣ K 10 7 6 5 4

Two notrump unusual. Here you choose two notrump rather than double, because you don't have much defense and would prefer partner didn't pass. Both two notrump and double will get partner to bid a minor, so you choose a bid which doesn't run the risk of a pass from partner.

No one vul

1 ♡ -Pass-1 ♠ -Pass
2 ♡ -Pass-Pass-?

♠ A 4 2
♡ 3
◇ A 10 8 7 5
♣ Q 7 6 5

Double. With decent defensive strength you don't mind if partner passes for business.

Both vul

1 ◇ -Pass-1 ♠ -Pass
2 ◇ -Pass-Pass-?

♠ 8
♡ K 10 8 7 5
◇ 4 2
♣ A 9 8 7 4

Double. You don't even consider an unusual notrump call. If partner preferred hearts, he would have to do so at the three level. Double would permit him to bid two hearts. No need to get partner too high for no reason. You use the unusual notrump only when it doesn't preempt partner's responses.

No one vul

1 ◇ -Pass-1 ♠ -Pass
2 ◇ -Pass-Pass-?

♠ 3 2
♡ K J 9 8 7
◇ 3
♣ Q 10 8 7 6

Here the chances that partner will make a penalty pass are substantial, and he will be disappointed in your hand for defensive purposes. Bid two hearts. Half a loaf is better than no loaf. Any bid can work out poorly.

You are trying to find a reasonable way to get involved, but safely. Two notrump, as noted, would get you unnecessarily high if partner preferred hearts rather than clubs.

No one vul

1 ◇ -Pass-1 ♠ -Pass
2 ◇ -Pass-Pass-?

♠ K 10 6 5
♡ Q J 8 4 2
◇ 3
♣ K 6 5

Two hearts. Safe suit, dangerous suit, doesn't count for as much when RHO has bid a suit as when he has bid one notrump. But the ability to bid at the two level rather than the three level does make a difference.

Both vul

1 ◇ -Pass-1 ♠ -Pass
2 ◇ -Pass-Pass-?

♠ K 2
♡ K 3 2
◇ 3 2
♣ A J 8 6 4 2

Dangerous to act. Two clubs the round earlier would have been safer than three clubs now. Vulnerable, it is surely right to pass throughout.

No one vul

1 ♣ -Pass-1 ♡ -Pass
2 ♣ -Pass-2 ♡ -Pass
Pass-?

♠ J 8 7 6 5
♡ A 4 2
◇ 4 2
♣ A 8 3

Two spades. A strong factor in this decision is that you have aces in both of their suits. This means you will be able to control the play somewhat. If you had the king of clubs instead there would be the serious danger that the defense would ruff off your club trick. Be aware that responder can hold a decent hand. He can have as much as nine or ten points but with no constructive bid available. Beware of these sequences where neither opponent makes a severely limiting bid.

No one vul

1 ♣ -Pass-1 ♠ -Pass
2 ♣ -Pass-2 ♠ -Pass
Pass-?

♠ A 2
♡ J 9 8 7 6
◇ K Q 5
♣ J 4 2

Pass. There is almost no hand which couldn't act over one club which becomes good enough to bid at the three level. The unlimited nature of their auction plus the fact that opener can hold either hearts or diamonds further dictates a pass. If you are still not convinced, realize that your club holding is about as bad as it possibly could be.

Vul vs. not

1 ◇ -Pass-1 ♡ -Pass
2 ♣ -Pass-2 ♡ -Pass
Pass-?

♠ Q 10 8 7 5
♡ A 9 7 6
◇ K 2
♣ 10 3

This sequence tells you nothing about whether or not you will have a fit. Too many things are wrong with this hand.

1. You have good defense against hearts.

2. There is no guarantee your partner is short in hearts. It is more likely that opener on your right is short in hearts. If so, you will have a hard time avoiding a lot of heart losers.

3. The vulnerability is the worst.

4. Each of the opponents can have some extras.

This hand can't be much better, or you would have bid earlier. In practice, you will almost never balance on this sequence unless you hold a good suit and a hand not worth an earlier overcall.

Vul vs. not

1 ◊ -Pass-1 ♡ -Pass
2 ♣ -Pass-2 ♡ -Pass
Pass-?

♠ A 10 8 7 6 5
♡ 4 2
◊ Q 10 6 3
♣ 7

Two spades. This hand doesn't quite make it as an overcall, although some would. But in the reopening position, your suit is good enough that opposite the normal values your partner should have, two spades will be safe. Note that you are bidding not on the fit you hope partner has, but on the high cards you hope partner has.

No one vul

1 ◊ -Pass-1 ♡ -Pass
2 ♣ -Pass-2 ♡ -Pass
Pass-?

♠ K Q J 10 7
♡ 3
◊ 10 7 6 5
♣ J 9 8

Another hand not up to an overcall but which is worth a reopening bid. But it's no bargain. You hope your good suit may keep you from getting doubled. Good opponents, may take a whack at you on general principles. Earlier in this book I told you to be very aggressive against good players when reopening. Let me amend this slightly. Do so when their one bid has been passed out. Do so when they have a fit. Do so when they have had a limited sequence, usually where responder bids one notrump. But do not be so hasty to reopen against one of those sequences where they appear to be competing against each other unless you can do so via a takeout double. On the sequence being discussed, there is only one unbid suit so a double would be unavailable for takeout in the traditional sense.

1 ◊ -Pass-1 ♠ -Pass
2 ♣ -Pass-2 ♠ -Pass
Pass-?

What hand can exist which can't bid after one diamond, but which can later bid after two spades?

No one vul

1 ♡ -Pass-1 ♠ -Pass
2 ◊ -Pass-2 ♠ -Pass
Pass-?

♠ 3
♡ A 10 6 5
◊ 4 2
♣ Q J 10 8 7 5

This is one of the rare hands which might pass after a one bid which later could bid at the three level. The difference here is that when RHO opened, this hand could not overcall at the one level. It would have had to overcall at the two level or perhaps to have made a weak jump overcall. Some would have chosen these actions. Nonetheless, it is possible to pass and then act at the three level against an unlimited misfit sequence. Note that if the opponents had bid

1 ♡ -Pass-2 ♡ -Pass
Pass-?

You would have been absolutely delighted to reopen with three clubs.

Both vul

1 ◊ -Pass-1 ♡ -Pass
2 ♣ -Pass-2 ♡ -Pass
Pass-?

♠ A 8 4 2   What does it mean when your opponents bid three
♡ 3   suits and you reopen with double? It doesn't seem likely
◊ A Q 8 3   that it's for takeout. On the other hand, if you are in the
♣ A J 9 7   reopening seat, you can't be doubling for penalty
because your LHO will hold the trump suit over you. It
is impossible that you will ever hold such good trumps with more tricks on the
side that you would want to double two hearts on this auction. You would have
been bidding earlier. If you doubt this, try concocting a hand. See if you wouldn't
do something over one diamond.

So if double isn't really for takeout, and it isn't for penalty showing a bunch of
trumps and tricks, then what is it, or does it even exist?

As with most bidding situations, if a bid exists, there is probably a meaning for
it. Some of the time you really have to work to find a meaning, and some of the
time there truly is no meaning. But if you persevere you can find an explanation
for almost everything except the ridiculous. The answer to what double would
mean can best be shown by the example had. You have a fine hand with values in
three suits and shortness in the last bid suit. It looks like a takeout double hand
except for the fact that two of your suits have already been bid. In fact, your double is a takeout double, but it is made with the expectation that partner will pass
and convert it to penalty. In effect, you are making the penalty double even
though holding a stiff heart. Partner will play you to have a good hand much like
the one you have and he will run to spades if he feels that best. He might even run
to clubs or diamonds! But what will happen about seventy percent of the time is
that partner will pass. Hearts are likely to be 6-5-1-1 or 6-4-2-1 around the table.
Partner can easily hold good trumps, and why not? If partner prefers, he can run
to spades. So it behooves you to be ready for them.

Here are a few hands partner may have?

No one vul

1 ◊ -Pass-1 ♡ -Pass
2 ♣ -Pass-2 ♡ -Pass
Pass-Dbl-Pass-?

♠ J 8 7   Pass.
♡ A J 9 7
◊ 10 3
♣ 8 6 5 4

♠ 10 8 7 5 2   Two spades.
♡ K J 5
◊ Q 3
♣ 10 4 2

♠ J 8 4 2   Two spades. The hearts aren't strong enough to pass.
♡ A 9 6 4
◊ 3
♣ 10 6 5 3

♠ Q 8 7
♥ Q 5 4
◊ Q 9 7 3
♣ 6 4 2

A true horror. Pass or two spades. The important thing is to know the kind of hand you are facing.

♠ K 4 2
♥ 8 6 5 4
◊ 2
♣ Q J 10 8 7

Three clubs could be the winning bid. Two spades is a reasonable choice also. Pass is out as the requirement is good hearts, not just four of them.

♠ Q 10 7 6
♥ A Q 2
◊ 10 9 4 2
♣ 7 3

Probably best to bid two spades. You have a good enough hand that you can expect to make it. If the opponents were vulnerable, you might chance a pass, but when you can expect to make something, it is usually better to play it.

♠ J 8 4 2
♥ K J 9 3
◊ J 2
♣ J 4 3

Pass. Even though holding four spades. Your offensive potential is not very good. The strength of your hand is hearts and that won't be much use in a spade contract. You can expect to take three heart tricks and perhaps one of your side jacks will be useful.

It is important to have a good hand when you reopen with double on one of those sequences which has just one unbid suit. Partner's options are limited, so you need a good hand to cater to those frequent times when partner doesn't have a useful hand.

The last common low level sequence you will encounter is when third seat opens and passes his partner's response.

Pass-Pass-1♥-Pass   or   Pass-Pass-1♠-Pass
1♠-Pass-Pass-?   2◊-Pass-Pass-?

Against these sequences, you should want to reopen, but because responder can have up to a near opener, you will have to be a bit cautious when reopening in a suit or in notrump. If you have the shape for a takeout double, do so fairly aggressively.

No one vul

Pass-Pass-1♣-Pass
1♠-Pass-Pass-?

♠ Q 10 8
♥ K J 4
◊ 7 6 5
♣ A Q 9 5

One notrump. You should treat this sequence similarly to when opener's bid was passed around to you: 1♠-Pass-Pass-1NT, but with an eye to safety. Just because opener didn't keep the bidding open doesn't mean he's psyched. He may have up to 13 balanced points with no particular future. If responder has a bit extra, one notrump could be in trouble. This means that the minimum values for one notrump after

Pass-Pass-1♣-Pass
1♠-Pass-Pass-1NT

must be a little more than the minimum values after

1♠-Pass-Pass-1NT.

You would prefer to have both suits stopped. But in any case, you must have opener's suit stopped.

Pass-Pass-1♣-Pass
1♥-Pass-Pass-?

Regardless of your hand, there are certain principles you have to be aware of. Opener here usually won't pass without three or more hearts, so you can treat this tentatively as a fit auction. But do not treat it as a limited auction. There's no danger that they will suddenly change their minds and procede to a game, but they are not limited in that one heart is as high as they can go.

Pass-Pass-1 ♡ -Pass
2 ◊ -Pass-Pass-?

Again, there are special considerations. This time opener does not promise more than a doubleton diamond by his pass, so there is not as strong a presumption of a fit. Also, responder promises more than minimal values. So the mere fact that they have stopped in two diamonds does not proclaim weakness. It is very dangerous to get involved here. Responder is not likely to have much in hearts or he would have tried some other approach rather than risk that two diamonds would be passed out. Do your opponents, for example, use Drury, where two clubs would show a good hand with heart support?

Whenever the opponents open in third seat and then pass partner's "forcing" bid you want to be careful about bidding a new suit. On the other hand, if you can make a takeout double, you will be on safer grounds because you can offer more than one potential resting spot.

One new possibility for you is that when third hand opens and passes his partner's response, you have the additional option of reopening with a natural bid in RHO's opened suit. After a one level response by responder, you will have to be reasonably careful when trying this because there is no presumption for you that responder has shortness in opener's suit. And when responder has made a two over one, you must be even more careful because of LHO's announced strength.

No one vul

Pass-Pass-1 ◊ -Pass
1 ♡ -Pass-Pass-?

♠ 4 2
♡ Q 8
◊ A Q 10 8 7 6
♣ K 9 5

With this good a suit, two diamonds would be reasonable. The important thing here is the recognition that two diamonds is a natural bid.

No one vul

Pass-Pass-1 ♡ -Pass
1 ♠ -Pass-Pass-?

♠ Q 7
♡ K J 8 7 5
◊ A 7 3
♣ K J 5

One notrump. Even though lacking a complete spade guard, it is a better action than two hearts. Your suit is not good enough to chance playing opposite a singleton. There is nothing in the auction to suggest partner will have a fit for you. Earlier there were examples where you reopened in RHO's suit on something like Q 10 8 7 3. But the situation then was that RHO had responded in the suit at the one level and his partner's rebid implied shortness in that suit. This was the sequence:

1 ♣ -Pass-1 ♠ -Pass
2 ♣ -Pass-Pass-?

On this sequence, opener could easily have a stiff spade and responder could have had as little as 10 8 7 3 to be bidding them. But when the auction is

Pass-Pass-1 ♡ -Pass
1 ♠ -Pass-Pass-?

. . . there are no such inferences.

Vul vs. not

Pass-Pass-1 ◊ -Pass
1 ♠ -Pass-Pass-?

♠ J 4 2
♡ K J 8 7
◊ 4 3
♣ A J 6 3

Double. Straightforward action. Any time you can offer a choice of suits, reopening with a double is much safer than the somewhat committal action of bidding a suit.

CHAPTER FOUR
Quiz

The Safety Factor in Reopening.

Throughout this book, I have made constant references to suits that are safe to bid and suits that are dangerous to bid. The concept of "safe suits" is very important in most aspects of low level competitive bidding. Understanding it is a big and necessary step in developing your competitive judgment.

This section is a short quiz devoted to a number of common auctions. No hands are involved. All you have to do is to determine how safe it is to bid any of the unbid suits in the given sequence.

Safeness of course is relative. Anything you bid may go for a ride on a given afternoon. But some bids may have more bad afternoons than others.

Let us score safeness in the following fashion: A, B, C, D, and F.

I don't want to use numbers because nothing is 100% safe nor is anything 100% doomed to disaster.

We will use as our range the following sequences.

1 ◊ -Pass-2 ◊ -Pass
Pass-?

♠ = A
♡ = A
◊ = 0
♣ = F

On the grading scale, both hearts and spades would get an A, and clubs would get an F. Notrump does not get graded because it would be natural only at the one level, and those situations are easily defined. Note that the opponents' suits are included in the scoring. Where it is conceivable that you might wish to bid one of them, I have given it a score. Where it is inconceivable that you would want to bid one of them, it has gotten a zero. For instance, after

1 ◊ -Pass-2 ◊ -Pass
Pass-?

. . . three diamonds as a natural bid does not exist. You may have some reason to concoct a reopening cue bid here, but that would be extremely unusual. The scores here are only for bids intended as natural.

1 ♣ -Pass-2 ♣ -Pass
Pass-?

♠ = A
♡ = A
◊ = B +
♣ = 0

When one club is raised, responder denies a major suit and tends to deny diamonds.

1 ◊ -Pass-2 ◊ -Pass
Pass-?

♠ = A
♡ = A
◊ = 0
♣ = F

The two diamond raise denies a major and implies club length. Even though clubs gets an F, you may still bid them if you have a good enough suit. The F is awarded because the two diamond bidder probably has length. If your suit can overcome the probable bad breaks, then go ahead. Note that most F suits must be bid at a higher level.

63

1 ♡ -Pass-2 ♡ -Pass
Pass-?

♠ = A −	Spades is demoted only slightly because responder could have ignored them to raise hearts. Clubs and diamonds have been elevated because responder does not as strongly promise strength in both of them as he did when the auction was 1 ◊ -Pass-2 ◊ and the lower rank-
♡ = 0	
◊ = D	
♣ = D	

ing suit was clubs. 1 ♡ -Pass-2 ♡ implies some minor suit length, but it could be in either minor, not necessarily both.

1 ♠ -Pass-2 ♠ -Pass
Pass-?

♠ = 0
♡ = D+
◊ = D+
♣ = D+

1 ♣ -Pass-1 ◊ -Pass
1 ♡ -Pass-2 ♡ -Pass
Pass-?

♠ = A	Just because a suit gets an A doesn't mean you can bid them. You have to have them. I've seen players bid them on a three card holding after this sequence. A match-point delicacy.
♡ = 0	
◊ = 0	
♣ = 0	

1 ♣ -Pass-1 ◊ -Pass
1 ♠ -Pass-2 ♠ -Pass
Pass-?

♠ = 0	Hearts gets a C only in theory. If you couldn't bid over one diamond, it is unlikely you would bid three hearts here. Neither opponent is likely to have hearts.
♡ = C	
◊ = 0	
♣ = 0	

1 ◊ -Pass-1NT-Pass
2 ♣ -Pass-Pass-?

♠ = A	Diamonds are rated only because it is conceivably possible for you to bid them. You and partner had better be on the same wave length, because it would be reasonable to play this bid as a very weak takeout double.
♡ = A	
◊ = F −	
♣ = 0	

1 ◊ -Pass-1NT-Pass
2 ♣ -Pass-2 ◊ -Pass
Pass-?

♠ = A	The usual. Responder has denied a major and opener is unlikely to have one.
♡ = A	
◊ = 0	
♣ = 0	

1 ◊ -Pass-1 ♡ -Pass
2 ♣ -Pass-Pass-?

♠ = B −	Responder has not denied four spades. They could be splitting poorly. Hearts is given an A only with the understanding that you have the proper suit for it, i.e., five or more *and* including good spots.
♡ = A	
◊ = 0	
♣ = 0	

When the opponents have found a fit or when responder has bid one notrump somewhere along the way, then you can make very accurate estimates of how safe it is to bid a particular suit. This is because the raise and the one notrump response show specific strength and carry strong implications about higher ranking suits which have been ignored. In similar fashion, you can derive information from opener's rebids, i.e. did he skip over any suits to bid one notrump (significant) or did he skip over any suits in order to raise partner (mildly significant)?

When the opponents do not have a fit and have not bid notrump along the way, then the safe suit and dangerous suit concept loses much of its significance. This is because you have far less information about the opponents' distribution. The raise and the one notrump bid offer you a wealth of positive and negative inferences. Other bids may be informative, but less so. Additionally, sequences not including raises or notrump are harder to interpret in terms of strength. Either opponent may have some extra values which leave him just short of making a stronger bid.

Continuing.

1♣-Pass-1♡-Pass
1♠-Pass-2♣-Pass
Pass-?

♠ =0   Diamonds are mentionable because both opponents
♡ =0   have shown length in two suits. Neither is likely to have
◇ =B+   length in a third. This is almost a "fit" auction by the
♣ =0   opponents.

1♣-Pass-1♡-Pass
1NT-Pass-2♣-Pass
Pass-?

♠ =A−   Any time the opponents have a fit, spades gets an A.
♡ =0
◇ =B+
♣ =0

1♣-Pass-1♡-Pass
1NT-Pass-Pass-?

♠ =B+   Responder could have spades. Note that his pass does
♡ =0   not deny up to a bad 11 points. As a matter of compari-
◇ =B−   son, he could have from five to 11 points whereas a one
♣ =0   notrump response to the club would have shown a far
                  narrower range, say seven to 10, or eight to 11. Note

also that when opener has rebid one notrump, bidding hearts gets a 0 on the grading scale. The one notrump bid shows two or three hearts, so if you have a five card heart suit, your partner will have 0, 1, or 2 rather than 2 or 3 which was the case after

1♣-Pass-1♡-Pass
2♣-Pass-Pass-?

1◇-Pass-1♡-Pass
1♠-Pass-2◇-Pass
Pass-?

♠ =0   Nothing special here. Clubs have to be bid at the three
♡ =0   level.
◇ =0
♣ =C

1 ◇ -Pass-1 ♡ -Pass
1NT-Pass-2 ◇ -Pass
Pass-?

♠ = A −
♡ = 0
◇ = 0
♣ = C

As usual, when your opponents have a fit, spades are fine.

1 ♡ -Pass-1NT-Pass
Pass-?

♠ = A −
♡ = 0
◇ = D
♣ = D

The classic situation of safe and dangerous suits. Responder hasn't spades or hearts, so must have minors.

1 ♣ -Pass-1 ♡ -Pass
2 ♣ -Pass-Pass-?

♠ = B −
♡ = A
◇ = B −
♣ = 0

These sequences where no one has clearly limited his hand are harder to judge. Consequently, it is more dangerous to act. Responder could have spades, opener could have diamonds. Strange that one of their bid suits, hearts, could be safer than an unbid suit.

1 ◇ -Pass-1 ♠ -Pass
2 ◇ -Pass-Pass-?

♠ = A −
♡ = B
◇ = 0
♣ = C

Spades here is demoted slightly because RHO is more likely to have five of them. This is because he didn't bid one heart. With four hearts and four spades, he would have responded one heart. All this is theoretical and probably not worth worrying about. Against undefined hands, reopening is more nervous, hence the B for hearts. Note that RHO could actually have four or five of them. With a five-five in the majors and less than nine points, he might have decided to pass two diamonds rather than get involved with a forcing two hearts.

1 ♡ -Pass-1NT-Pass
2 ♡ -Pass-Pass-?

♠ = B +
♡ = 0
◇ = D
♣ = D

No fit, but RHO hasn't spades and is limited. Minors potentially dangerous.

1 ♡ -Pass-2 ♣ -Pass
2 ♡ -Pass-Pass-?

♠ = C
♡ = 0
◇ = D
♣ = 0

Not a sequence you are likely to run into. Be very suspicious of it. They could have two decent hands with a misfit and be most happy to hear from you.

1 ♣ -Pass-1 ♠ -Pass
2 ♣ -Pass-Pass-?

♠ = A
♡ = B
◇ = B −
♣ = 0

With the right suit, spades is safe. Other suits subject to the vagaries of this undefined sequence.

66

1♣-Pass-1◊-Pass
2♣-Pass-Pass-?

♠ = A –   This is one of the few undefined sequences your
♡ = A –   opponents can have in which you can bid just about
◊ = A –   anything you want. Opener doesn't have a major and
♣ = 0   responder is unlikely to. Note the previous sequence.
That one spade response preempted opener so that his
rebidding options are seriously restricted. Look at the difference.

1♣-Pass-1◊   Opener can bid just about anything he pleases.

1♣-Pass-1♠   Opener can not rebid hearts or diamonds with most
                               minimal opening hands.
On the sequence of

                         1♣-Pass-1♠-Pass
                         2♣

. . . opener can have four hearts or four diamonds. The two club rebid is often a
least of evils choice. But after

                         1♣-Pass-1◊-Pass

. . . opener will have no trouble selecting a bid. Two clubs if chosen will be
because it is a good descriptive bid rather than the best of a bad lot.

So when you hear the auction

                         1♣-Pass-1◊-Pass
                         2♣-Pass-Pass

. . . you can feel that opener at least won't have any special surprises for you.
Responder usually doesn't have a major on this sequence because he would bid it
in preference to one diamond. Usually—not always. In any case, hearts and
spades gets their highest score ever for an undefined auction.

One comment about reopening with two diamonds. There is no sequence
where you would ever reopen in a suit bid on your left. When you reopen in a
previously bid suit, it will be one bid on your right. Ninety-nine percent of the
time the sequence will be something like

                         1♣-1♠
                         2♣

or

                         1◊-1♠
                         2♣

. . . and you will reopen with two spades. If opener rebids one notrump, you will
not reopen with two spades.

1♣-Pass-1♡-Pass
2♣-Pass-2♡-Pass
Pass-?

♠ = B   Opener won't have four spades but may have dia-
♡ = 0   monds. When considering your action, remember that
◊ = D   opener often has a stiff heart. If responder has a stiff
♣ = 0   club, the defense can initiate a cross ruff

1 ◊ -Pass-1 ♡ -Pass
1NT-Pass-2 ♡ -Pass
Pass-?

♠ = A −
♡ = 0
◊ = 0
♣ = C

Clubs is slightly elevated here because LHO might have bid them. This isn't truely significant, but this sequence is the only one where responder can bid a new suit and not create a force.

1 ♣ -Pass-1 ♡ -Pass
1 ♠ -Pass-2 ♡ -Pass
Pass-?

♠ = 0
♡ = 0
◊ = C
♣ = 0

If you couldn't bid one diamond, how in the world can you bid three diamonds? Theoretically, the suit is not unduly dangerous. But bridge-wise, it's impossible.

1 ◊ -Pass-1 ♡ -Pass
2 ♣ -Pass-2 ♡ -Pass
Pass-?

♠ = B
♡ = 0
◊ = 0
♣ = 0

The main thing to remember is that both opponents can have some unannounced extras. Responder can have as much as

♠ K 8 7
♡ A J 9 7 6 5
◊ Q 2
♣ 4 3

. . . and still come up with the weak sounding one heart-two heart sequence. These auctions which include no clearly limited and defining bids are always suspect.

The clear point to be derived from these examples is that when the opponents have a fit, it is both safe and desirable for you to compete. When the opponents don't have a fit, they may have made a limited and definitive bid such as one notrump which gives you enough information so as to know whether or not to balance. And if there is no fit and their values are unclear, then you are pretty much on your own when reopening. As long as you identify the type of sequence you are up against and apply when possible the safe suit, dangerous suit rule, you will be judging well.

PART II

RESPONDING TO THE REOPENING BID

When someone reopens the bidding, the frequent effect is that of starting a small scale war in which everyone gets involved. This is especially the case when both sides have a fit or when opener thinks he has a good hand and decides to continue. Both sides will be called upon to make some delicate decisions with huge bushels of matchpoints, money, or IMPs hanging in the balance.

On other occasions, the reopener's side will have enough to get to and make a game. Or perhaps they will have enough that they will be allowed an uncontested auction which stops short of game.

The latter situation where the reopener's side has the majority of the values is fairly easy to judge and I don't intend to spend much time on it. It is the other category in which both sides have some values that I will discuss in detail.

Before getting into the specific auctions, I want to give you a few very important rules.

On those hands where you do not have enough values to make a strong bid, such as a jump or a cue bid, the following rules should apply.

1. Fight like crazy throughout the one and two levels.
2. If your first bid must be made at the three level, do so on any excuse.
3. If you have already made a bid, continue to contest at the two level, but go to the three level with caution.

The point of these rules is that you want to fight strenuously to establish that you have a fit, and then leave the final decision to partner. If you refuse to bid on marginal hands, your partner will be locked out of the auction on many hands which belong to your side.

CHAPTER V

Partner doubles and opener passes.

This is the easiest case of all. The only question here is how much you need to make more than a minimum response. Here are your strong responses and a few comments on each.

1. The jump to two of a major.

Inasmuch as partner's double can be rather light, you should have a decent hand to make this invitational jump. Generally speaking this jump shows from 11 to 13 points. Some good tens might even qualify. Basic to this is the fact that if you have the values to jump, your suit will be lousy, else you would have been worth an overcall.

Vul vs. not

1♣-Pass-Pass-Dbl
Pass-?

♠ Q 8 7 6 5   Typical maximum jump to two spades. This hand is
♡ K Q 3   not quite an overcall because of the questionable queens
♢ Q 8   and the spotless suit.
♣ K J 4

No one vul

1♢-Pass-Pass-Dbl
Pass-?

♠ K 3   A minimum two heart bid. Good useful high cards
♡ 10 7 6 5 4   with a five card suit.
♢ A 2
♣ K 9 7 5

No one vul

1♢-Pass-Pass-Dbl
Pass-?

♠ Q 9 8 7   Two spades. This does not guarantee a five card suit.
♡ A 6   With suitable values, even this poorish suit is acceptable.
♢ 10 6 5 4
♣ A J 5

2. The jump to two diamonds.

This bid does guarantee a five card suit, else you would bid a major or one notrump. Your suit won't be too good or you would have overcalled.

No one vul

1♣-Pass-Pass-Dbl
Pass-?

♠ K 8 7   Two diamonds. Random five card suit plus no major
♡ A J 3   plus a decent hand.
♢ Q 10 6 5 4
♣ 9 3

70

3. The jump to three hearts (after a one spade opening).

This shows slightly more than jumps to the two level, and it shows a five card suit or a good four card suit.

4. The jump to three of a minor.

This also shows a hand better than jumps to the two level, and it shows a good five card suit. The reason these minor suit jumps show good suits is that you are probably going to three notrump if partner can bid it. Jumps to the two level in a major tended to deny good suits because with a good suit plus the appropriate values you would have overcalled. But you could easily have a good hand and a good minor suit and have passed because an overcall would have been at the two level.

1 ♡ -Pass-Pass-Dbl
Pass-?

♠ K 3
♡ 8 7 6
◊ A Q 10 6 5
♣ Q J 3

Three diamonds. Had you held the same hand with spades, you would have overcalled, so the hand would not have existed. But with this actual hand, you would not have overcalled two diamonds after one heart. Thus it is possible to pass an opening bid by RHO when holding good hands with good suits, if RHO's suit is higher ranking than yours.

5. The jump to two notrump.

This is invitational, showing 12 to 14 high card points, and partner is expected to continue with most twelve counts.

1 ♠ -Pass-Pass-Dbl
Pass-?

♠ Q 10 8 7
♡ K 3
◊ Q J 4
♣ A J 5 3

About right for two notrump. If you really want to bid more, remember that partner can have as little as

♠ 6
♡ Q 8 6 5
◊ A 8 5 2
♣ Q 6 4 2

Two notrump would be quite high enough. As long as you trust partner to continue with a decent 12 points, it is sufficient to invite partner. Don't hang him.

6. The jump to three notrump.

Very unusual, but it could happen. Probably a hand just short of a notrump overcall.

1 ♡ -Pass-Pass-Dbl
Pass-?

♠ Q 2
♡ K J 6
◊ Q J 8 6 5
♣ A Q 7

Three notrump. This is the wrong kind of hand on which to overcall initially, but is too good to merely invite. Don't think three notrump will be cold. It may not be. But it will make on many hands where partner would rightly pass two notrump.

7. The cue bid.

Even rarer. The most likely possibilities are hands like these.

1 ♡ -Pass-Pass-Dbl
Pass-?

♠ 8 6 5 4   Looking for four card spade support.
♡ A J 8 3
◊ A K 2
♣ 7 3

1 ◊ -Pass-Pass-Dbl
Pass-?

♠ Q 7 6 5   Looking for a major suit.
♡ A J 6 5
◊ A 10 5 4
♣ 3

1 ♡ -Pass-Pass-Dbl
Pass-?

♠ A J 2   Looking for a heart stopper for notrump.
♡ 8 6 5 4
◊ A K J
♣ Q 10 7

I don't intend to discuss the cue bid any further here. Whatever your treatment will be, fine. However, I offer a couple of questions for your partnership discussion.
  1. Is a cue bid game forcing?
  2. If not, does the cue bidder promise to bid again?
  3. Does the cue bid guarantee a major suit?

8. The one notrump response.

While this is not a strong bid, it does show some values. The upper range is around 11 points and might even be more if partner had passed originally. The lower range is sometimes dictated by necessity, but it should seldom stray below seven or eight points. One point here is that when the bidding has been:

1 ♣ -Pass-Pass-Dbl
Pass-?

. . . one notrump will be a bit more constructive than when the bidding has gone

1 ♠ -Pass-Pass-Dbl
Pass-?

The reason for this is that you had more options after one club. You could have bid anything else at the one level.

♠ Q 10 8   With this hand for instance, if you were responding to
♡ J 7 6   one club, pass, pass, double, pass, you would bid one
◊ J 9 6 4   diamond rather than one notrump. But if opener's suit
♣ Q 10 7   had been one spade, you might choose one notrump.
                      Your alternative would be two diamonds.

9. The penalty pass.

One of your options is to pass partner's double converting it to penalty. This is often a winning action, but before passing, consider:

1. Partner does not need much for a reopening double.
2. How good are your spots in opener's suit? Q 7 6 4 2 is not a particularly good holding, while K J 9 7 is.
3. Do you have any offensive potential of your own? Perhaps you have a game.

No one vul

1 ◊ -Pass-Pass-Dbl
Pass-?

♠ A 8 7 6
♡ 3
◊ Q 9 7 4 2
♣ J 9 7

One spade. On any close hand, you should lean toward playing rather than defending.

No one vul

1 ♡ -Pass-Pass-Dbl
Pass-?

♠ K 3
♡ A 8 4 3 2
◊ Q 10 7
♣ Q 9 5

One notrump. You have bad spots. Opposite a light takeout double, you have little or no chance of beating one heart.

Vul vs. not

1 ♣ -Pass-Pass-Dbl
Pass-?

♠ J 8 7 4 2
♡ Q 2
◊ 3
♣ A Q 8 7 6

Far better to declare than defend. Bid at least two spades. Passing would be seriously wrong.

Both vul

1 ♠ -Pass-Pass-Dbl
Pass-?

♠ K 10 9 7 5
♡ Q J
◊ K 3 2
♣ A 10 7

Pass and expect to beat them, but don't expect to get rich. These spade spots have substantial value.

Both vul

Pass-1 ♠ -Pass-Pass
Dbl-Pass-?

♠ K J 9 3
♡ K 5 4
◊ K Q 3
♣ 10 6 5

Reasonable to pass. The alternative is one notrump because partner is a passed hand.

As a conventional aside here, if opener redoubles, I suggest you play pass as still being for business.

No one vul
1♦-Pass-Pass-Dbl
Pass-?

♠ 4 2
♡ 10 7 5
♦ K J 4
♣ Q 8 7 6 5

One diamond. The clubs aren't good enough to pass and the hand isn't good enough to bid one notrump. You should have eightish points to do this over one club.

Not vul vs. vul
1♣-Pass-Pass-Dbl
Pass-?

♠ 10 7 6 5
♡ 4 2
♦ 3 2
♣ A J 8 6 5

This hand is intended to test your resolve to bid. If you have a suit to bid at the one level, you need to be pretty sure to make a penalty pass. Bid one spade.

Both vul
1♦-Pass-Pass-Dbl
Pass-?

♠ J 8 7
♡ 10 9 3
♦ 4 2
♣ K J 9 7 5

Pass. But only because there is no reasonable alternative. Whatever you bid, your partner will get you too high. At least you can hope to beat them. If your clubs were K J 4 3 2, I would feel this problem to be insoluble.

CHAPTER SIX

Partner Reopens With Double and Opener Rebids.

This is the first of the many situations which will separate the successful from the unsuccessful and getting the best possible results will depend on an understanding of certain guidelines. Remember those rules you received a few moments earlier. Fight like mad through the one and two levels and occasionally at the three level. Then quit. Let's see how it works.

No one vul

1♣-Pass-Pass-Dbl
1♡-?

♠ Q 10 8 7
♡ K 2
◊ K 9 8 7
♣ 10 5 4

It's clear to bid one spade here. Every one of your high cards is working. This hand is quite good enough to take further action. For instance, if the auction continues

1♣-Pass-Pass-Dbl
1♡-1♠-Pass-Pass
2♣-?

You should bid two diamonds and still feel as though you have extras.

No one vul

1◊-Pass-Pass-Dbl
1NT-?

♠ J 8 7 5 4
♡ K 4 2
◊ 10 7 5
♣ Q 3

Two spades. You have no wasted cards and you have a fifth spade. This hand is not so good however, that you will take any more voluntary action. Partner shouldn't credit you with very much here. With a good hand, you might have overcalled one spade or doubled one notrump. The important principle here is that when either defender knows a fit exists, he should do everything possible to share that information with partner. And partner should allow for that.

Vul vs. not

1♡-Pass-Pass-Dbl
1NT-?

♠ K 8 7
♡ K 8 7
◊ A 10 8 7 5
♣ J 2

This hand is close to a penalty double. But you probably shouldn't for a number of reasons.

1. It's almost always better to play in a reasonable contract than to make a speculative double.

2. The opponents aren't vulnerable.

3. You would like better hearts. Perhaps K 10 8. Even with this reasonable hand, you might not beat them, or they might run to two hearts. Now you would have to bid three diamonds.

No one vul

1♡-Pass-Pass-Dbl
2♡-?

♠ K J 8 7   Two spades. Strive to bid when possible. Even though
♡ A 9 6 5   you have some defense against hearts, it is not over-
◊ 4 2   whelming.
♣ 10 7 5

A very important point regarding reopening sequences is this. On some
reopening auctions game is possible, while on others, game is impossible or
highly unlikely. Here partner is not a passed hand so game is not out of the question. In such circumstances, you have added reason to bid on marginal hands. By
comparison, if partner had passed originally, you would not expect a game opposite this hand. It would still be right to bid two spades, but you would have low-
ered expectations or hopes.

Both vul

1◊-Pass-Pass-Dbl
2◊-?

♠ K J 8 7 5   If you want to bid two spades, that's okay, but best
♡ 4 2   only to want to. You should pass. It's not that two
◊ 10 6 5   spades will be a bad spot, but the bid shows minimum
♣ 9 4 3   values that partner should be able to expect, and this
                         hand falls short of them.

Both vul

1◊-Pass-Pass-Dbl
2◊-?

♠ K J 8 7 5   Up to minimum values. It is very important to com-
♡ Q 2   pete with these hands. Opposite an assortment of hands
◊ 10 6 5   like these, partner will have to pass two diamonds when
♣ J 6 4   you should be either making a partscore or at least
                         pushing them higher.

♠ Q 6 4 2   ♠ A 6 4   ♠ 10 9 2
♡ K 10 7 5   ♡ J 9 5 4   ♡ A K 4 3
◊ J 2   ◊ 4 2   ◊ 7
♣ A 9 7   ♣ K Q 8 3   ♣ A 8 5 3 2

        ♠ A Q 2   ♠ 9 4 2
        ♡ K 7 6 3   ♡ A J 6 3
        ◊ J 4 2   ◊ K 4
        ♣ K 10 5   ♣ K Q 3 2

No one vul

1◊-Pass-Pass-Dbl
2♣-?

♠ Q 10 7 5   Two spades. As good as this hand is, it isn't good
♡ A 4 2   enough to jump. In order to introduce your suit, it is
◊ A 9 7 6   necessary frequently to do so on marginal values. The
♣ 8 6   price you pay for this is that your range becomes rather
                        wide. Two spades here turns out to show from a six
count with a five bagger up to 11 or even a terrible 12 count with a four bagger.
The price you pay is that on occasion you miss a game. What you get in return is

a large number of partscores and small sets in your favor. In the long run, your sacrifice in definition is many times returned in results.

Vul vs. not

1 ◊ -Pass-Pass-Dbl
1 ♡ -?

♠ J 8 7 6 5
♡ K 3
◊ A 10 6
♣ Q 5 2

One spade. You are willing to take the push to two spades, but not higher unless helped by partner. Had opener not bid one heart, you might have jumped to two spades. But given that one spade is voluntary, it is sufficient. Not that a free bid guarantees the earth.

Both vul

1 ♣ -Pass-Pass-Dbl
2 ♣ -?

♠ Q 2
♡ J 10 8 7 5
◊ A J 9 5 4
♣ 8

Bid two hearts. If opener continues to three clubs, you will compete with three diamonds. This apparently violates the principle of not competing at the three level when you have already taken a bid. But when you are introducing a new suit, it is part of the search for a fit rather than confirming one.

Vul vs. not

1 ◊ -Pass-Pass-Dbl
2 ◊ -?

♠ 4 2
♡ K 10 9 7 6
◊ 3
♣ A 10 9 6 5

Two hearts. If opener continues to three diamonds, you should bid three hearts. This sequence is very rare and to bid in this fashion requires good distribution and a good suit. Considering that you weren't able to jump or overcall, there won't be many hands in this family.

No one vul

1 ◊ -Pass-Pass-Dbl
2 ♣ -2 ♠ -3 ♣ -Pass
Pass-?

♠ Q 10 4 3 2
♡ Q J 3
◊ Q 8 7
♣ K 2

Very doubtful that you should continue. You have soft cards and bad shape.

No one vul

Pass-1 ♡ -Pass-Pass
Dbl-Pass-?

♠ K J 7 3
♡ Q 8 5
◊ K Q
♣ Q 7 6 5

One spade only. Partner is a passed hand. Try to buy this hand as low as possible.

No one vul
Pass-1 ◊ -Pass-Pass
Dbl-2 ◊ -2 ♠ -Pass
Pass-3 ♣ -Dbl-3 ◊
Pass-Pass-?

♠ K J 7 3   Very likely you should pass this. After partner's pass
♡ Q 8 5   you have no game, so you are involved in a partscore
◊ K Q   decision only. The only thing you can consider is dou-
♣ Q 7 6 5   ble, but your chances of beating it are minimal. When
                           you doubled three clubs, you expected they would run
to diamonds, but hoped not. But they did. Partner has had two chances to act
after your two spade call and passed both times. You should do so also.

Both vul
1 ◊ -Pass-Pass-Dbl
2 ◊ -?

♠ K Q 9 7   Three spades. Partner is still unlimited. Game is pos-
♡ Q 8   sible. The important point here is that this hand is not
◊ K 5 4   worth either a direct game bid or a cue bid.
♣ K J 7 6

No one vul
1 ♡ -Pass-Pass-Dbl
Pass-1 ♠ -Pass-Pass
2 ♡ -?

♠ A Q 10 8   Two spades. It's curious that you would bid and rebid
♡ 4 3 2   a four card suit and never mention a five card suit. But
◊ 7   there is a slight danger that partner won't have adequate
♣ 8 6 5 4 2   club support. This plus the fact that he does need spade
                           support suggests sticking with the known fit. If you had
four bad spades, you might not try this. Also, if you had a singleton heart, you
might fear the tap and choose to bid clubs first.

No one vul
1 ♡ -Pass-Pass-Dbl
2 ♡ -?

♠ K 8 7   A minimum three diamond bid. You take this action
♡ Q J 8   because it is important to get your suit in. Had the auc-
◊ Q J 8 7 5   tion been:
♣ 9 7   1 ♣ -Pass-Pass-Dbl
                           2 ♣ -2 ◊ -Pass-Pass
                           3 ♣ -?
You would not continue to three diamonds. Having once expressed your values,
you should subside.

When opener rebids, your notrump bids will acquire a stronger flavor than
when opener passes. Inasmuch as you don't have to get involved, a free notrump
bid shows substantial values. When partner doubled, he was hoping to find a fit,
and notrump was not something he particularly wanted to hear. Considering
how few high card points partner needs for a reopening double, you will need
about nine or more for one notrump and twelvish for a non-jump bid of two
notrump.

No one vul

1♦-Pass-Pass-Dbl
1♡-?

♠ Q 8 7
♡ Q 9 5
♦ K 5 4
♣ J 9 7 5

Pass. If you must, one notrump at matchpoints, but I don't care for it.

Both vul

1♦-Pass-Pass-Dbl
1♠-?

♠ Q 7
♡ J 5 4
♦ K 10 7 5
♣ A 6 4 2

One notrump. Not much more than a minimum. Note that partner has promised something in spades so you don't need a full stopper. But you shouldn't be doing it on a stiff either.

No one vul

1♦-Pass-Pass-Dbl
1♡-?

♠ K 5 4
♡ 4 2
♦ A J 9 7 5
♣ A 10 5

One notrump. Getting close to a maximum. With this good a hand, you can fudge a bit on the heart stopper. Normally, you would like at least 10 x of opener's second suit.

No one vul

1♠-Pass-Pass-Dbl
2♠-?

♠ Q 9 7 5
♡ K J 7
♦ K J 7
♣ Q 10 6

Two notrump. But not happily. This is really a crummy hand. Your alternative is double and that is not unreasonable. But you would rather have some fast tricks.

There will be times where you want to make a penalty double. Some thoughts on this.
1. Would it be better to play it yourself?
2. Am I hanging partner?
3. Is it close?
4. What is the vulnerability?

Both vul

1♡-Pass-Pass-Dbl
2♡-?

♠ A 8 5 4
♡ K J 9 7
♦ Q 8
♣ J 10 3

With the opponents vulnerable, a double is very reasonable. You have trump tricks, which is the first criterion for a low level double, and you have an ace. Note that you have heart spots which are sure to promote to winners. Compare with the next hand.

Both vul

1♡-Pass-Pass-Dbl
2♡-?

♠ Q J 9 7
♡ A 6 5 4 2
◇ Q 3
♣ Q 4

This hand offers only one sure trick plus some kickers. Not nearly as useful as the previous hand. Bid two spades.

No one vul

1◇-Pass-Pass-Dbl
2♣-?

♠ K 4 2
♡ A 3
◇ Q J 9 6 4
♣ K 5 4

Not unreasonable to double this. You intend to lead a trump. Furthermore, you may get lucky and hear LHO go back to diamonds. Yum.

Both vul

1♡-Pass-Pass-Dbl
1NT-?

♠ Q 10 8 3
♡ Q 10 7 2
◇ A 3
♣ K J 4

Double. You have a good lead available, the spade three, and you have declarer's main suit locked up. Even if partner has one of those shapely minimums, declarer will have trouble developing his tricks.

CHAPTER SEVEN

Partner Bids a Suit and Opener Passes.

When this happens you will have fewer options than when partner doubled. These options include:
1. The simple raise.
2. Bidding notrump.
3. Bidding a new suit.
4. Cue bidding and jump raises.
5. Passing.

1. The simple raise.

The raise is one of your more likely actions and it will be most welcome to partner. The range for this is about the same whether partner's suit was bid at the one level or the two level. When opener passes, your range is from a good eight to a bad 12. The reason that the range is so large is that you have fewer techniques available when the other side opens. Having to put science aside means that on many hands where you would normally shilly-shally around you can't. You just have to raise, that being your only option. As you will see later, the range changes when opener rebids.

No one vul

1 ♣ -Pass-Pass-1 ♠
Pass-?

♠ K 8 7
♡ A 10 9 5
◇ 4 2
♣ Q 9 7 3

Two spades. Slightly better than a minimum. One notrump would be an error and passing would be worse.

Vul vs. not

1 ♡ -Pass-Pass-1 ♠
Pass-?

♠ J 8 7
♡ K 10 9 7
◇ K 5 4
♣ Q J 3

One notrump. A reopening bid at the one level does not guarantee the same quality suit as an overcall. While J 8 7 of spades is adequate support, the rest of your hand suggests notrump. If you had any unstopped suit at all you should not be so quick to give up the raise.

Both vul

1 ♣ -Pass-Pass-1 ◇
Pass-?

♠ Q 8
♡ K 5 4
◇ K 9 7 5
♣ Q J 6 3

One notrump. When partner reopens with one diamond, it is less imperative to raise than if partner had reopened with a major.

Both vul
1 ◇ -Pass-Pass-1 ♠
Pass-?

♠ Q 10 7 5   This is about the maximum you can have for a simple
♡ K 5 4   raise. Bid two spades.
◇ K 9 5
♣ K 8 3

Both vul
1 ◇ -Pass-Pass-1 ♡
Pass-?

♠ K J 9 7 5   Two hearts. One spade would be non-forcing and
♡ Q J 3   runs the risk of playing in an inferior trump suit. One of
◇ K 2   the most frustrating things you can have happen is to
♣ 9 6 3   reopen and have partner fail to raise, as per this hand.

No one vul
1 ♡ -Pass-Pass-2 ♣
Pass-?

♠ A 8 7   Three clubs. But very minimum. This hand makes me
♡ 10 6 5 4   think perhaps the minimum to raise should be a good
◇ K 10 5   nine rather than the good eight I suggested earlier.
♣ Q 9 7

Both vul
1 ♠ -Pass-Pass-2 ◇
Pass-?

♠ K 5   Three diamonds. Close to a maximum. That opening
♡ 4 3 2   one spade bid really does make it difficult for you to bid
◇ A 9 7   accurately. It takes away so much room. Partner's range
♣ A 10 8 6 5   for two diamonds is quite large, as is your range. Fortunately, you won't be involved in too many game auctions so the lack of definition won't hurt and you will be in your best suit.

2. Bidding notrump.

Any amount of notrump shows ranges similar to those shown on other
sequences.

One notrump shows nine to a crummy 12. Two notrump non-jump shows 11
or 12. Two notrump jump shows 12 to 14.

Understand that the edge of each of these ranges is tempered by such pluses and
minuses as spot cards, fit for partner, etc.

All of these bids show stoppers, although at the one level, it may be suspect.

No one vul
1 ◇ -Pass-Pass-1 ♠
Pass-?

♠ 8   One notrump. This is not because you have a single-
♡ Q 10 7   ton spade. It is because you have some values worth
◇ K J 8 3   showing. With no ace of clubs, you would pass.
♣ A 5 4 3 2

Both vul
1♣-Pass-Pass-1♠
Pass-?

♠ J 7
♡ K Q 9 7
◇ K Q 10 5
♣ Q 8 6

Two notrump. Nothing special. You could have a bit more. Note that the softness of your cards, i.e. queens and jacks is poor. But it is of far less consequence when RHO passes than when he rebids his suit. True, he may have good clubs, but there is no guarantee, and LHO may choose not to lead them. He may decide to be brilliant and lead a heart or a diamond.

No one vul
1♡-Pass-Pass-2♣
Pass-?

♠ Q 7
♡ K 9 3 2
◇ A J 9 7
♣ Q 10 7

Two notrump. About average. Three clubs would be a conservative alternative.

Both vul
1♠-Pass-Pass-2◇
Pass-?

♠ A 7 6 4
♡ K Q 6 4
◇ 9
♣ K J 8 3

Two notrump is enough. You actually have extra values, but getting tricks will be difficult if partner has a minimum, or good hand lacking in fast tricks. Your spade spots are poor. You would be far happier to have the spade nine. Plus you have poor diamonds. You could bid two notrump and hear partner bid three notrump, and then go down quite a few. Give partner

♠ J 3
♡ A 2
◇ K Q J 8 5 2
♣ Q 9 2

. . . and he will bid three in a flash. And you will have no play. This hand very much shows those pluses and minuses I mentioned when discussing notrump ranges.

3. Bidding a new suit.

Once in a while, partner will reopen and you will bid a new suit. There are five situations where this might occur, and they are rather unlikely.

a. Partner reopens at the one level and you bid a new suit at the one level.

No one vul
1♠-Pass-Pass-1♡
Pass-?

♠ J 8 7 6 5
♡ 3
◇ A J 8
♣ Q 10 6 4

One spade. A hand not worth overcalling on. Probably a poor suit. And no fit for hearts. An unlikely auction.

b. Partner reopens at the one level and you bid a new suit at the two level.
No one vul
1◇-Pass-Pass-1♡
Pass-?

♠ K 3
♡ J 2
◇ 10 7 5
♣ K Q 10 8 7 4

Two clubs. You need a decent suit for this. And you deny support for partner. Given the good suit, you won't have too much else.

c. Partner reopens at the two level and you bid a suit at the two level which is lower ranking than opener's.
No one vul
1♡-Pass-Pass-2♣
Pass-?

♠ 9 8 2
♡ Q 3
◇ K J 10 8 6 4
♣ Q 3

Bid two diamonds. The same as after partner reopens at the one level. You have a decent suit that wasn't worth a two level overcall and no fit for partner.

No one vul
1♠-Pass-Pass-2♣
Pass-?

♠ 8 7
♡ K 3
◇ Q J 8 6 4 3
♣ A 5 4

Raise to three clubs. Two diamonds would deny support for partner.

d. Partner reopens at the two level and you bid two of a suit higher ranking than opener's.
Almost inconceivable. To do this would require a good suit, and with that you would surely have been able to make a *one* level overcall or a weak jump overcall. Perhaps it should be a cue bid in support of partner.

Both vul
1◇-Pass-Pass-2♣
Pass-?

♠ A Q 2
♡ 8 7 6 5 3
◇ 4 2
♣ A Q 8

Should it be two hearts natural, two spades forcing as a club cue bid, a very conservative three clubs, or a cue bid of two diamonds? Frankly, I can't remember ever having heard this auction. But it's worth discussing if you have a serious partnership.

e. Finally, the last possibility is the most unlikely of all. **Partner reopens at the two level, and you bid a new suit at the three level.**

1 ♡ -Pass-Pass-2 ◊   Hard to imagine.
Pass-3 ♣

4. Cue Bidding and Jump Raises.

Lastly, you will have some strong hands to handle. These will be of two types.
1. A good fit for partner.
2. A good hand with no fit or stopper.

You won't have any other good hands, or they would have overcalled or doubled earlier.

When you have a good fit for partner, there will be two cases.
1. Unbalanced, which is defined as shape plus four trumps for partner.
2. Balanced, which is defined as three card support or four card support but no shape.

When partner's suit is a major, it is easy to raise with unbalanced shape. Just raise the appropriate amount.

No one vul
1 ♣ -Pass-Pass-1 ♡
Pass-?

♠ K J 7   A minimum three heart bid. More would be unkind
♡ Q 10 5 4   to partner. Note that partner will not expect you to be
◊ 4 2   short in opener's suit. Given the values you are show-
♣ A Q 7 3   ing, you would have overcalled or doubled with short-
                 ness in opener's suit.

Both vul
1 ◊ -Pass-Pass-1 ♠
Pass-?

♠ K J 7 6   Four spades. Too good to leave the decision to part-
♡ 3   ner. There are those who would have overcalled one
◊ 10 7 5 4 2   spade.
♣ A K 9

No one vul
1 ♡ -Pass-Pass-1 ♠
Pass-?

♠ Q J 8 7   Treat this as unbalanced and bid three spades. But be
♡ Q 8   aware that it's a slight overbid.
◊ K 10 8 7 5
♣ A 5

Both vul
1 ♠ -Pass-Pass-2 ♡
Pass-?

♠ A 8 7 5   Four hearts. Partner has a good five card suit, and
♡ J 10 5   modest values. Your shape plus good controls is worth
◊ 3   four hearts. Don't raise to three and force partner to
♣ A 10 9 5 4   make an unnecessary guess.

No one vul
1♡-Pass-Pass-2♣
Pass-?

♠ K 8 7   Hands like this are very difficult. Anything could be
♡ J 10 5 4 2   right. I would try four clubs. This almost always guar-
◊ 3   antees a stiff somewhere. Perhaps three diamonds
♣ A Q 9 7   should be a splinter bid. I can't think of a natural mean-
                       ing for it.

This leaves the case where you have a good balanced hand with a fit for partner
and the case where you have a good balanced hand but no idea what to do. Since
both are usually solved by making a cue bid and then clarifying it, I will treat
both situations at once via examples.

No one vul
1♣-Pass-Pass-1♠
Pass-?

♠ Q 10 8   This is not as good as it looks. Bid two clubs, intend-
♡ A 5 4   ing to
◊ K J 8 7   1. Pass two spades.
♣ K 6 2   2. Preference to two spades if partner bids two hearts
                       or diamonds.
    3. Raise two notrump to three notrump.
I would strongly suggest here that you borrow or buy a copy of *Overcalls**. It
contains a thorough discussion of cue bidding sequences, which can easily be
adapted to this situation. You would need only adjust the ranges to suit reopening
auctions as opposed to overcalling auctions.

The point of this hand is that you do not wish to get partner too high. Nothing
is worse than voluntarily bidding to the three level on balanced hands and going
down one. When it's your hand, you must go plus.

Both vul
1♡-Pass-Pass-1♠
Pass-?

♠ K J 8 7   Again, two hearts intending to play in two spades if
♡ 8 6 5   possible. If partner bids two notrump, you may con-
◊ A 5 4   sider passing although three spades rates to be better. I
♣ A 4 2   think partner can pass three spades. Good point to
                       discuss.

No one vul
1◊-Pass-Pass-1♡
Pass-?

♠ K J 7   Typical of the good hands you may have which do
♡ Q 2   not include a fit or a stopper. Bid two diamonds intend-
◊ 8 6 5   ing to
♣ A K J 7 6   1. Pass two hearts.
                       2. Bid three notrump over two notrump.
    3. Bid three clubs over two spades.
Note that this is not an overcall of two clubs over one diamond.

The Complete Book on Overcalls in Contract Bridge by Mike Lawrence

No one vul
1♣-Pass-Pass-1♦
Pass-?

♠ J 7 2
♡ K Q 10
◇ A Q J
♣ 8 6 5 4

Two clubs, intending to return to two spades or raise to three notrump. You won't have very many good hands which don't include a fit for partner when the opening bid was one club. You would usually have been able to bid after the opening call. Here you might have doubled one club for takeout. Not vulnerable I would have tried that, although I've no quarrel with a pass.

Both vul
1♠-Pass-Pass-2◇
Pass-?

♠ 8 6 5
♡ A Q J
◇ 10 3
♣ A Q 8 7 5

The higher ranking their suit, the more likely you will have a random good balanced hand. This is because there are many hands with values which could only be shown by overcalling at the two level. This hand could not overcall two clubs over one spade. But if the black suits were reversed, you would overcall one spade over any other opening bid. With the actual hand and auction, you should try two spades intending to raise to three notrump or to pass three diamonds. Perhaps this is a three club bid implying a good hand with club strength, diamond tolerance and no spade stopper. If you have that agreement, then this hand is easy. It's theoretical though and I have never had such understandings in the formal sense. If it came up at the table, I would feel nervous about it.

5. When partner reopens and opener passes, one of your options is to pass.

While this is obvious, it is worth mentioning. There are some hands where you may feel like bidding but either can't or shouldn't. Here are some typical examples.

No one vul
1♣-Pass-Pass-1♠
Pass-?

♠ K Q 8 7
♡ J 5 4
◇ 8 6 5
♣ J 9 7

Pass. A raise should show a good eight. This hand doesn't make it. The fine spade support does not compensate for the poor distribution and lack of useful cards.

Both vul
1♡-Pass-Pass-1♠
Pass-?

♠ 10
♡ J 6 5
◇ 4 3 2
♣ K J 10 8 7 5

You know clubs is better than spades, but it is unlikely partner would pass two clubs. Better to pass. When you won't be able to stop, don't get started.

No one vul
1 ◊ -Pass-Pass-1 ♡
Pass-?

♠ K J 7
♡ 4 2
◊ 8 6 3
♣ A Q 8 6 2

Still best to pass. Even with this much, game is most unlikely. No reason to suppose clubs from your side is better than hearts from his side.

Both vul
1 ♡ -Pass-Pass-1 ♠
Pass-?

♠ 10 3
♡ 8 6 4
◊ A Q 6 4
♣ A J 8 3

Again. A good hand, but no convenient bid. If the hearts were as good as J x x or 10 x x x, or even 10 x x, you might chance one notrump. As it is, you should probably pass.

No one vul
1 ◊ -Pass-Pass-1 ♠
Pass-?

♠ 3
♡ K 7 6 5
◊ 8 5 4 2
♣ A K Q 8

Possibly one notrump. You want better diamonds, but you have compensating values. In part, you are running because of the stiff spade. Note the previous hand which had a doubleton spade.

No one vul
1 ♡ -Pass-Pass-1 ♠
Pass-?

♠ 9 2
♡ 8 6 5
◊ A Q 6 2
♣ A K 5 4

Too good to pass. Try two hearts, intending to pass two spades. If partner bids three clubs or diamonds, you will have another problem. In practice, I've never had this hand and auction.

CHAPTER EIGHT

Partner Reopens with a Suit and Opener Rebids.

As when opener passes, you have a number of options plus the additional one of doubling opener. The fact that opener has rebid changes things significantly. Here are your options, plus a look at the differences that occur as opposed to when opener passed.

1. The simple raise.
2. Bidding notrump.
3. Bidding a new suit.
4. Cue bidding and the jump raise.
5. The penalty double.
6. Passing.

1. The simple raise.

The simple raise of partner's suit is the easiest method you have of establishing a basis for competition. This remains true whether opener has rebid or not. But there is a change in the values shown by the raise. When opener passes, the raise is defined as eight to 11. But when opener intervenes, it becomes incumbent on you to raise far more aggressively. This is because failure to raise runs the risk that you may be shut out of the auction. It's not that you will be missing any games. It is that you will be missing all kinds of partscores. Compare these two auctions:

1 ◊ -Pass-Pass-1 ♠   1 ◊ -Pass-Pass-1 ♠
Pass-?   2 ♣ -?

In the first sequence, partner's one spade bid may buy the contract. You are in live contention for a partscore. A raise by you is encouraging with an eye toward getting to game.

The second sequence is much different. If you pass, the opponents may buy the hand for two clubs on hands where you might have a partscore of your own. True, partner may have enough to bid further. But against that, if LHO raises to three clubs, neither partner nor you will be able to continue. And, if partner has an in-between hand, needing only to know of support from you, then he may have to pass when he could have gone on had you raised.

The upshot of this is that when opener competes, a "free" raise by you shows less than a non-free raise. This is contrary to most concepts of "free" bids, but necessary if you are not going to be robbed blind.

No one vul

1 ♣ -Pass-Pass-1 ♠
2 ♣ -?

♠ Q 10 8	Two spades. You would pass if opener had passed
♡ K 3 2	also. It's very important to establish a fit. More values
◊ Q 10 9 5	would be nice, but the fit is more important than the
♣ 4 3 2	odd queen or two.

Both vul
1 ♠ -Pass-Pass-2 ◇
2 ♡ -?

♠ A 10 8 7 5
♡ 4 2
◇ Q J 9
♣ 10 6 5

Three diamonds. Another minimum which would not have acted over a pass. If you are worried that you may push them to a game, don't be. Once opener has bid two hearts, they will get there regardless of your action, should they choose to do so.

No one vul
1 ◇ -Pass-Pass-1 ♠
2 ◇ -?

♠ 10 6 5
♡ K Q 9 7
◇ K 5 4
♣ K 6 2

Two spades. The upper range of the raise remains the same. You could even have a little more than this. You may lose some games now and then by having such a wide range for two spades, but you will hold your own on partscore hands. The return vs. gain will be substantially in your favor.

No one vul
1 ♠ -Pass-Pass-2 ♡
2 ♠ -?

♠ Q 8
♡ J 9 7
◇ K 8 7 5
♣ K 6 5 4

This one sequence is rather special. Most of the time when you raise partner's suit from the two level to the three level, he will either pass or look for three notrump. The one thing he won't do is continue voluntarily to the four level. This is because in all other cases, his suit is a minor, and there are no bonuses for getting to the four level. In this auction, partner's suit is hearts. If you raise, partner may well go on to four hearts. This sequence doesn't allow for game tries so partner will have to guess. This means that you should not raise to three hearts on bad hands.

Some players solve hands like this one by bidding three hearts while folding up their cards, or perhaps bidding in an unenthusiastic tone. Conversely, with good hands, they bid three hearts with interest, enthusiasm, and a warm smile. Works pretty well. Unfortunately, for the rest of us, it is best to pass this particular hand. It's close though, and if you do bid, it won't necessarily be wrong.

2. Bidding notrump.

Notrump ranges remain the same as when opener passed. But there are additional considerations when he rebids.

When opener rebids a new suit, notrump by you will require two stoppers, not just one. And if opener rebids his suit, he will have a much better than average suit. You will be subject to an especially effective defense, so you may want to reconsider some marginal hands.

No one vul
1 ♡ -Pass-Pass-1 ♠
2 ♡ -?

♠ J 7
♡ Q 9 8
◇ K Q 10 7
♣ K Q 10 9

Very dangerous to bid with this hand. It looks like you have values to bid at least two notrump, but if you visualize opener's hand, you will see why you would be lucky to make even one notrump, let alone two or three.

90

Opener rates to have a good six card or longer suit, and at least one additional ace.

♠ K 3
♡ A K 10 7 5 4
◇ A J 3
♣ 5 2

This is about an average two heart rebid by opener.

Now if you bid two notrump, you will get a heart lead and will quickly lose five hearts, the ace of diamonds, and probably a spade as well.

I would probably bid two notrump anyway, but would hate it. Perhaps two spades is right. Maybe double, or even pass. No one said bridge was easy.

No one vul

1♡-Pass-Pass-1♠
2♡-?

♠ K 2   You could try two notrump with this. You have better
♡ J 7 4 2   help in spades plus you have a good diamond suit which
◇ A Q 10 9 3   could easily come home. Here you have two reasonable
♣ Q 10   sources of tricks. The last hand had no such hope.

Both vul

1◇-Pass-Pass-1♡
2◇-?

♠ Q 8 7   Two notrump again. Here you have a second stopper
♡ 10 2   plus a suit which could provide tricks. Don't consider
◇ A Q 3   doubling.
♣ K J 9 8 7

No one vul

1♣-Pass-Pass-1♡
1♠-?

♠ Q 10 3   One notrump. Useful to note that RHO has four
♡ 10 4   spades and a club suit of unclear length. You need stop-
◇ K J 9 8 3   pers in both suits or if you have a maximum, one and
♣ K 10 7   one-half stoppers.

Both vul

1◇-Pass-Pass-1♡
2♣-?

♠ J 8 7 6 2   Two notrump I suppose. While neither of opener's
♡ Q 5   suits presents an enormous threat, the opening leader
◇ K 10 3   will be able to select the right lead almost without excep-
♣ A Q 2   tion. Opener is likely to be five-five or perhaps five-
               four. Note that in the previous hand, opener had four
spades, but the club suit was of undetermined length, ranging from three to six.

When opener rebids, it will be even more unlikely that you will bid new suits than it was when opener passed. When opener rebids a new suit, there will be only one suit remaining, and when opener rebids his suit, that may make it impossible for you to bid your suit at a convenient level.

1♡-Pass-Pass-1♠   The two heart bid makes it awkward to show a
2♡-?   minor.

3. Bidding a new suit.

Whatever principles you have adopted for showing new suits when opener has passed with work when opener rebids.

4. Cue bidding and jump raises.

When opener rebids, there will be far more effect on the way you treat your strong raises and your cue bids. Those hands with shape and support will still jump raise, but the other hands will become more difficult to handle. Opener's rebid will frequently have the effect of taking away your cue bid, or will force you to make it a level higher. Sometimes your hand just isn't that good.

No one vul

1♡-Pass-Pass-1♠
2♡-?

♠ Q 10 8 7　　　　　Three spades is enough. The jump still shows a good
♡ 6 5 4　　　　　　hand with four trumps and useful distribution.
◊ A K J 8 3
♣ 10

Both vul

1◊-Pass-Pass-1♠
2◊-?

♠ K J 7　　　　　　Had opener passed, you would have cue bid two dia-
♡ K Q 8 6　　　　　monds and been content to stop in two spades. Opener's
◊ Q 2　　　　　　　rebid has stolen your cue bid and leaves you with an
♣ Q 10 6 3　　　　　awkward problem. You can
　　　　　　　　　　1. Jump to three spades. This hand has the approximate values, but lacks the fourth trump and has poor shape.
　　2. You can cue bid. This will get you too high on a number of occasions.
　　3. You can raise to two spades, which will cause you to miss a few games.
If partner were a passed hand, I would choose the simple raise. Here partner has not passed, but I'm not at all convinced that only two spades isn't best.
　　1. It will be a very poor result to get to three spades voluntarily and go down. You just can't afford minus scores when the hand belongs to your side.
　　2. Your diamond queen is wasted. Effectively, you are no longer playing with a 40 point deck. You are playing with a 38 point deck.
One important point of this hand is that when opener rebids his suit, a cue bid by you must include a fit for partner. You can't have a hand good enough to go exploring at the three level unless you have some idea where you are going to play.

No one vul

1♡-Pass-Pass-1♠
2♡-?

♠ J 3　　　　　　　This is a good hand. But where is it going? If you cue
♡ 8 6 2　　　　　　bid, you are not going to know what to do over three
◊ A K 10 4　　　　　spades, and you don't have values to make three
♣ A J 8 3　　　　　notrump worthwhile. I would suggest two spades or
　　　　　　　　　　pass. Note that partner is not barred from rebidding.

Partner with

♠ K Q 10 8 4 2
♥ 3
♦ J 6 3
♣ K 10 2

. . . would bid one spade over one heart and if opener rebid two hearts, your partner would continue to two spades. He would be counting on you to have a good hand without a clear bid. Something like the one you actually have. More on this later.

No one vul

1♠-Pass-Pass-2♣
2♠-?

♠ 8 6 5
♥ A J 9 7
♦ A K J 3
♣ 4 2

This hand carries the situation of the previous hand to extremes. There is almost no way you can hold this hand and hear the given sequence. But if you should ever find yourself with this problem, you might actually try passing. Your only real alternative is three clubs. If you are afraid of missing a game, try constructing a few hands for partner. You'll find the only games available are in hearts or diamonds and there is no way to explore these possibilities. Three clubs by you will usually end the auction. If you pass though, partner may reopen again expecting you to have a good hand of this approximate description. If he does bid again, he will be pleased to find you with extras.

Once again, the possibility of assigning some significance to three hearts or diamonds arises. Perhaps one of these bids is the answer. What would it mean? Unclear. It should deny support, but it should show a tolerance. Otherwise how could you bid at the three level on a hand which couldn't overcall at the two level? Because either of these bids could push you to four clubs, you will need a good hand.

On some sequences, your new suit will allow you to get to three of partner's suit, so you could do it on less. This sequence for example won't force you past three diamonds:

1♥-Pass-Pass-2♦
2♥-3♣

I am not prepared to offer answers to what new suits should mean if you choose to treat them as semi-artificial or completely artificial. But I'm willing to offer the problem for your consideration. When selecting your treatment, you may wish to recognize such factors as
  1. Is partner a passed hand?
  2. Is it IMP's or matchpoints?
  3. Could your suit have been bid at the one level?
  4. Could your suit have been bid at the two level?
  5. Is your suit higher ranking or lower ranking than partner's? If lower, it will permit partner to return to his suit at the same level.
  6. Is your bid forcing?

Both vul
1♡-Pass-Pass-2♣
2♡-?

♠ K 2	Three hearts. Good enough to try for three notrump.
♡ 8 6 5	Even five clubs is possible. You have a club fit and you
◊ A K J 9 7	have excellent chances for fast tricks if partner can stop
♣ K J 4	hearts.

Vul vs. not
1♠-Pass-Pass-2◊
2♠-?

♠ 8 6 5 4	Even though you don't have a true fit, your fast tricks
♡ A Q	plus diamond help make this hand worth a cue bid.
◊ Q J	
♣ A 6 5 4 2	

Some of the time, opener will rebid a new suit, thus opening up some extra possibilities for you. When opener rebids his own suit, it makes it difficult for you to cue bid because that action automatically gets you to the three level. But when opener rebids a new suit, you can often cue bid his first suit and save an entire level of bidding.

No one vul
1♡-Pass-Pass-1♠
2◊-?

♠ K J 7	This is the same hand offered a few pages back. Then,
♡ K Q 8 6	RHO opened and rebid in diamonds. The only cue bid
◊ Q 2	you had was three diamonds, and this was rejected.
♣ Q 10 6 3	Here you have an extra option. You can bid two hearts
	and quit at *two* spades if that is partner's choice. Note

the enormous difference in actions available to you when opener rebids a new suit as opposed to the same suit.

Both vul
1♠-Pass-Pass-2◊
2♡-?

♠ 8 6 2	Two spades. Again, the economy of space. You can
♡ A 9 7	show a good hand and still not get past three diamonds
◊ K J 7	if partner is minimum. Note that your cue bid says
♣ A J 9 3	nothing about your holding in that suit.

No one vul
1♡-Pass-Pass-1♠
2♣-?

♠ 8 6	Back to the same theme. What should two diamonds
♡ A Q 10 7	mean? It looks like you should do something and
◊ A Q 6 5	neither two spades nor two hearts seems quite right.
♣ 4 3 2	

Both vul
1 ◇ -Pass-Pass-1 ♠
2 ♣ -?

♠ Q 10 9 7   Two diamonds. The jump raise shows both four card
♡ A 5 4   support plus good distribution. This hand has support
◇ K J 7   only.
♣ K 6 2

Both vul
1 ♡ -Pass-Pass-1 ♠
2 ♡ -?

♠ K Q 8   Very reasonable to treat these spades as four card sup-
♡ A 6 5 4   port and jump to three spades. Partner has five spades,
◇ 2   or else he would have doubled for takeout. You draw
♣ K 6 5 4 2   this inference from the fact that your partner is known
                    to be short in hearts. If you had a similar hand with a
stiff heart, you would have no assurances as to partner's length in spades.

5. The penalty double.
When opener rebids, you may wish to double for penalties. The usual criteria
apply. Should you prefer to try for a contract of your own? Are you allowing for
the minimums partner may have?

No one vul
1 ♡ -Pass-Pass-1 ♠
2 ♡ -?

♠ J 8 2   Two spades. Don't take extreme positions. Two
♡ A J 6 4   spades should be safe and two hearts doubled doesn't
◇ K 10 7   rate to be more than one down. If you held the heart
♣ Q 5 4   nine against vulnerable opponents, a matchpoint double
                    would be reasonable.

Vul vs. not
1 ♠ -Pass-Pass-2 ♣
2 ♠ -?

♠ K J 3 2   Three notrump. This should be cold. Note that you
♡ K 3   can count on a better minimum from partner when he
◇ A 6 5 4   reopens at the two level than you could when he
♣ Q J 3   reopens with a double.

No one vul
1 ◇ -Pass-Pass-1 ♠
2 ◇ -?

♠ 3 2   This is the kind of hand you want when you double
♡ A 9 7 5   them. Good trumps, adequate values otherwise, no fit,
◇ K J 9 3   and no worry that game exists. If there is a game for
♣ K 5 4   your side, the penalty will be that much more for you.

Both vul
1♡-Pass-Pass-2♣
2♡-?

♠ K 8 7 5   Exactly the kind of hand you shouldn't double with.
♡ Q 6 5 4 2   You have no heart spots, and your partner has not
◇ K 9 7   promised that much. His normal values will include 11
♣ 3   high card points with a trick or two for defense. Had
                 partner opened with one club and the auction gone like
                 this

                 1♣-1♡-1♠-Pass
                 2♣-2♡-?

. . . then you would have a fine double. The reopening two club bid tends to be
limited to about 11 to 14. On the second sequence partner's values are on the
order of 12 to 17. Par would be an additional king or an additional defensive trick
or trick and a half. Furthermore, when the opener opens and then rebids two
hearts, he shows a better hand than the person who overcalls and then rebids his
suit.

No one vul
1♣-Pass-Pass-1♠
1NT-?

♠ Q 9 7   Two spades. As usual, try to play in a reasonable con-
♡ A 8 6 5   tract rather than make a close double. Be especially con-
◇ A J 9 5   cerned about opener's suit in a situation like this one.
♣ 10 7   It's almost never right to double when you can't control
                 that suit.

6. Passing.

Finally, your last option is to pass. Usually, this shows lack of a good hand but
as we've seen, there are some quite good hands which can't act intelligently. One
important point here is that you should not act on unclear hands unless you have
maximum values for that action.

No one vul
1♣-Pass-Pass-1♡
2♣-?

♠ Q J 7   No reason to do anything. If partner can't act again,
♡ 10 6   this hand has no future.
◇ K J 8 4 2
♣ Q 6 5

Both vul
1♡-Pass-Pass-2♣
2♡-?

♠ A 8 7   Three clubs. Unusual with only two clubs. Because of
♡ 8 3 2   this flaw, you require a maximum to try it.
◇ K 10 9 8 3
♣ K J

No one vul
1♡-Pass-Pass-2♣
2◇-?

♠ K J 9 8
♡ Q 6 4 2
◇ K 8 3
♣ Q 5

The values are too slow for two notrump and the clubs too poor to raise. Two spades would be far too committal, regardless of what it means. Pass.

Both vul
1♡-Pass-Pass-2♣
2♡-?

♠ Q J 8
♡ 8 6 5 2
◇ A K Q 7
♣ 4 3

Another good hand with no safe way to enter. Double would be horrible. That requires sure trump tricks, not just four pups.

Both vul
1♠-Pass-Pass-2♡
2♠-?

♠ J 8 7
♡ Q 2
◇ A J 8 5
♣ K 10 9 7

With no obvious bid available, you go quietly. Any time you don't know what to do, you need extra values to try an experiment.

No one vul
1♡-Pass-Pass-2♣
2◇-?

♠ K J 7
♡ Q J 3
◇ K 6 5 4
♣ 8 6 3

Pass. If your clubs and hearts were interchanged, you would raise. As it is, this hand is not nearly worth two notrump.

PART III
CONTINUING THE AUCTION

A lot of space has been devoted to what reopener's partner should do in the case where one of a suit was passed around to the balancer. The reason was that this is the only reopening sequence in which game is likely to exist and which permits much room for partnership discussion. For this reason I am going to devote more attention to how the reopener should continue. This is the only type of sequence which warrants such attention. Space won't permit a thorough inspection of all the cases, but there are quite a few generalities worth discussing.

CHAPTER NINE
If Your Reopening Bid Was Double

When you have doubled for takeout, you will far more often continue the auction than if your reopening bid was a simple bid of a suit. This is because your range for the double is so enormous. Your minimum is a shapely seven and your maximum can be as much as a super 25 or even more. Having doubled, it is necessary to catch up on the strength.

Whether or not you continue will frequently depend on whether partner has made a simple forced response, a free bid, a jump, a cue bid, or a bid of any number of notrump.

1. If partner's bid is minimum, i.e. simply answering your double, a raise by you will show values such that game is possible opposite the maximum partner may have. Inasmuch as partner can have ten or even 11 points and still make a simple response, a raise by you should show a good 14 or so. Note that this is somewhat less than what you would show if your double was immediately after the opening bid. Other bids by you will show similar sound values but will still not be up to the standards that would be required for an immediate takeout double and rebid.

No one vul

1♣-Pass-Pass-Dbl
Pass-1♡-Pass-?

♠ K J 8 7
♡ Q J 6 2
◇ A 4 3
♣ 10 7

A normal decent hand. Nothing special here. Pass.

No one vul

1♡-Pass-Pass-Dbl
Pass-1♠-Pass-?

♠ K J 3
♡ A 2
◇ K 10 9 7
♣ A 6 4 2

Pass. Partner won't have both five spades and the ten points you need for game. He would jump. If you had a fourth spade, you would have an average raise to two spades. That fourth trump is extremely significant.

Both vul

1◇-Pass-Pass-Dbl
Pass-1♠-Pass-?

♠ Q 10 8 7
♡ A K 4 2
◇ 3
♣ K 9 7 6

The good shape and well coordinated high cards suggest a raise. Two spades.

Both vul
1♥-Pass-Pass-Dbl
Pass-1♠-Pass-?

♠ K J 8 7
♥ 3
♦ A Q 10 7
♣ A J 9 7

Three spades. Had you doubled an opening one heart bid at your *right* and heard partner bid one spade, you would raise to two.

Both vul
Pass-1♥-Pass-Pass
Dbl-Pass-1♠-Pass
-?

♠ J 10 8 7
♥ 3
♦ A K 10 6
♣ Q J 9 3

Two spades. You would not do this normally, but having passed originally, you can afford to raise. This caters to the possibility that partner was being conservative. He knows he is facing a passed hand, so he might have a little extra. He won't expect more from you.

No one vul
1♦-Pass-Pass-Dbl
Pass-1♥-Pass-?

♠ K Q 10 8 7
♥ A 10 5
♦ 3
♣ K Q 7 5

One spade. This shows more than a minimum opening bid, but does not guarantee the earth.

Both vul
1♦-Pass-Pass-Dbl
Pass-1♠-Pass-?

♠ A 10 5
♥ K Q J 8 7
♦ 3
♣ A Q 6 5

Two hearts. Because you doubled, and then bid your suit at a higher level than was necessary, you do show extras. On the previous hand, you doubled and bid one spade. Here you could have bid one heart but doubled and then bid two hearts. This sequence shows a good hand.

No one vul
1♦-Pass-Pass-Dbl
Pass-1♥-Pass-?

♠ J 8 7
♥ K J 7
♦ A Q 9
♣ A J 10 5

You will remember that the reopening one notrump range varied according to the suit opened. Over one spade, one notrump showed 12-16 and over one club, it showed 12-14. If you double first, you are showing a hand slightly better than whatever one notrump would have shown depending on the suit opened. Bid one notrump.

No one vul
1♥-Pass-Pass-Dbl
Pass-2♣-Pass-?

♠ K 9 7 5
♥ K 2
♦ A 9 5
♣ K 10 8 7

Pass. Any further action would be wrong. If partner had responded one spade, you might be talked into going to two spades if pushed. But this hand is not good enough to volunteer for the three level.

99

Both vul
1 ♡ -Pass-Pass-Dbl
Pass-2 ♣ -Pass-?

♠ K Q 7 4
♡ A J 3
♢ A J 6 4
♣ 10 2

Two clubs wasn't what you wanted to hear. Perhaps one spade or one notrump would have been better. At least on this hand. The point is, that having doubled, you can't try two notrump. That would show more. Double was a reasonable action which seems to have backfired. But not necessarily. Two clubs could be all right. Don't make it worse. Pass.

Should opener's partner decide to get involved, a raise by you need not show quite as good a hand. In this situation, you can raise with less than normal values if you have good trumps. This is in keeping with the theory that in competitive auctions it is important to establish that your side has a good fit.

No one vul
1 ♣ -Pass-Pass-Dbl
Pass-1 ♡ -2 ♣ -?

♠ A 5 4
♡ Q J 10 7
♢ A 8 6 3
♣ 4 2

You would not raise if RHO had passed. But he didn't. You raise here to show good trumps and a bit more than some of the real minnies you could have. Your partner can have a hand worth a competitive bid, but he might not want to rebid 9 6 4 2 of hearts and find you with Q 8 7.

When partner's bid has been voluntary, you shouldn't get too excited. Remember that partner will strive to bid on any excuse. All his bid means is that he has a suit of sorts and isn't completely broke.

If the auction becomes competitive, you can be a little freer in raising him, and if his suit is a minor, you can play him for a bit more than if his suit is a major.

No one vul
1 ♣ -Pass-Pass-Dbl
1 ♡ -1 ♠ -2 ♡ -?

♠ A 10 8 7
♡ J 9 5
♢ A J 8 2
♣ 9 3

Two spades. You have nothing wasted and you have a fourth spade. You should not be as quick to push to the three level. The two level is sort of a dog eat dog world where no one is sure what's going on. But when you get higher, things become better defined and the doubling starts. This doesn't mean you should never compete at the three level, just don't be too wanton about it. There is much to be said for pushing the opponents up there and letting them have it.

Both vul
1 ♢ -Pass-Pass-Dbl
1 ♡ -1 ♠ -Pass-?

♠ Q 10 3 2
♡ A 9 5
♢ A 2
♣ Q 10 6 3

Pass. Partner's maximum is about the same regardless of whether the one spade is free or not. You don't have to raise.

No one vul
1 ♡ -Pass-Pass-Dbl
2 ♡ -2 ♠ -Pass-?

♠ K Q 8
♡ 3 2
♦ K J 7 3
♣ A 9 4 3

Pass. Two spades doesn't show nearly enough to get you excited with this hand.

Both vul
1 ♣ -Pass-Pass-Dbl
2 ♣ -2 ♡ -Pass-?

♠ K J 7
♡ Q J 3 2
♦ A Q 10 3
♣ 4 2

Pass again. Getting close, but still not quite worth a bid. Give partner as much as:

♠ 8 6 5
♡ A K 10 6 4
♦ K 4 2
♣ 9 8

. . . and game will depend on a spade finesse. With that hand, he might have overcalled one heart. He is more likely to have something like

♠ Q 4 2·
♡ K 10 8 5 3
♦ K J 3
♣ 8 7

Three hearts is the maximum, and once in a while two hearts will be all.

Both vul
1 ♡ -Pass-Pass-Dbl
2 ♡ -3 ♣ -Pass-?

♠ 10 8 6 4
♡ K 2
♦ A K J 7
♣ K J 6

You could try three notrump with this. It has good chances. The important point is that partner ought not to bid a minor suit freely without some genuine values. Had partner bid two spades instead, you would have a clear pass.

There is a family of hands for which description clearly must start with a take-out double, but which are awkward to handle after partner's response.

These hands will usually be those where you have good three card support for partner, or where you want to bid notrump but have no stopper. Usually these hands can be handled with a cue bid.

No one vul
1 ♣ -Pass-Pass-Dbl
Pass-1 ♡ -Pass-?

♠ A Q 8
♡ K 8 7
♦ A K Q 9
♣ 10 5 4

Two clubs. This is typical of the problem hand. You have good values. You haven't another suit to bid. You can't bid notrump. Most of the time when you cue bid, you will have a balanced hand.

If partner bids two hearts, you will pass. So if partner has enough to make game opposite this hand, he must not make that simple rebid.

Both vul
1 ♡ -Pass-Pass-Dbl
Pass-1 ♠ -Pass-?

♠ K 7
♡ 8 6 5
◊ A K J 9
♣ A K Q 8

Two hearts. You are hoping partner can bid notrump. If he bids two spades, you will have a very difficult decision.

No one vul
1 ◊ -Pass-Pass-Dbl
Pass-1 ♡ -Pass-?

♠ K Q 9
♡ Q 10 8 7
◊ A 3 2
♣ A K J

You have the values to jump to three hearts, but your shape stinks. Losers all over. You could cue bid two diamonds and not get higher than two hearts.

This hand is not as good as it looks. Opposite

♠ 8 7 2
♡ A 6 4 2
◊ 10 7 5
♣ 9 5 4

You could end up losing seven tricks.

2. When partner jumps, the only thing you need to know is his range. You will bid according to that range. Your auction will continue very much as if you had doubled the opening bid at your right and partner gave you a jump response. The only differences are:

1. Partner's jump shows more when responding to a reopening double than when responding to an immediate double.

2. If partner jumps in a major suit, it is very likely to be a poor five card suit or a ho-hum four card suit. With values for the jump, he might have overcalled with a good suit.

If partner cue bids, you treat it similarly to cue bidding in response to a takeout double. Questions for your partnership are

1. Does the cue bidder guarantee another bid?
2. Is it forcing to game?
3. Is it forcing until a suit is agreed on?

Note that whatever partner has, he will not have a hand worth an overcall or a takeout double. It is useful to remember the hands that partner can't have.

3. If partner bids some number of notrump, you should expect him to have a better hand than when responding to a direct takeout double. This is because your reopening double doesn't show that much. He will need good hands to aspire to any number of notrump.

No one vul
1 ♠ -Pass-Pass-Dbl
Pass-1NT-Pass-?

♠ 8 7
♡ K J 9 6
◊ A Q 10 5
♣ A J 4

Raise to two notrump. Partner's spade holding will be useful on this sequence because he is behind the bidder. K Q 7 or Q J 5 2 or Q 10 6 3 will be two stoppers on this auction. Had you doubled directly these holdings could easily be worth one trick only as they would be under the bidder.

Both vul
1♣-Pass-Pass-Dbl
Pass-1NT-Pass-?

♠ K J 9 6
♡ A Q 10 5
◇ A J 4
♣ 8 7

Three notrump. Partner should have a better hand for one notrump after an opening one club bid than after an opening one spade bid. This and the previous hand are the same. The change in the sequence dictates the change in how you should treat it.

No one vul
1◇-Pass-Pass-Dbl
Pass-2NT-Pass-?

♠ K Q 8 7
♡ A 9 5
◇ 10 2
♣ K 10 3 2

An easy three notrump. Partner wants to know if you have a decent hand. You do. Considering you could have doubled with an ace less, you have plenty to accept.

Both vul
Pass-1♡-Pass-Pass
Dbl-Pass-2NT-Pass
-?

♠ J 10 8 7
♡ 3
◇ K Q 10 9 7
♣ A 10 3

Given that you are a passed hand, you should feel you are very close to a maximum. You have a fine source of tricks. Three notrump.

No one vul
1◇-Pass-Pass-Dbl
2◇-2NT-Pass-?

♠ Q 9 7
♡ K J 8 2
◇ 4 2
♣ A Q 8 6

Pass. Partner is under pressure and may have had to stretch slightly. You have a slow hand without many obvious winners. If partner has only one stopper, you may already be too high.

4. When opener rebids and partner passes, you will frequently pass as well. But some of the time you will have enough to try again. If it had been your intention to double and then bid a suit, you should probably do so in spite of partner's pass. If your shape and values warrant, you can double again, still for takeout. If you doubled, intending to bid notrump, you should think twice about it. Partner can be weak, and opener's rebid implies a better than average hand or suit.

No one vul
1♣-Pass-Pass-Dbl
2♣-Pass-Pass-?

♠ A 10 7 3
♡ A J 9 5
◇ K J 7 6
♣ 3

Double again. It won't take much to make a part score and you may push them one trick higher. You have about six points more than a minimum. Note that partner can bid at the two level.

No one vul
1 ◇ -Pass-Pass-Dbl
2 ♣ -Pass-2 ◇ -?

♠ K Q 10 8 7
♡ A 10 4
◇ 3
♣ K Q 9 3

You can bid two spades. But it's close.

Both vul
1 ♡ -Pass-Pass-Dbl
2 ♣ -Pass-Pass-?

♠ A Q 10 8 7
♡ 3
◇ A Q 9 8
♣ A 10 4

Double. If partner bids two diamonds, now bid two spades.

Both vul
1 ◇ -Pass-Pass-Dbl
2 ◇ -Pass-Pass-?

♠ A J 7
♡ A Q 2
◇ 3 2
♣ A J 7 4 2

Double again. You may end up in a three-three major suit fit, but the alternative of three clubs is too dangerous. Perhaps partner can pass for penalty.

Vul vs. not
1 ◇ -Pass-Pass-Dbl
2 ♣ -Pass-Pass-?

♠ A Q 8
♡ K 10 7
◇ A J 9
♣ Q 8 6 4

Pass. You had intended to rebid one notrump over one heart or one spade by partner. Here partner couldn't drag up a bid. You haven't nearly enough to bid two notrump and the hand doesn't rate a second double.

No one vul
1 ♡ -Pass-Pass-Dbl
2 ♡ -Pass-Pass-?

♠ Q 8 7
♡ A 9 5
◇ K Q J 7
♣ K Q 7

You would do well to pass. With hearts being rebid, they pose a very serious threat to a notrump contract. Before the rebid, you were sort of hoping to find a heart honor in partner's hand. Now you don't expect to find one, and opener has extra length as well. Your high cards might see you through a second double, but you have so many losers. Pass is best.

CHAPTER TEN

If You Have Reopened by Bidding

If your reopening action has been to bid a suit, you will have somewhat different problems in the later rounds than when you reopened with double.

When you doubled, most of your subsequent decisions were to raise or to pass. Sometimes when you had a strong hand you bid notrump or a new suit.

When you reopen in a suit however, most of your decisions will be whether to compete in your own suit (perhaps partner has raised) or to introduce a new suit. Note that you will seldom have a strong hand.

Looking back, we see that partner's options include:

1. Raising our suit.
2. Bidding notrump.
3. Bidding a new suit.
4. Jump raises.
5. Cue bidding.
6. Doubling.
7. Passing.

1. When partner raises your suit, there will be times when you will want to bid further. You may wish to make a game try, or you may wish to bid further simply because the opponents have done so. In either case, you should note whether or not partner made a free raise. Remember, if opener passes, partner's raise should show a decent hand. But if opener has rebid, partner may have stretched some to raise. He would do this in order to tell you that he does have a fit for you.

No one vul

1♣-Pass-Pass-1♠
Pass-2♠-Pass-?

♠ Q 9 8 7 5
♡ A Q 3
◇ K Q 5 4
♣ 9

Three diamonds. Partner's raise shows a fair hand, eight to 11, so game is possible. You would not try this if you had opened and partner raised as the values for this raise would be about six to nine. Note that this is not a particularly strong hand. It's not worth doubling first and following with one spade. But when partner raises, it improves substantially. It is the added value of a fit which makes this hand strong enough to make a game try.

No one vul

1♣-Pass-Pass-1♠
2♣-2♠-Pass-?

♠ Q 9 8 7 5
♡ A Q 3
◇ K Q 5 4
♣ 9

Same hand. Different auction. Pass. Partner's competitive raise may be lighter than if opener had passed. Give partner a little room.

No one vul
1♣-Pass-Pass-1♠
2♣-2♠-3♣-?

♠ Q 9 8 7 5
♡ A Q 3
◊ K Q 5 4
♣ 9

Same hand. Yet another auction. This sequence suggests more than either of the prior two that partner has nothing wasted in clubs. I would bid three spades which is not a game try. But it's close. If you want to try with three diamonds, it could work.

Not vul vs. vul
1♡-Pass-Pass-1♠
2♡-2♠-3◊-?

♠ 10 8 7 6 5 4
♡ K 9 8
◊ 3
♣ A J 4

Three spades. You have a good offensive hand. This should not be interpreted as forward going.

No one vul
1♡-Pass-Pass-1♠
Pass-2♠-Pass-?

♠ A K 8 7 5
♡ 8 6 4
◊ A Q 8
♣ K 8

This is a trap hand. You have too much for the original one spade bid. Better to have started with double. Had you bid one spade and been lucky enough to hear partner raise, you should just bid four spades directly, or perhaps investigate three notrump by bidding three hearts.

Both vul
1◊-Pass-Pass-1♡
Pass-2♡-Pass-?

♠ A 10 8 6
♡ Q 10 9 4 3 2
◊ 3
♣ A 10

Four hearts. This is the sort of distributional hand which starts with a suit bid. Partner's raise so improves the hand that you go directly to game.

Vul vs. not
1◊-Pass-Pass-2♣
Pass-3♣-Pass-?

♠ 10 7
♡ A 8 7
◊ K 9
♣ A Q 10 8 7 5

Three notrump. It is more likely that you will have a strongish hand when you reopen at the two level rather than the one level. This is because it is more difficult to handle decent minor suit hands than decent major suit hands. Also, since it is harder to make five of a minor, you don't worry as much about missing a game.

Vul vs. not
1♡-Pass-Pass-2◊
Pass-3◊-Pass-?

♠ A 8 7
♡ 5 4 2
◊ K Q 10 9 6
♣ K 8

Pass. Straightforward. You need too much from partner to try three notrump. If you were sure that four diamonds were safe, then you could consider trying for three notrump, but four diamonds is hardly a lock. You do not want to trade a secure plus for a minus score.

Getting to four diamonds and going down just because you wanted to try for an odds against game is not good bridge.

Both vul

1 ♡ -Pass-Pass-2 ♣
Pass-3 ♣ -Pass-?

♠ A 4 2
♡ 4 2
◊ A 8
♣ K Q 9 6 5 4

This is a very reasonable hand to try for three notrump. You have good chances of nine tricks, and if it turns out partner has a minny or no heart stopper, you will have a play for four clubs. You are not automatically giving up a plus score to try for game. Bid three hearts.

Both vul

1 ♡ -Pass-Pass-2 ♣
2 ♡ -3 ♣ -Pass-?

♠ A 4 2
♡ 4 2
◊ A 8
♣ K Q 8 6 5 4

Same hand. Different sequence again. Partner can be somewhat lighter for this free raise than if opener had passed. Also, opener's two heart rebid implies a better suit. Three notrump will be less likely. You can try for it but your chances are sufficiently diminished that on balance, pass will be best.

No one vul

1 ♡ -Pass-Pass-2 ♣
2 ◊ -3 ♣ -3 ◊ -?

♠ K Q 4
♡ 4
◊ 10 7 5
♣ A Q 10 8 7 5

As a general rule, you should almost never compete to the four level. This hand looks good for clubs. Partner has short diamonds, you have a good trump suit, a stiff heart, and a strong holding in your fragment suit, spades. Yet it is not at all clear that you should bid. It may be right, but it's not clear. Partner rates to have some heart strength, and he may have a doubleton diamond.

Both vul

1 ♠ -Pass-Pass-2 ◊
2 ♡ -3 ◊ -3 ♡ -?

♠ Q 2
♡ Q 7
◊ K Q J 6 4
♣ K J 8 7

A good example of what not to bid with. Losers all over. Pass. What has happened here is a good example of reopening when you are worried about a major suit. Here, hearts were a concern. Not a great concern, as partner could easily hold them, but this time it seems, he doesn't.

It would not be surprising to see opener go on to game and make an overtrick. It was right for you to reopen. It just didn't work this time.

2. When partner bids one notrump, you will be able to count on him for decent values. You won't often have enough to raise him, but you may have enough distribution to introduce another suit or to rebid your own. If you rebid a major suit, you will need six of them. If you rebid a minor suit, which can only be diamonds, you ought to have six, but might do it with a five-bagger.

No one vul

1 ◇ -Pass-Pass-1 ♡
Pass-1NT-Pass-?

♠ K 3
♡ K Q J 10 4
◇ J 3
♣ A 10 8 4

You have a minimum raise to two notrump. You should almost never concern yourself with opener's suit. Partner frequently has two or more stoppers. If you did not have the ten of hearts, you would probably pass. As it is, your suit rates to take four tricks opposite a stiff or doubleton heart. Under no circumstances rebid two hearts.

No one vul

1 ◇ -Pass-Pass-1 ♠
Pass-1NT-Pass-?

♠ K 10 8 7 5
♡ 3
◇ J 2
♣ A 9 8 6 3

Two clubs. This shows nothing extra. Just bidding out your hand.

Not vul vs. vul

1 ♣ -Pass-Pass-1 ♠
Pass-1NT-Pass-?

♠ A 10 6 5 4
♡ 3
◇ Q 10 9 5
♣ K 6 4

Two diamonds. You should be worried about the heart suit. RHO couldn't respond one heart, but he will probably lead one. Partner has about ten points and didn't overcall, so he won't have good hearts.

Both vul

1 ◇ -Pass-Pass-1 ♡
Pass-1NT-Pass-?

♠ K Q 7
♡ Q J 4 3 2
◇ 4
♣ Q 8 6 5

Pass. You don't want to play a four-three club fit, and if partner returns to hearts, he is likely to have only two. As both of your suits are poor, you should not want to play in one of them. Diamonds could be a problem, but partner can easily have a five bagger.

♠ A 8 6
♡ 9 3
◇ K J 10 5 3
♣ J 7 4

One notrump is going to be better than two clubs or two hearts. The defense may err and set up partner's diamonds.

If partner jumps in notrump, you will have a systemic consideration. That is, if you bid again, is it forcing or not forcing?

1 ♣ -Pass-Pass-1 ♠
Pass-2NT-Pass-3 ♠

Is this signoff or forcing? What would it mean if you bid three hearts instead? Whatever you decide, you will often wish you were doing the other. Myself, I play these rebids as forcing. But it is not a common situation. Pick an understanding and stick to it.

On balanced hands, you go to game when your side has sufficient points or tricks. Partner should have something worth around 13 if he jumped and 11 to 12 if he didn't.

On second thought. If the auction is:

1♠-Pass-Pass-2♣
Pass-2NT-Pass-3♣

. . . you can treat it as non-forcing.

Perhaps you should play that if you reopen at the two level, and partner bids two notrump, a rebid of your suit or a lower suit is non-forcing. A good area to discuss with partner. I admit, I've never talked about these sequences to anyone.

No one vul

1♦-Pass-Pass-1♠
Pass-2NT-Pass-?

♠ A 10 8 7 6 5	You have values for game, but it is not clearly in
♡ K J 4	spades. If three spades is forcing, you can bid that and
◊ 3	leave the decision to partner.
♣ Q J 4	

No one vul

1♡-Pass-Pass-1♠
Pass-2NT-Pass-?

♠ Q J 10 8 7 4	Whatever your system calls for. Three spades if it's
♡ 3	not forcing. If it is forcing, I would bid four spades on
◊ 4 2	the theory that as long as I can't stop in three, I'd rather
♣ A 8 6 5	play in four spades than in two notrump.

Both vul

1◊-Pass-Pass-1♠
Pass-2NT-Pass-?

♠ Q 10 8 7 5	Three notrump. No misfit. Help for all suits, and a bit
♡ K Q 4	more than a minimum.
◊ J 2	
♣ K 10 7	

No one vul

Pass-1◊-Pass-Pass
1♠-Pass-2NT-Pass
-?

♠ Q 10 8 7 5	If I had not already passed originally, I would pass
♡ K Q 4	now. But inasmuch as I did pass earlier, I would treat
◊ 8 3	this as enough to go on to game.
♣ K 9 4	

No one vul

1♡-Pass-Pass-2♣
Pass-2NT-Pass-?

♠ 8 3	Three notrump. You have a good source of tricks.
♡ 10 5	Hands like this seldom make just two. You would raise
◊ 8 6	to three with one fewer club. Partner ought not to have
♣ A K J 9 8 5 4	a stiff club. It's possible though and if so, you may go
	down a lot.

3. When you reopen with a suit bid and partner introduces a new suit, your bids will depend on your systemic understandings. Is this new suit natural or is it some sort of force implying a partial fit? As I said earlier, these sequences do not come up very often in the natural sense, but if treated as artificial, they might become useful. We can take a look at some hands and see what to do opposite both treatments. Remember that if it's natural, it will be a hand which could not overcall because it was deficient in either suit quality or values.

No one vul
1♣-Pass-Pass-1♡
Pass-1♠-Pass-?

♠ Q 8	If natural,
♡ A 10 6 5 4	Pass. You need more to bid one notrump. Remember,
◊ K 10 7	partner couldn't overcall at the one level. It is not
♣ Q 8 4	unreasonable to play new suits at the one level as
	natural.

If artificial,
One notrump. Partner will have a goodish hand which did not have an available bid the round before. He does have spades, although perhaps only four. He probably does not have a full club stopper:

> ♠ K J 7 6
> ♡ 3 2
> ◊ A Q 9 6
> ♣ J 7 3

No one vul
1◊-Pass-Pass-2♣
Pass-2♡-Pass-?

♠ A Q 3	If natural,
♡ Q 2	Not likely to be natural. Partner needs a good hand to
◊ 8 6 3	justify two level action and he couldn't overcall. But, if
♣ K J 10 8 7	it is, pass.

If artificial,
You have a decent hand but no diamond stopper. Bid two spades.

Vul vs. not
1♠-Pass-Pass-2♣
Pass-2♡-Pass-?

♠ 8 2	If natural,
♡ 10 2	It could be because partner would have had to over-
◊ A 6 4 2	call at the two level. On this sequence, he can have a
♣ A Q J 9 7	pretty good hand. You should pass.

If artificial,
You don't have enough to bid three diamonds. That would force the auction to a higher level which two spades on the previous hand did not. Bid three clubs.

Both vul
1♠-Pass-Pass-2♣
Pass-2◊-Pass-?

♠ K 10 7   If natural, pass.
♡ 8 6 3   If artificial,
◊ 4 2   Two notrump. It seems like an overbid, but if you
♣ K Q J 10 3   write down a bunch of hands, you'll find that on almost
                 all of them, you would have bid one notrump instead of
two clubs whenever holding the required 12 to 16.

As you can see, it gets involved. If partner's bid is natural, your action will be
fairly clear cut. But it won't come up very often. If it's artificial then you may
have more opportunity to use it and you may get some good results and some
confusing results. Decide how you want to treat this and proceed. In either case,
it will not come up that frequently.

4. When partner makes a jump raise, your decision will be one of simple evaluation. You bid again, or you pass.

Both vul
1♣-Pass-Pass-1♠
Pass-3♠-Pass-?

♠ Q 10 8 7 5   Pass, but close to going on. Partner's raise shows a
♡ K 6 2   good hand with four trumps and with distribution. He
◊ A 9 5   will have length in clubs, else he would have acted ear-
♣ 4 3   lier, so he will be short in either hearts or diamonds.

Vul vs. not
1♡-Pass-Pass-1♠
2◊-3♠-Pass-?

♠ K Q 8 7   Clear to continue. Though holding only four spades,
♡ A 6 5 4   your values are solid. Good trumps, an ace, and a stiff.
◊ 3
♣ 10 8 5 4

Both vul
1♡-Pass-Pass-2♣
Pass-4♣-Pass-?

♠ 9 8 5   Five clubs. So many extras. Partner almost surely has
♡ 2   a stiff else he would have cue bid trying for three
◊ A 6 3   notrump.
♣ K Q 9 7 5 3

An aside here. If partner jumped in another suit, it could be treated as a
splinter, showing good trumps plus a singleton. If that were the case, then the
jump to four clubs would deny a singleton. Or, you could treat the suit jump as
showing a splinter with game forcing values and the jump raise as probably
showing a singleton but just worth an invitation.

No one vul
1♡-Pass-Pass-2♣
Pass-4♣-Pass-?

♠ 7   Pass. Partner has a stiff diamond which is not going
♡ Q 8 6 4   to do you much good. You know partner's shortness is
◊ K J 7   in diamonds because
♣ K J 8 7 5   1. If it were hearts, he would have bid earlier.
               2. If spades, the opponents would have been bidding
               them.

1♠-Pass-Pass-2♣   There is good reason to play that after the double, the
Dbl-4♣-Pass-?   jump to four clubs is preemptive. Another point worth
                   discussing.

5. **When partner cue bids**, the auction frequently becomes involved. His cue bid
can be based on a good hand with a fit or he can be looking for three notrump.
And if you play new suits as artificial, (see page 000), there are even more
considerations.

Because the concept of a new suit being forcing has not spread particularly past
these pages, I'm going to assume that new suits would have been natural. Therefore, it won't be possible to draw any inferences from partner's lack of bidding a
new suit.

No one vul
1♣-Pass-Pass-1♠
Pass-2♣-Pass-?

♠ J 8 7 6 5   With a minimum, bid two spades. This does not
♡ K Q 6   imply a good suit.
◊ K 5 4
♣ 7 6

Both vul
1♡-Pass-Pass-1♠
Pass-2♡-Pass-?

♠ K J 9 7   Again, two spades. Sometimes you are forced into
♡ 8 6 5 4   rebidding a four card suit. Partner should be wary of
◊ A Q 2   this possibility. Especially when the cue bid doesn't
♣ 8 6   leave you with any room.

Vul vs. not
1♣-Pass-Pass-1♠
Pass-2♣-Pass-?

♠ Q 8 6 5 4   Two diamonds. You do not show a good hand with
♡ 3 2   this. You are merely describing your hand. Partner's cue
◊ A Q 8 6   bid is forcing to two spades, so he will bid again. If you
♣ 4 2   had the same shape with a good hand, you would bid
               two diamonds to show your shape and would bid again
               later to show extra strength.

No one vul

1♣-Pass-Pass-1♦
Pass-2♣-Pass-?

♠ A K 8 7 5
♡ 8 6 4
◇ A J 5
♣ 4 2

Two diamonds. You can't rebid two spades as partner might pass. Three spades would show a better suit and a distributional hand. Two diamonds is a waiting bid. Whatever partner does, you will insist on game.

Both vul

1♣-Pass-Pass-1♡
Pass-2♣-Pass-?

♠ 8 7 6
♡ K Q 10 8 5
◇ 4 2
♣ K 9 8

Two hearts. Not enough values to show a club stopper. A minimum hand.

Both vul

1◇-Pass-Pass-1♡
Pass-2◇-Pass-?

♠ J 8
♡ A Q 9 5 4
◇ K J 3
♣ Q 4 3

Two notrump. A decent hand with balanced shape and stoppers. Don't worry about lack of a spade stop. There's almost no way you will reopen in a suit and hold stoppers in all the other suits.

Both vul

1♣-Pass-Pass-1♠
Pass-2♣-Pass-?

♠ Q J 9 8 6 2
♡ A Q 2
◇ K 3
♣ 9 7

Three spades. You show a six card suit with opening bid strength. You can't have more than this as you probably would have reopened with a jump to two spades.

No one vul

1◇-Pass-Pass-1♠
Pass-2◇-Pass-?

♠ K J 8 7 5
♡ 4 2
◇ 9
♣ A Q 10 8 7

Three clubs. This shows better than a minimum and implies five spades plus four or more clubs.

Both vul

1♡-Pass-Pass-1♠
Pass-2♡-Pass-?

♠ J 9 8 7 6
♡ 4 2
◇ 3
♣ A J 9 7 5

Two spades. You need more than a bare minimum for three clubs.

Both vul

1♣-Pass-Pass-1♦
Pass-2♣-Pass-?

♠ K J 8 7 5   Three diamonds would be a good bid if intended to
♡ 3   show two good five card suits. The upper strength of
◊ A Q 10 4 3   your hand is limited so partner won't expect a huge
♣ 9 7   hand. As two diamonds is forcing, the jump must show
some additional features.

No one vul

1◊-Pass-Pass-1♠
Pass-2◊-Pass-?

♠ A J 9 7 5   In my book on overcalls, I recommended that after an
♡ K 5 4   overcall, if partner cue bid, you could with adequate
◊ Q 2   values, re-cue to show a half stopper or more in the
♣ K 4 2   opponent's suit. This treatment is not suggested when
balancing because whenever partner bids notrump, the
lead will be through your half stopper and its value will be diminished. On this
hand, I would try either two hearts or three clubs. Either should be safe. It is
unlikely that partner will go crazy over your new suit, although it could happen.
An alternative call would be two notrump, which works on many hands. Partner
will expect a full stop however and if he goes to three notrump and they run diamonds, it's your fault, not his.

Perhaps a re-cue by you should show a good hand with nothing in the suit.
Two or three small would be your most likely holding.

Questions you may wish to discuss are:

1. If you bid two notrump in response to a cue bid, is it forcing to game?

2. Is it forcing at all, or should you jump to three notrump with much more
than a minimum?

3. If two notrump is not forcing, what does it mean when the cue bidder
returns to reopener's suit?
i.e.

1♣-Pass-Pass-1♦
Pass-2♣-Pass-2NT
Pass-3♣-Pass-?

It seems logical that this last sequence should be forcing. After all, the cue bid was
a game try and it elicited a strength response. The problem is really which game
to play, not shall we play one at all.

6. When partner doubles.

The next area is a rather emotional one. What do you do when partner doubles? Now this doesn't sound like it ought to be an emotional decision, but when
you have reopened on absolute garbage, and partner makes an agonized double,
it can be almost traumatic.

Or you have reopened with a dog and partner doubles with such enthusiasm
that the person at the next table turns his hearing aid down two levels. Of all the
bids partner can make, the quality of his hand is most clearly defined by the range
and intensity of both the time and volume of partner's double. This is not always
true. Some people are careful to express their opinions in a level voice and do so
with an even temper. But it's hard.

Assuming you can properly ignore the extraneous input from partner, your decisions to sit or run will depend on a number of factors.

1. Your defensive potential
2. Your offensive potential
3. How safe it is to run if you don't like the double

The vulnerability is not as important a consideration as you might think because partner knew what it was when he doubled.

No one vul

1♣-Pass-Pass-1♠
2♣-Dbl-Pass-?

♠ J 10 8 7 5
♡ A 3 2
◊ K J 9 3
♣ 4

An easy pass. One of the criteria is your defensive potential which is quite good. You have an ace and your diamond holding can easily be worthwhile. You even have a club. The only bad feature of this hand is the weak spades. Partner may lead the king from his king doubleton. But even this is not necessarily bad. Considering that you will often reopen in a bad suit, you should not feel that partner will get off to a bad lead. Partner will appreciate that your suit can be bad. He will be doubling on trump tricks and something on the side.

No one vul

1◊-Pass-Pass-1♠
2◊-Dbl-Pass-?

♠ A 9 8 6 4 2
♡ A 3
◊ 8 2
♣ J 7 3

In spite of six spades, this hand is a one hundred percent pass. You have two aces. Guaranteed tricks.

Both vul

1◊-Pass-Pass-1♠
2◊-Dbl-Pass-?

♠ J 10 9 7 6 5
♡ Q 10 8
◊ 3
♣ A.8 6

Getting close to running back to spades. You have weak defense and a good suit. But it's not a lock either way. Pass and two spades are about even. Partner will be short in spades, but against that, you haven't shown more than four of them. Note that mere possession of a six or seven bagger is not grounds for running.

No one vul

1◊-Pass-Pass-1♠
2◊-Dbl-Pass-?

♠ A Q 5 4 3 2
♡ 8 6 5
◊ 3
♣ 10 5 4

Pass. Partner will get off to a good lead which is a major consideration on very close hands. Also, you have less offensive potential than on the previous hand.

Both vul

1♡-Pass-Pas-1♠
2♡-Dbl-Pass-?

♠ K 10 8 6 5
♡ — —
◊ K 7 6 5
♣ 10 9 4 2

One of the reasons you didn't double for takeout was so you wouldn't have to defend one heart doubled. As your reward for this anticipation, you now have to decide whether to sit for two hearts doubled. You should pass, if for no other reason than that there is no sure way to escape. Even if you could, there's no guarantee that it would be the right decision. For example, two notrump would be an unusual bid at this stage and partner should work out its meaning. But if he has no four card minor, it won't be of much value for him to know what you have.

Both vul

1◊-Pass-Pass-1♠
2◊-Dbl-Pass-?

♠ K Q J 8 7 6
♡ 7 5 4 3
◊ 2
♣ Q 3

An easy two spades. For a change though, you can hope to make something. Only if partner puts down an incredible diamond holding will he have no useful side suit values. The reason you don't bid two hearts is that there is the danger of playing in a four-three fit. If partner has no spades and four hearts, you will have done the wrong thing. But that's unlikely. With an outstanding suit and a weak one, it is often best to play in the six-one fit. Anyway, partner is allowed to have two spades.

No one vul

1◊-Pass-Pass-1♠
2◊-Dbl-Pass-?

♠ 8 7 6 5 4 2
♡ K 10 9 7
◊ 3
♣ K 2

Two hearts. Compare with the previous hand.

Both vul

1◊-Pass-Pass-1♠
2♣-Dbl-Pass-?

♠ A K Q 10 8
♡ J 6 5 4
◊ 8 6 2
♣ 3

Pass. You have fine defense. Yanking the double with this hand is a typical unnecessary error.

No one vul

1◊-Pass-Pass-1♠
2♣-Dbl-Pass-?

♠ A 10 8 7 5
♡ K Q 9 8 3
◊ 4
♣ 3 2

This is a difficult decision. It is not at all clear to run to two hearts. Declarer is going to run into bad splits in both of his suits. The reason you might run are:

1. You expect to get a plus score. You aren't running totally from fear.

2. Game is possible if partner can raise hearts.

3. Partner is going to lead a spade. You would far prefer a heart.

As against all this, you may find that passing is your last plus score. If you weren't sure what to do, that's just about right.

No one vul

1 ◊ -Pass-Pass-1 ♠
2 ◊ -Dbl-Pass-?

♠ Q J 8 4 2   With no apparent defensive trick and an easy way
♡ Q J 7 3 2   out, you should run. Two hearts.
◊ 3
♣ 9 7

No one vul

1 ◊ -Pass-Pass-1 ♡
1NT-Dbl-Pass-?

♠ 10 8 7   Pass. Partner should have a good hand plus some
♡ J 9 5 4 2   hearts or he should have an excellent hand. Also, he
◊ 8 7   should hold at least one stopper in diamonds. You won't
♣ A Q 9   always beat one notrump, but you have a better chance
                        at beating it then guessing what else would be better.

When you have reopened on a weak hand and partner doubles something or
another, you will often regret having bid. C'est la vie. The one thing you mustn't
do is run solely because you have a weak hand. When you don't think you can
beat them, you run only when you have something sensible to run to.

Both vul

1♡ -Pass-Pass-1 ♠
1NT-Dbl-Pass-?

♠ J 8 7 6 5   With a minimum hand and knowing partner will lead
♡ 3   spades, you have an easy run to two clubs.
◊ 8 7
♣ K Q 10 9 7

Both vul

1♠ -Pass-Pass-2 ♣
2♡ -Dbl-Pass-?

♠ 8 3   Pass. There are two clear reasons not to run to three
♡ 7 3   clubs.
◊ A K   1. It will probably go down.
♣ J 9 8 7 6 5 4   2. You have very good defense against hearts. Very
                        likely you will get two diamond tricks. The only bad
                        feature of this hand is that partner will lead a club. Even
                        so, it does not have to work out badly.

No one vul

1 ◊ -Pass-Pass-2 ♣
2 ◊ -Dbl-Pass-?

♠ 10 8 7 5   I made the statement much earlier that a reopening
♡ K 9 7   bid at the two level should show around ten working
◊ — —   points. This should be qualified slightly. If you have
♣ Q 10 8 6 5 4   only a five card suit and your hand is rather ordinary,
                        i.e. balanced, you will need about ten points. When you
have excellent distribution, you can shade the requirements somewhat. This hand
may have shaded the requirements somewhat and then some, but it was a reasonable effort. Matchpointwise, it is a typical action bid.

Having heard partner double, you should have no part of it. Run to two spades. Partner will expect more, but he won't expect much more. If you had the same shape with the A J 9 of hearts instead of the K 9 7, you could give thought to passing.

Vul vs. not

1♡-Pass-Pass-2♣
2♡-Dbl-Pass-?

♠ Q 6   Pass. Not because you hope to beat it. Pass because
♡ 7   your chances of making three clubs are lousy. At IMPs,
◇ K J 4   you might not have bothered to reopen.
♣ Q 9 7 6 5 4 2

Vul vs. not

1♠-Pass-Pass-2♣
2♠-Dbl-Pass-?

♠ — —   Pass. This time you have defense. Auctions like this
♡ 8 6 5   are a little unfair because you may have gotten some
◇ 9 6 5   help from partner. I know that when I'm the opener and
♣ A K 8 6 5 3 2   I decide to rebid two spades, I can usually tell from
                         LHO's double whether he has J 8 6 4 as opposed to K J
10 8 7. So can the doubler's partner. How easy on this example hand to do the right thing, whatever it is. Perhaps there should be a rule that you must hesitate ten seconds before making a penalty double.

Somehow, I don't think that one would fly.

7. When partner passes.

The last group of sequences occurs when partner passes your reopening bid. This can happen when opener rebids or when opener passes and his partner gets back in. The question is whether you should continue and if so, how much do you show?

In deciding your action, there are a number of points to consider:

1. If your partner has a fit for you he has not got much of a hand.

2. There are forty points in the deck, and if the opponents are not showing strength, your side has as much as twenty of them, partner's silence notwithstanding.

3. You can usually gauge partner's values fairly accurately, and if they are significant, you can determine why they weren't worth bidding.

4. A further bid by you should not be interpreted as showing a good hand. It is merely an effort to show some additional feature of your hand and still counts on partner to produce something.

No one vul

1♣-Pass-Pass-1♡
2♣-Pass-Pass-?

♠ 8 7   Two diamonds. Partner is marked for some values.
♡ A 10 8 5 4   He didn't overcall one spade, he didn't raise hearts and
◇ K Q 9 7   he didn't whack two clubs.
♣ 8 3

        ♠ K 8 7 5   ♠ J 10 6 4 2
        ♡ J 2   ♡ K 3
        ◇ A 6 5 4   ◇ J 10 5
        ♣ Q 10 7   ♣ K 4 2

These hands are typical of what you might find. Note that on the first of these hands, partner should give no thought to raising diamonds, and if the opponents push to three clubs, he should pass again.

Both vul

1♡ -Pass-Pass-1♠
2♡ -Pass-Pass-?

♠ Q J 9 8 7 5	Two spades. Still bidding partner's values, but show-
♡ 4 2	ing a good suit. Your upper range is limited by your fail-
◇ A Q 8	ure to take a stronger initial action.
♣ 10 7	

Both vul

1♡ -Pass-Pass-1♠
2♡ -Pass-Pass-?

♠ A Q 8 6 5	Double. This shows slight extra values above those
♡ 3	already shown. Partner will play you to have a hand
◇ K 6 5 4	with five spades, short hearts, support for the other
♣ Q 10 8	suits, and values similar to these or more. Double is
	very flexible. Partner may be able to pass this. He could
	have any of these hands:

♠ J 2	He can pass.
♡ K J 8 7	
◇ Q 9 3	
♣ K 7 6 4	

♠ J 9 4	He can bid two spades.
♡ Q 8 7 5	
◇ J 9 3	
♣ K 5 4	

♠ 9 2	He can bid three clubs.
♡ J 7 6 4	
◇ Q 2	
♣ A 9 7 5 4	

♠ 9 2	He can take two aspirin and call me. Not collect.
♡ 10 8 6 4	
◇ Q 8 3	
♣ K 7 5 4	

Seriously, this last hand is not likely. You will be able to compete successfully at least 95 percent of the time with reopener's given hand.

No one vul

1♡ -Pass-Pass-2◇
2♡ -Pass-Pass-?

♠ K 7	Pass. When you reopen at the two level, you show a
♡ 4 2	decent five card suit, so on this sequence you have only
◇ A Q 8 7 6 5	one additional trump. Also, you show a decent hand, so
♣ K 7 3	you have only slight additional values.
	So dangerous to rebid a suit at the three level.

Both vul
1♡-Pass-Pass-2◊
2♡-Pass-Pass-?

♠ A 9 7
♡ 8 7
◊ K Q J 10 8 7
♣ 4 3 2

Three diamonds. The hand is not as good as the previous but the suit is solid. Here you are rebidding partner's values.

No one vul
1♡-Pass-Pass-2♣
2♡-Pass-Pass-?

♠ J 10 8 7
♡ 3
◊ 9 2
♣ A Q 10 6 5 4

Two spades. Not promising extra values. Promising useful distribution. If it were possible to rebid two clubs at your second opportunity, you would still bid two spades. As a general rule, it is usually safer to introduce a second suit than it is to rebid the first. Note that if the opponents go on to three hearts, your partner will be able to judge whether to compete in spades or to double or to pass. If you pass, the opponents will have bought it and if you bid three clubs, partner will have no idea what to do if they continue.

Both vul
1♡-Pass-Pass-2◊
2♡-Pass-Pass-?

♠ 8 3
♡ 2
◊ A Q 10 6 3
♣ K 9 8 6 5

Three clubs. To bid a new suit at the three level requires a five card suit, but not that much in values. All you are doing is describing your hand within the framework that you expect your side to have about 20 points.

If partner has a good hand he should appreciate that you are counting on it.

No one vul
1♠-Pass-Pass-2♣
2♠-Pass-Pass-?

♠ 8
♡ 4 2
◊ Q 10 9 3
♣ A Q 9 6 5 4

This is an excellent systemic hand. Two notrump unusual. Having shown clubs, you can now show diamonds and at the same time not get past three clubs if partner prefers them. Partner will credit you with this shape and will return to three clubs with three diamonds and two clubs. Note how well this treatment works if partner has four or more diamonds.

Both vul
1♠-Pass-Pass-2♣
2♠-Pass-Pass-?

♠ 3
♡ K 10 8 7
◊ 4 2
♣ A J 10 8 7 5

Very difficult. You should want to bid in the worst way. Here are your options and the merits and flaws in each:

1. Pass. Safe but you will lose many part score decisions and a few games when four hearts is on.

2. Double. This will get you to hearts when it is right. But partner may pass for penalty, and you haven't the defense partner will expect, or he will bid diamonds

which will create further problems.

3. You can bid three clubs which runs the risk of playing in the wrong suit. You won't be down a lot, but three clubs down one when four hearts is cold would be bad.

4. You can bid three hearts, but since this is a reverse, partner will expect you to have a better hand and may play you for another heart. If he has to return to clubs, you will have gotten a trick too high for no reason. Also, partner might raise you to four hearts with only three card support. This is not the hand for a four-three fit.

5. You can bid two notrump unusual and then go to three hearts if partner bids three diamonds. This would show four hearts only, but would also show a better hand. If you end up in clubs, you will once again have squandered a level of bidding. There is also the nightmarish occasion when partner jumps in diamonds.

Holding the above hand, I would definitely bid at matchpoints and depending on my mood would select from three clubs or two notrump. At IMPs there are too many dangers to getting involved and I would either pass or try three clubs.

Both vul
1 ♡ -Pass-Pass-2 ♣
2 ♡ -Pass-Pass-?

♠ K 8 7
♡ 3
◊ Q 10 8
♣ A J 9 6 5 4

Double. A decent hand with either this shape or a 3-1-4-5 with good clubs and poor diamonds. Partner can sit, support you, or try a new suit according to his hand. You need more than just shape for this action as partner can convert your takeout double to penalties. You will need some defensive values to make this work. Remember that partner didn't double two hearts so his defensive strength is limited. The hand you have is a normal minimum.

No one vul
1 ♣ -Pass-Pass-1 ◊
1 ♣ -Pass-Pass-?

♠ K 8 7
♡ 4 2
◊ A Q 10 8 7
♣ A 9 4

One notrump. This does not show a huge hand (16-17) as you would not have started with one diamond. All it shows is a sound hand of this approximate description.

Both vul
1 ♣ -Pass-Pass-1 ♠
Pass-Pass-2 ♣ -?

♠ Q J 9 8 6 4
♡ 4 2
◊ A Q 8
♣ 8 7

You've seen this hand before. Opener rebid two clubs and you continued on with two spades. On the sequence here, it is both safer and more dangerous for you to bid again. Safe because they are raising clubs, which suggests that partner's values are elsewhere. But dangerous in that RHO has *some* values which decreases the total that you were hoping existed for your side. Also, opener may be able to double you on the basis of his partner's delayed raise. On balance, you should bid two spades but less enthusiastically than before.

No one vul

1 ♡ -Pass-Pass-1 ♠
Pass-Pass-2 ♡ -?

♠ Q 10 8 7 5
♡ 3
◇ A 5 4
♣ K J 9 8

Double. A takeout double showing moderate values, five spades, and shape. There is less chance on this sequence that partner will be passing for penalty than if opener had rebid two hearts.

No one vul

1 ♣ -Pass-Pass-1 ♡
Pass-Pass-1 ♠ -?

♠ 3
♡ K Q 8 7 5
◇ A 9 8 4
♣ K 10 6

Double. You were worried about spades when you reopened. Perhaps the opponents have gotten back together. But maybe not. Double shows this hand and allows partner a range of options including the additional one of playing in clubs. Your expected shape is exactly the one you have.

Both vul

1 ♣ -Pass-Pass-1 ♡
Pass-Pass-1 ♠ -?

♠ 8 7
♡ K J 9 7 6
◇ K Q 8 7 5
♣ 4

Two diamonds or pass. Opener hasn't denied some extras and RHO's bid shows something. Note that when RHO passed he showed zero to five. On a good day your partner has all of that five. But when RHO bids he shows something which decreases by that much what you can hope to find in partner's hand. Two diamonds is reasonable but not altogether safe. For this you ought to have four very good diamonds or a five card suit. More often than not, you are going to play in your second suit, so it should be reasonable.

No one vul

1 ◇ -Pass-Pass-1 ♠
Pass-Pass-1NT-?

Of all the bids RHO can make, this should most have the effect of discouraging you. Whatever you do, you can't depend on partner as heavily as on most other sequences. You will need a good suit or distribution to act. No speculation.

CHAPTER ELEVEN

Finding the Best Contract

So far, an enormous amount of space has been devoted to the reopening action itself, and a large amount of space to the complete auction which ensued when partner reopened after the opening bid was passed out.

The reason that so much time was spent in this one area is that it is the only reopening sequence which lends itself to a constructive auction.

When the bidding goes:

$$1 \clubsuit \text{-Pass-Pass-Dbl} \qquad \text{or}$$
$$1 \spadesuit \text{-Pass-Pass-2} \clubsuit \qquad \text{etc.}$$

. . . the reopening side may have a game and that possibility suggests that their bidding cater to such likelihood.

On the other hand, when was the last time you got to game after a sequence like one of these:

$$1 \clubsuit \text{-Pass-1} \spadesuit \text{-Pass}$$
$$2 \clubsuit \text{-Pass-Pass-?}$$

or

$$1 \spadesuit \text{-Pass-1NT-Pass}$$
$$2 \spadesuit \text{-Pass-Pass-?}$$

or	or
$1 \heartsuit$ -Pass-1 $\spadesuit$ -Pass	$1 \spadesuit$ -Pass-1NT-Pass
$2 \clubsuit$ -Pass-Pass-?	Pass-?
or	or even
$1 \spadesuit$ -Pass-1NT-Pass	$1 \diamondsuit$ -Pass-1NT-Pass
$2 \clubsuit$ -Pass-2 $\spadesuit$ -Pass	Pass-?
Pass-?	

It just doesn't happen. If you make a game, it's an accident, and if you bid it and make it, it's almost worth writing home about.

For this reason, when your partner reopens on any sequence other than after an opening one bid, your goal as a partnership will very seldom be to outbid the opponents. Instead, it will be simply to get the opponents one trick higher. Very seldom will you raise partner's bid. Very seldom will you do more than make a simple response to his takeout double. Perhaps you will make a penalty double. It will be rare. Jumps and cue bids? Forget them. Conceivably, you might use them when the opponents have had a "fit" auction and partner reopens. But it will require an exceptional hand.

Since the remaining sequences were discussed earlier in terms of how well the opponents' hands fit, we will do so here as well.

First, the fit auctions where the opponents have found a positive fit and partner has reopened. These are the only sequences where the opponents can have an exchange and then stop in which your side may feel the hand is yours. Bear in mind that the opponents will think it belongs to them. Consequently, there will often be more bidding by both sides and good judgment will be required as the auction advances.

Let's see how reopener's partner will react to various situations:

1. When the opponents have found a fit after a one-suited auction.

No one vul

1♣-Pass-2♣-Pass
Pass-Dbl-Pass-?

♠ Q 8 7 5   Two spades. This is not a good hand. Partner didn't
♡ J 4   act over one club, so this hand is going nowhere. You
◊ K 10 7 6   will not compete if the opponents go on to three clubs.
♣ Q 9 7

No one vul

1♣-Pass-2♣-Pass
Pass-Dbl-Pass-?

♠ Q 10 8 7 5   Two spades. This hand is still not going to take a sec-
♡ K 8 5   ond bid. You have the all time worst possible holding in
◊ Q 10 7   the opponents' suit, Q x, and you have otherwise only a
♣ Q 3   collection of junk. Partner will almost always be bidding your values. Not often will you have a queen more
or less than partner thinks you have. The only thing you can have which he won't
know about is extra distribution. You might have extra length in your good suit.
You might have a second suit. You might have a stiff in their suit rather than a
doubleton. Your honor cards may be very well combined rather than scattered
loosely about the hand. It is these extra qualities that should give you cause to
rebid or to bid strongly rather than the mere possession of some number of
points. This example hand has wasted points in clubs, soft cards otherwise, and
has only one extra feature, the fifth spade.

No one vul

1♣-Pass-2♣-Pass
Pass-Dbl-Pass-?

♠ K 10 7 6   For a change, you have a good hand. So good in fact
♡ K 4 3   that you might have bid over two clubs. But as good as
◊ K 10 6 5 4   this hand is, you should content yourself with a simple
♣ 3   two spades. The reason you don't bid diamonds is
involved. This hand is good enough that you will con-
sider bidding again. If the opponents compete to three clubs, you will take a
second bid.

If you start now with two diamonds and the opponents go on to three clubs
you will have to bid three diamonds or pass. Spades will be lost. Or if you can't
stand it, you can bid three spades and perhaps have partner stick you back in four
diamonds. You will have managed to get one trick higher than necessary for no
reason at all.

Bidding two and then three diamonds in addition to losing the spade suit, also
runs the risk of playing in a five-two fit. It wouldn't be so terrible to miss a spade
fit if diamonds turned out to be adequate, but sometimes they won't be, and you
won't know until the dummy hits.

It would be reasonable for partner to reopen with double on

♠ Q J 8 3
♡ Q 10 9 2
◇ A 9
♣ 10 5 4

. . . and diamonds could work out poorly. Given your actual hand, you might make a game. You won't bid it of course, but you should at least find the right suit.

If partner's hand should be

♠ J 9 5
♡ A 10 6 4
◇ A 9 3 2
♣ J 8

. . . then diamonds will be right. How can you tell? You can't. If your bid were going to end the auction, you would guess and you would probably guess diamonds. On this hand however, there is likely going to be more bidding and you will get a second chance. The solution is to start with two spades and subsequently bid three diamonds.

Won't this mislead partner? It shouldn't. When he doubles, he promises at least three spades, so if you had five spades and four diamonds, you could just rebid spades. If you do bid two spades and then three diamonds, partner should not correct to spades unless they are better than diamonds or unless he has four of each. With equal three card holdings he should leave it in diamonds. Only when partner has three spades and two diamonds will you get to a bad contract and that would require partner to have a pretty strange hand.

No one vul

1 ◇ -Pass-2 ◇ -Pass
Pass-Dbl-3 ◇ -?

♠ K J 4 2
♡ K 9 7 6
◇ Q 8 2
♣ Q 3

Pass. Had responder passed, you would have guessed two hearts or spades and not bid again. Your goal would be to get them to the three level. That's been done. Accept it. For you to bid would require a hand with values and shape, not just a flat and soft 11 count.

No one vul

1 ◇ -Pass-2 ◇ -Pass
Pass-Dbl-3 ◇ -?

♠ K 10 5
♡ Q 10 8 7 5
◇ 9 6 4
♣ A 3

Three hearts. With responder rebidding, there is a good chance of finding partner with a stiff diamond. If opener has three diamonds and responder five of them, you are in trouble because it means opener is four-four in the majors. In any event, this hand is pure enough to warrant a bid.

Both vul

1 ◇ -Pass-2 ◇ -Pass
Pass-Dbl-Pass-?

♠ J 8 7 5
♡ J 2
◇ Q 8
♣ K 10 8 7 5

Two spades. You have a poor hand. Don't make the mistake of bidding three clubs. Better to bid two spades which is both cheaper and assured of a decent fit than three clubs which is higher and which may be facing a

125

doubleton. The fact that you have two diamonds leaves open the possibility that partner has three. This means partner's double can be a bit off-shape. The one thing partner does need is three cards in each major suit. If he has a flaw it will be in the length of the unbid minor. With bad hands like this, it is incumbent to get the auction over with as quickly and safely as possible. You will remember that clubs is a dangerous suit which responder may hold when raising diamonds. Here the lower level of two spades plus its inherent safety more than overcomes the extra length in clubs.

No one vul

1 ♡ -Pass-2 ♡ -Pass
Pass-Dbl-Pass-?

♠ K J 10 8
♡ 9 7 5
◇ A J 9 7 5
♣ 3

This is another good hand which presents special problems. First, you might consider jumping to three spades. I wouldn't do that because when partner reopens, I feel he is entitled to the benefit of the doubt. So if you don't jump, your choices are two spades and three diamonds.

This hand is good enough to compete further so you have to decide if you want to:
1. Bid three diamonds and then three spades if given the opportunity.
2. Bid two spades and then three or four diamonds.
3. Two spades followed by three spades, ignoring the diamond suit totally.

It's easy to reject choice two, because you may get too high. Silly to be bidding four diamonds when three spades is likely to be best. I would also reject choice one because there is some chance that three diamonds could get passed out. You have three hearts and enough high cards that three diamonds might buy it. This means you should not offer a choice of suits.

This leaves two spades followed by a rebid of spades. Heart leads won't bother you because you can take the tap in dummy. A club is unlikely to be led, and even so, it is unlikely that the opponents will be able to establish a forcing game. Note also, that if the auction should go

1 ♡ -Pass-2 ♡ -Pass
Pass-Dbl-Pass-2 ♠
Pass-Pass-3 ♣ -?

. . . you can bid three diamonds after all.

No one vul

1 ♠ -Pass-2 ♠ -Pass
Pass-Dbl-Pass-?

♠ 3 2
♡ Q 10 8 7
◇ K 3
♣ K 9 7 6 5

When all of your choices are at the same level, you may as well bid your best suit. Three clubs. Note that when the opponents own the spade suit, you will almost never bid again if they compete to three spades because you would have to go to the four level to do so. That would require an exceptional hand. You would need a five-five hand or a good six card suit, plus you would need reason to expect the hand to play well.

No one vul

1♠-Pass-2♠-Pass
Pass-Dbl-Pass-3◊
Pass-Pass-3♠-?

♠ Q 4
♡ 3
◊ K 10 8 7 5
♣ K J 9 6 4

Very dangerous, even with this hand to go on to four clubs. You will probably be off the first two spades and some number of aces. You could easily be doubled. Be happy to have pushed them up to the three level. If your major suits were reversed it would be okay to bid four clubs. Now your shape would be improved by one trick and the heart queen would be worth something which the spade queen is not.

Both vul

1♠-Pass-2♠-Pass
Pass-Dbl-Pass-3♡
3♠-Pass-Pass-?

♠ 8 6 5
♡ A J 9 7 6 5
◊ K 6 5
♣ Q 2

Even this hand is dangerous. You can easily have two spade losers plus whatever else. You would have been happier had responder bid three spades because that would have increased the chances of your catching a stiff spade in partner's hand. Considering that if you bid four hearts you will be doubled, you have to be right. Best to pass. If you were not vulnerable, you could consider four hearts as a save, but that would assume that three spades was going to make.

The important thing about this hand is that you must resolve not to hang partner. Taking a second bid smacks of being a genius.

No one vul

1♠-Pass-2♠-Pass
Pass-2NT-Pass-?

♠ Q J 7 5
♡ J 9 7 6
◊ Q 10
♣ K 9 7

Three clubs. Nothing much here. You have a crummy hand but it does include honors in partner's suits. Don't pass whatever you do. You will neither bid again nor will you double if they go to three spades. With partner showing the minors, the opponents probably have an unknown number of heart tricks. A double would require some additional tricks. Another ace or the heart king plus the spade nine. Partner will be in there on as little as

♠ 2
♡ 8 3
◊ K 9 8 6 4
♣ Q 10 8 6 3

He's bidding your values. You have unexceptional defense, unexceptional high cards and an unexceptional fit. When partner reopens, you should bid three clubs, and if the opponents bid three spades you should pass with no second thoughts. If you bid anything at all or even think of bidding over three spades, you are being too busy. Partner doesn't need the aggravation. He stuck his neck out and got them up a trick. Give him a break. Note that if you do double, there is almost no hand on which partner will pull. If they make it, partner will be properly disappointed, whatever he has.

Both vul
1♥-Pass-2♥-Pass
Pass-2NT-Pass-?

♠ K 10 8 6 5
♥ 2
♦ K 10 8 7
♣ Q J 4

Three diamonds. If they go on to three hearts, you should pass. The fact that the opponents have gone quietly so far suggests that responder does not have too many hearts. Three probably, four maybe, but not more, which means your partner may well have a 1-4-4-4 or a 1-3-4-5 pattern. If this is the case, then your spades and partner's heart length will both be useful defensively.

Both vul
1♥-Pass-♥-Pass
Pass-2NT-Pass-?

♠ A 6 4 2
♥ 3
♦ K 10 8 7 5
♣ Q 10 3

Three diamonds only, but be willing to compete four. Everything you have is working. It's not that you have extra high cards, it's that the ones you have are all in the right place. You have the spade ace, a stiff heart, a fifth diamond and useful clubs. Even the club ten can come into its own. It could turn out to be worth more than the spade king!

No one vul
1♥-Pass-2♥-Pass
Pass-2NT-Pass-?

♠ A K 8 7
♥ K 10 9 6
♦ 8 6 5
♣ 4 2

Three diamonds. If they bid three hearts, you can consider doubling. But remember that partner is on lead. If he hasn't a clear lead, he may lead a diamond which you don't want. You would like a spade lead, but you're not likely to get it. Even though you have a potential four tricks, double should be reserved for a bad declarer. A good declarer will expect things to be breaking poorly and will have made allowances for that when he bid three hearts. Likewise, if it is responder who bids three hearts, he will have some reason for it.

No one vul
1♥-Pass-2♥-Pass
Pass-2♠-Pass-?

When partner reopens in a suit, you will almost never bid. Whatever high cards you have, he is bidding them. Notrump is out of the question unless you have some fantastic hand, and it will be obvious. About 85% of the time you will pass partner's bid. On those occasions when you do bid, it will be to raise when you have magic, or when you have a terrible holding in partner's suit you will introduce a super suit of your own which you couldn't show earlier.

Note that when partner reopens in a suit which could have been bid at the one level, he has either a bad hand, a bad suit, or even both.

No one vul
1♡ -Pass-2♡ -Pass
Pass-2♠ -Pass-?

♠ K 8 7
♡ Q 10 6
◊ A J 5 3
♣ Q 9 6

Pass now and forever. Partner knows about the high cards. You have nothing extra.

Not vul vs. vul
1♡ -Pass-2♡ -Pass
Pass-2♠ -Pass-Pass
3♡ -Pass-Pass-?

♠ K 4 3 2
♡ J 3
◊ K 8 7 5
♣ A 6 4

Pass again. There are very few hands which will make three spades which couldn't act over one heart.

♠ Q 10 7 6
♡ 10 6 5
◊ A 10 4
♣ K 5 2

This hand makes three spades about one time in five. Mathematicians need not correct this estimate. On the other hand, partner has gotten them to three hearts which also makes about one time in five. Note that I gave partner good working cards with nothing wasted, and two spades is not assured, let alone three.

Vul vs. vul
1♡ -Pass-2♡ -Pass
Pass-2♠ -3♡ -?

♠ J 10 8 7
♡ 8 6 5 4
◊ A Q
♣ K 8 7

Three spades. A fourth trump and everything else both working and prime. When you take the push, you should never expect to have a fast two losers in their suit. It gives the defense too quick a start and it's hard to catch up.

Vul vs. vul
1♡ -Pass-2♡ -Pass
Pass-2♠ -3♡ -?

♠ K Q 10 8
♡ J 2
◊ A 9 7
♣ Q 10 6 4

An exceptional case where you might accept the push on a hand where you have two losers. You have good enough trumps that you are unlikely to get doubled, plus a good enough hand otherwise to hold down side suit losers. Had responder passed two spades, you would have done so also. This hand is nothing wonderful.

No one vul
1♠ -Pass-2♠ -Pass
Pass-3♡ -Pass-?

♠ K 8 7
♡ K J 9 7
◊ K Q 2
♣ Q 9 7

Again. Pass now and again if they compete. God knows what partner has, but he is obviously counting on you for a lot. The only good thing you really have is good hearts. If opener has psyched, you lose, but it would be wrong to bid anything on this assumption.

No one vul

1 ◇ -Pass-2 ◇ -Pass
Pass-2 ♠ -Pass-?

♠ 4 2
♡ A 8 7 5
◇ K 10 7
♣ A 8 5 4

Pass. Partner appears to be short in diamonds so he probably has five spades. If he is 4-2-2-5 he is in trouble. It's not up to you to get him out of it. Pass. I don't really think two notrump exists in this auction, but if it does, this isn't the hand for it.

No one vul

1 ◇ -Pass-2 ◇ -Pass
Pass-2 ♡ -Pass-?

♠ Q J 8 2
♡ 4
◇ J 8 6
♣ K J 7 6 5

This is an almost impossible hand. Partner is probably 3-5-2-3 but it's not a lock. I would pass and hope the opponents save us. If they double, you can redouble for takeout. Note that partner's heart suit isn't very good. He passed earlier.

Both vul

1 ♡ -Pass-2 ♡ -Pass
Pass-2 ♠ -Pass-?

♠ 3 2
♡ J 8 7
◇ K 2
♣ K Q 10 9 7 5

Partner looks to be short in hearts. Run to three clubs. This is a little unusual, but you are the only one who knows the nature of your values. You haven't the spade support partner is looking for, and this time you can offer a good alternative.

No one vul

1 ◇ -Pass-2 ◇ -Pass
Pass-2 ♠ -3 ◇ -Pass
Pass-3 ♡ -Pass-?

♠ K 7 6
♡ Q J 5 4
◇ 8 6 4
♣ A 5 4

As good as this hand is, you haven't got a game. Partner passed one diamond and is merely expressing additional distributional values and is counting on you for the high cards.

♠ Q 10 8 4 2
♡ A 9 6 3 2
◇ J
♣ Q 5

Perhaps less.

Both vul

1 ♣ -Pass-2 ♣ -Pass
Pass-2 ♠ -3 ♣ -Pass
Pass-3 ◇ -Pass-?

♠ K 9 5
♡ K 10 8 6 5
◇ Q J 4 2
♣ 8

Pass. You have the diamonds and the stiff club partner expects. You are missing the high cards he would like. Your stiff club suggests partner is counting on it so he may have a four card diamond suit. If so, he will have a stiff heart which he will try to sneak past the defense at an early opportunity. Remembering that he did not overcall the opening bid, you can place partner with a weak five-five in spades and diamonds, or a hand like this:

♠ J 10 8 6 4
♡ 3
◇ A K 10 3
♣ J 5 4

This hand would be exciting at matchpoints. At IMPs it would be too dangerous unless you clearly needed a swing. The potential six IMPs would be worth trying for.

There is no 5-4-2-2 hand which partner can have. The doubleton club would suggest two fast losers and would not offer enough chance of finding a good fit.

Both vul

1 ♡ -Pass-2 ♡ -Pass
Pass-2 ♠ -Pass-?

♠ A 10 8 7	Three spades. A very rare hand which can invite part-
♡ A 4 3 2	ner when he has reopened. If you think this is conserva-
◇ K J 8	tive, I would suggest that it is actually average for a
♣ 7 2	raise. Opposite

♠ Q 9 6 4 2
♡ 8
◇ 10 9 6 3
♣ A 8 5

. . . four spades would go down if you lost the diamond finesse or if you lost two spade tricks. With the hand I have given partner, he would pass your raise, but he should have misgivings about it. If he had the spade king instead of the queen, or the queen-jack, or either minor suit queen, he would continue to four. If you give partner sufficient room in general when he reopens, then he will have enough confidence to bid four when holding

♠ Q 9 6 4 2
♡ 8
◇ Q 10 4 2
♣ K 9 7

. . . or similar useful minimums.

Note that a new suit by you is natural. When the opponents have both bid and then subsided, your side won't have very many games. Your auctions will seldom require constructive sequences. This is not at all like the situation which existed when opener's bid was passed to partner who reopened in a suit. With

♠ A 10 8 7
♡ A 4 3 2
◇ K J 8
♣ 7 2

. . . when the bidding went

1 ♡ -Pass-2 ♡ -Pass
Pass-2 ♠ -Pass-?

. . . three diamonds would be natural. There is no way it should be confused with

1 ♠ -Pass-Pass-2 ♡
Pass-3 ◇

1♠-Pass-2♠-Pass
Pass-3♣-Pass-?

Regardless of your hand, you should pass except in very rare circumstances. If partner can get them to the three level, that should be good enough.

1♠-Pass-2♠-Pass
Pass-3♣-3♠-?

You would have to bid four clubs.

1♡-Pass-2♡-Pass
Pass-2♠-3♡-?

You can bid three spades. The gist of this is simple. If you almost never have the hand to raise partner's two level action to the three level, you will have even fewer hands that warrant raising partner's three level action to the four level.

There are some additional points worth noting here.

1. Partner's two level bids are in safe suits.

2. Partner's three level bids are in dangerous suits.

3. A reopening bid in a safe suit can be and often is made with absolute cheese and a bad four card suit.

4. A reopening bid in a dangerous suit requires a decent suit plus some expectations.

If all of this makes it sound like it's okay to raise partner's three level reopening action, it is and it isn't. The differences in what you can expect were pointed out to help you with your decision when your hand qualified. But against all of this, you must remember that you will be at the four level against an opening bid plus a response.

1♠-Pass-2♠-Pass
Pass-3◊-3♠-?

♠ Q 8 7
♡ K J 3
◊ K 9 5
♣ A 10 6 5

Pass. As always, you need your cards to be working and, or, you need unexpected shape. This is a random piece of garbage. Any time you have a wasted king or queen in the opponents' suit, you should almost always forget the whole thing. These cards are part of the high cards partner is expecting, but as they are worthless, your hand will be that much less than he was hoping for.

1♠-Pass-2♠-Pass
Pass-3♣-3♠-?

♠ 8 7 5
♡ 9 5 4
◊ A K J 9
♣ K Q 2

This is typical of the hand that goes on to four clubs and which goes down a trick. You then discover that you could have taken two clubs and two diamonds and a diamond ruff to beat three spades. I wouldn't blame anyone for bidding four clubs because you have super trumps plus a source of tricks, but it is worth noting the hand type. If you had another spade and one less heart, that might be worth two full tricks. One less spade loser in partner's hand, and one less heart loser in yours. Watch out for balanced hands.

132

Both vul
1 ♡ -Pass-2 ♡ -Pass
Pass-3 ♣ -3 ♡ -?

♠ J 8 7
♡ 2
◊ A K 10 6 5
♣ J 10 8 3

Reasonable to bid four clubs. Good shape with useful working values. Typical of what you need to raise. With one less club and another spade, you would pass.

Both vul
1 ♡ -Pass-2 ♡ -Pass
Pass-3 ◊ -Pass-?

♠ A 6 5 4
♡ J 10 6 2
◊ K Q 3
♣ A 2

The kind of good hand which can try three notrump. But it comes with no guarantee. If it looks automatic, consider where your tricks are coming from. If partner has six diamonds to the ace and the opponents are kind enough to set up a heart trick, you'll be okay. But if they switch to a club or spade, whichever is to their advantage, then you will need partner to have a king in addition to a sixth diamond. Slow cards like queens or a queen-jack will not produce the trick fast enough. If partner has a seventh diamond things will be okay unless he is missing the ace.

This hand is as fine a hand as partner could ever expect to find and game is still not a sure thing. Remember this when you are thinking of bidding three notrump on some similiar auctions. Ask yourself where the tricks are coming from.

There is an important point to be made here. You have four hearts, the opponents' suit. Partner likely has a stiff. Why did he not reopen with a double? The answer is that he is probably worried about this shape and poor spades is a possible reason. Why didn't he bid two notrump for the minors? Probably because his diamonds were so much better or longer than clubs. This means he will have a long if not good diamond suit.

When partner reopens at the three level, he needs a five card suit about 95% of the time, but at the two level, he can frequently have a four card suit.

Your length in the opponents' suit will often give you a clue. After

1 ♡ -Pass-2 ♡ -Pass
Pass-2 ♠

. . . if your hand includes a singleton heart, you can assume partner has heart length and consequently may have a four card spade suit.

If your hand has three or four hearts, it means partner is short, so one of his options was to double. If he doesn't double but bids two spades, it means he has either five spades or some shape not appropriate for a double.

The hand being discussed a moment ago:

♠ A 6 5 4
♡ J 10 6 2   1 ♡ -Pass-2 ♡ -Pass
◊ K Q 3   Pass-3 ◊
♣ A 2

This suggests partner has a stiff heart. If you work out partner's distributions, he will surely have a sixth or seventh diamond. What shape can he have which includes a singleton heart and only five diamonds which would not either double or bid two notrump as his reopening call?

2. When the opponents have found a fit after a two-suited auction.

No one vul

1♣-Pass-1♡-Pass
2♡-Pass-Pass-Dbl
Pass-?

When the opponents have had a two-suited auction, you are less likely to be involved in bidding after partner's reopening bid than when they have had a one-suited auction. This is for a number of reasons:

1. Both you and partner have passed up a chance to act at the one level thus limiting your hands.

2. There are only two suits remaining for you to compete in, not three.

3. The range of the one heart bidder's hand is wider than that of a hand which raises opener's suit. The one heart bidder can have up to a crummy 11 which wasn't worth another bid.

4. The opponents may be on a four-three fit which means that when you hold three of their raised suit, you can't be as sure of shortness in partner's hand.

5. The opponents' defense will be better because they have more options as to the opening lead and subsequent play.

Given all of this, you will need to exercise more caution about responding to partner's bid. You will answer his double, but you won't take many second efforts. Note that as long as the opponents have an established fit, the possibility of further action by you does exist. Later when we get into balancing against non-fit auctions, you will see the meaning of true abstinence.

No one vul

1◊-Pass-1♡-Pass
2♡-Pass-Pass-Dbl
Pass-?

♠ K Q 7 3
♡ Q 6 5
◊ A 4 2
♣ Q 8 6

Two spades. No further bidding by you. You have the wasted heart queen and terrible shape. Partner may have three hearts and your diamond holding is poor. Both hearts and diamonds are vulnerable to attack and the defense can take their pick. Partner hasn't much and is trusting you not to get too excited. Don't disappoint him.

What does he have? These are all possible:

♠ 10 8 6 2
♡ K 8
◊ J 10 7
♣ A J 9 7

which may or may not produce two spades.

♠ A 9 4 2
♡ 9 7 4
◊ 10 6
♣ K 10 9 3

maybe two spades, maybe not.

♠ J 6 4 2
♡ J 7
◊ 10 9 3
♣ A K J 2

which may produce three spades against soft defense.

This last hand won't exist too often because if partner has it, the opponents have auctioned it up to two hearts on 16 high card points. Partner is more likely to have one of the first two hands.

134

No one vul
1♣-Pass-1♠-Pass
2♦-Pass-Pass-Dbl
Pass-?

♠ K 3 2   Three hearts only. You won't have more than this or
♡ A 10 6 5 4   you would have overcalled. As it is, quite a few players
◊ Q 8 7   would overcall so they wouldn't have this decision.
♣ Q 6   Note that partner has a choice of reopening bids avail-
                 able. He can double, or he can choose an unusual no-
trump. Which raises another problem. Should two notrump be for the unbid suits
or should it be for the minors, ignoring the fact that clubs have been bid? It can be
played either way efficiently, so your partnership needs only to choose one and
stick to it. Here are the advantages of both ways.

If you play it for the minors, regardless of the auction, you will not lose
opener's suit if it belongs to your side.

If you play it as takeout, then you can play that double is for takeout with a
balanced hand and which includes some defense. Two notrump would show a
distributional hand which would not want to hear partner converting for penalty.
If you play it this way, you can make the distinction only when it doesn't cost
you a level of bidding.

No one vul
1♣-Pass-1♡-Pass
2♡-Pass-Pass-Dbl
Pass-?

♠ J 9 8 7 5   Two spades. I wouldn't be caught dead passing this
♡ 3   hand earlier, but this isn't a commonly held view. So for
◊ A Q 6 2   some the problem is valid. If they bid three hearts, you
♣ K 4 3   can bid three spades. The usual criteria. Good shape,
                 extra trump, and all working cards. Again, it's not that
you have a lot of points, it's that they are all of value. Note that you are violating
a basic rule of balancing. You've pushed them to the three level, and that is
usually your goal. When you bid again, it is because you hope to make your bid,
or at least come close. You are not expecting to push them any higher. At matchpoints especially, you may get doubled on speculation, so you need to be on firm
ground for this second push.

No one vul
1♣-Pass-1♡-Pass
2♡-Pass-Pass-2♠
Pass-?

♠ Q 8 7   Pass. The theme remains the same. Good hands are
♡ K J 8 7   not necessarily just a bunch of points. Your hearts are
◊ K Q J   wasted, your club queen questionable, and you have
♣ Q 8 6   losers all over. In the unlikely event they go to three
                 hearts, you can double if you wish, but it's a little
greedy. Note partner is short in hearts so probably has five spades. At IMPs, he
should for sure because he doesn't have enough points to bid without spade
length. And, because partner is short in hearts, he can't expect you to have spade
length. At matchpoints of course, anything seems to go, so partner may be in
there on nothing more substantial than a wing and a prayer. Your hand has

answered that prayer. He is also praying that you pass two spades. You should answer that one too.

No one vul

1♣-Pass-1♡-Pass
2♡-Pass-Pass-2♠
3♣-?

♠ K 8 7 6   Pass. This sequence confirms that opener has only
♡ 10 6 5   three hearts so there is a good chance your partner has
◊ A Q 7 5   three also. You have the spade support partner was hop-
♣ J 2   ing for but not the heart shortness. The defense will be
good because opener has options. Note that your diamond holding, while good, is likely not facing four card length. Partner might have doubled with four diamonds and his spade length. No guarantee that he may have five spades and four diamonds, but it is possible.

1♣-Pass-1♡-Pass   Can't exist. Partner would have acted over one club.
1♠-Pass-2♠-Pass
Pass-3◊

1♣-Pass-1◊-Pass   Not likely, but possible. Don't bother looking at your
1♡-Pass-2♡-Pass   hand. Pass. Partner didn't bid over one club or one
Pass-2♠   heart. No matter what you have, you will be lucky to
make it. Note that opener has not psyched and responder has bid twice. Responder might have made a marginal initial response, but he wouldn't bid again without values. Too dangerous. He would pass one heart.

Not vs. vul

1◊-Pass-1♠-Pass
1NT-Pass-2◊-Pass
Pass-Dbl-Pass-?

♠ Q 10 8 7   Two hearts. Even though this is a fit sequence, it is
♡ K 9 6 4   not safe to be involved. The one notrump rebid implies
◊ J 2   a mild dislike of spades, so there is danger there of a
♣ K 6 5   ruff, and the rebid also shows solid values. Opener was
not counting on distribution to justify his opening bid. While neither of the unbid suits is likely to split poorly, the defensive nature of opener's hand suggests your goal be only to push once. You won't be as quick to bid on after this auction as after some other "fit" auctions.

1◊-Pass-1♡-Pass
1NT-Pass-2◊-Pass
Pass-Dbl-Pass-?

♠ K 8 7   Two spades. Some reopening doubles may imply a
♡ Q 10 6 4 2   tolerance for one of the opponent's bid suits. But this is
◊ J 3   not one of them. Opener's rebid shows two or more
♣ Q 9 3   hearts. They will not be playable. Two spades is your
only alternative and it could be expensive. You really have a poor hand. Partner deserved better.

When the opponents have bid two suits, there remain only two for your side. When partner reopens with a double, he will frequently find you with no unbid four card suit and you will have to select from two three-baggers. Here you have two unbid three card suits and you bid two spades because it's lower than three clubs. It could be worse. You could have two spades and three clubs.

Not vs. vul

1 ♦ -Pass-1 ♡ -Pass
1NT-Pass-2 ♦ -Pass
Pass-Dbl-Pass-?

♠ A J 9
♡ Q 6 5 4
♦ Q 2
♣ 9 6 5 4

You could bid three clubs showing your suit, or you could bid two spades hoping not to get doubled. Spades are probably three-three on this sequence. Neither opponent rates to have four. With your spade and club high cards reversed, you should bid clubs. In any case, holding this hand, you would be happy to concede 100.

3. When the opponents have conducted a preference auction.

When the opponents have a semi-fit sequence where someone takes a preference, your side will be unlikely to do more than offer one effort at reopening. Pushing the opponents a trick higher, or going down a trick undoubled are your usual goals. The times you actually make something will be rather rare.

If it sounds to you as though every area of bidding is introduced with various warnings, it is probably true. But it is also true that as the opponents' auction becomes less fit oriented, your chances of making something are reduced accordingly and the dangers to you increased. Consequently, your goals become diminished as do the number of hands on which you compete. At the end of this chapter, I'll present a list of the auctions and what your expectations and goals should be against each. In the meantime, you should be developing a feel for when you can compete and when you can't, and the gradations of safety in between.

No one vul

LHO		RHO	YOU
1 ♦	Pass	1 ♠	Pass
2 ♣	Pass	2 ♦	Pass
Pass	2 ♡	Pass	?

♠ K 8 7
♡ J 4 2
♦ Q J 3
♣ K 9 6 5

On many preference auctions, the opponents will have bid three suits, partner reopening in the fourth. When this happens, partner will be in serious jeopardy. He will be right or he will be wrong. When he's wrong, there is no escape. Here, it does appear that partner got away with it. You have three hearts which is the first thing that should catch your eye and you have a hodge-podge, some of which may be useful. The spade king should not be over-evaluated as opener can have the spade ace.

Of passing interest is the fact that you have three diamonds. Partner has two or three diamonds also, and is not particularly expecting you to be short. It looks as if partner has a five card heart suit. No matter, whatever he has, it's his business. Sometimes though, it is useful to know, hence the exercise.

Obviously, this is not the hand to act with. Pass throughout.

No one vul

LHO		RHO	YOU
1 ♡	Pass	1 ♠	Pass
2 ♣	Pass	2 ♡	Pass
Pass	Dbl	Pass	?

Either a penalty double or a takeout double. Look at your heart length. Hard to imagine anything other than penalty.

Vul vs. not

RHO	YOU	LHO	
1♢	Pass	1NT	Pass
2♣	Pass	Pass	2♡
Pass	?		

♠ Q 8 7
♡ Q 10 6 5
♢ K 8 3
♣ K 9 5

As this is almost a fit auction, you can be a little optimistic about making something. With a good hand, you could raise. This is not a good enough hand.

No one vul

RHO	YOU	LHO	
1 ♢	Pass	1NT	Pass
2♣	Pass	Pass	Dbl
Pass	?		

♠ K J 9 7
♡ K J 4 2
♢ K 3
♣ 9 6 4

Again, they can have a fit so you can hope to make something. It would not be outlandish to cue bid two diamonds and raise either major suit by partner to three. Partner won't misconstrue two diamonds as natural because he will hold a few himself. Note that partner can actually hold a decent hand. If he is 4-4-4-1 he would not have been able to act over one notrump. The stiff club would preclude a takeout double. With the actual auction, he was given a second chance. If you had one more heart and one less spade, you could jump to three hearts.

No one vul

LHO		RHO	YOU
1 ♢	Pass	1NT	Pass
2♣	Pass	2 ♢	Pass
Pass	2♡	Pass	?

♠ J 10 8 7 5
♡ K 4 2
♢ Q 3
♣ A 6 5

Pass. Partner will reopen quite freely after this auction. Both majors are safe. Note that when responder bids one notrump and takes a preference to diamonds, he has three or four of them whereas if he bids one spade and takes a preference to diamonds, he may have a doubleton.

When opponents bid in this fashion, your side can usually compete with impunity in a safe suit at the two level, but responder's high cards will keep you from competing too high.

As usual, almost no amount of high cards will be worth a raise. Partner knows about them. He is interested in the quality of them, the quality of your trump support, and some unexpectedly good distribution.

This hand is the routine pass.

Both vul

LHO		RHO	YOU
1 ◇	Pass	1NT	Pass
2 ♣	Pass	2 ◇	Pass
Pass	Dbl	Pass	?

♠ A 10 8 7
♡ K J 6 4
◇ 8 6 4
♣ K 2

This is a takeout double, but because partner could have acted over one diamond, he is limited in strength. Compare to two hands ago where partner's double of two clubs was not limited by his previous pass. Bid two spades and consider bidding three hearts if the auction continues.

No one vul

RHO	YOU	LHO	
1 ♡	Pass	1 ♠	Pass
2 ♣	Pass	Pass	2 ◇
Pass	?		

♠ A 10 8 7
♡ K 9 8 6 2
◇ Q 10 5
♣ 4

Pass. Partner is probably looking at four or even five clubs and is bidding on your shape as well as your strength. You have what he expects.

Both vul

RHO	YOU	LHO	
1 ♡	Pass	1 ♠	Pass
2 ♣	Pass	Pass	Dbl
Pass	?		

♠ Q 10 6 3
♡ A 7 5
◇ Q 10 2
♣ J 8 3

Two spades. This may look like a curious bid, but it's quite logical. Partner is making a takeout double, and the suits can only be diamonds and spades. He has something like

♠ A J 9 2   ♠ K J 8 4
♡ Q 6 4   or   ♡ 10 3 2
◇ K 9 8 7 3   ◇ A K J 9
♣ 6   ♣ 5 4

He must have four spades as you will bid them any time you have four. With one of the opponents announcing length in spades, partner shouldn't be trying to get you into a four-three fit.

No one vul

RHO	YOU	LHO	
1 ♡	Pass	1 ♠	Pass
2 ♣	Pass	Pass	Dbl
Pass	?		

♠ 8 6 5
♡ K J 5 4
◇ 3 2
♣ K 10 9 7

Pass. There is not much else you can do. But do so expecting to beat them. Partner can have anything from a weak 4-4-4-1 to a good 4-2-5-2. In the first case, you are minus 180 instead of 300 and in the second case you are plus a bunch.

No one vul

RHO YOU LHO

1♡   Pass   1♠   Pass
2♣   Pass   Pass 2♠
Pass ?

♠ K 8 5
♡ A Q 6 2
◇ K 8 4 3
♣ 9 2

Three spades. Partner has made a natural reopening bid and you have only to judge whether or how high to raise. The sequence by opener frequently shows a stiff spade so partner is hoping to find you with two or three of them. You have the maximum number of spades (in practice) plus you have extra working values. Note that responder's auction is unclear in terms of high cards. He could have from five to ten. From partner's viewpoint, this leaves a wide range of values that can be in your hand. This time you have the goods. Tell him.

No one vul

1♡-Pass-1♠-Pass
2♣-Pass-Pass-2♠
Pass-?

♠ 9
♡ Q 10 8 7
◇ K 9 8 7 5
♣ Q J 4

Pass. You haven't got what partner wants, but you haven't anything better to offer. Opener's pass suggests he hasn't more than one spade himself, so that improves the chances that partner has a good suit. If his trump suit divides five-one or even six-zero, partner will be better off scrambling for tricks in spades than you would be scrambling for tricks in diamonds or notrump.

Responder isn't going to have six of them very often. He would rebid them.

On this hand and auction, partner rates to have something like

♠ K J 8 7 5 2
♡ 9 3
◇ A 6 4
♣ K 2

No one vul

RHO YOU LHO

1♣   Pass   1♡   Pass
1NT Pass 2◇   Pass
2♡   Pass Pass 2♠
Pass ?

Don't look. Just pass. An action in the fourth suit is dangerous and unilateral. Partner has whatever he has and is counting on you to have certain values. He looked at his hand and determined what he expected you to have and then decided that it was enough to bid two spades. He has a much better idea of your hand than you do of his. Pass.

No one vul

1♡-Pass-2♣-Pass
2◇-Pass-2♡-Pass
Pass-2♠-Pass-?

A pretty amazing auction. Partner reopened after the opponents showed strength. Your best result will be to have them compete to three hearts and not leave you in two spades. Hard to imagine why partner suddenly got interested. I would expect that his hand indicates that you have a spade fit with him so he must have long hearts. If you don't have some spade support plus short hearts then your partner has done something wrong.

When the opponents end in a suit contract, but have not shown a fit, you will be cautious out of respect for their potential misfit. When they bid like this:

$$1 \clubsuit - 1 \spadesuit$$
$$2 \clubsuit - Pass$$

. . . they frequently have matching singletons and are able to establish an immediate cross ruff. Both your decision to reopen and your decisions to compete when partner reopens should show cognizance of this misfit and what it means to you.

No one vul

1♣-Pass-1♠-Pass
2♣-Pass-Pass-2♡
Pass-?

♠ K J 8 7   Pass. So often the right action with good balanced
♡ K 6 5   hands. Two hearts will go down a fair percentage of the
◊ Q 10 7   time if the opponents can ruff off all your black suit
♣ K 9 5   winners. But lest you think notrump would be better,
             consider that they would set up and run the club suit.
You would rather have a couple of aces so as to control the tempo of the defense.

4. Bidding naturally in a suit the opponents have bid.

No one vul

1◊-Pass-1♡-Pass
2◊-Pass-Pass-2♡
Pass-?

This is a natural bid, and as we saw on page 55 partner can make this bid on some pretty poor hands and suits.

As a conventional aside here, many players have adopted this convention. When opener bids a minor suit, and responder bids a suit at the one level, a bid of either of the opponents suits is natural. It is not a cue bid.

1♣-Pass-1♡-2♣   is natural
1♣-Pass-1♡-2♡   is also natural

This is because opener often opens in a short minor and responder often responds in a bad four card suit. It is an effective strategy to overcall naturally in either suit. If you don't like this, you might try using natural bids in responder's suit only. You can be sure that if you don't misuse this treatment, you will create serious problems for the opposition.

There is little loss to your side because you still have the takeout double and the unusual notrump, plus your overcalls. Seldom will you want to have a cue bid in the traditional sense.

Why not wait and bid later? Because like all overcalls, one of the main advantages is that it makes it harder for the opponents to get together. Why let them conduct their nice one-over-one-over-one sequences with some preferences and or raises and no interference.

Some typical hands for this treatment:

1♣-Pass-1♡-?

Not vul

♠ A 3   two hearts
♡ K Q 10 9 7 5
◊ 10 9 3
♣ 5 4

♠ 3   two hearts
♡ A Q 10 9 3
◊ A J 6 4
♣ 9 5 3

♠ A K   two hearts
♡ Q J 10 8 7 5
◊ K 6 3
♣ 4 2

♠ A 3   Two clubs. Because clubs have been bid over you,
♡ 4 3   you need a better suit than when the suit was bid on
◊ K 9 7   your right. For this reason, you could just play natural
♣ K Q J 9 7 5   bids in RHO's suit. For that matter, there is a second
                         reason. It is easily conceivable that you would want to
play a cue bid of LHO's suit had some special meaning. I said a moment ago that
the takeout double and the unusual notrump were still available and would probably suffice, but a case can be made to play that a cue bid of LHO's suit can fill a
system gap. Perhaps it could show six cards in the unbid minor and four cards in
the unbid major, if such combinations existed. Whatever.

I do remain firm in saying that you don't need *both* cue bids.

The purpose for this digression was to point out that if you use this convention,
then when partner passes and reopens in a previously bid suit, he will not have
some of the good hands shown as examples. He will have a genuine balancing
hand without the values of an overcall. Probably his suit will be on the weakish
side although he could have a good suit with no side high cards. You will usually
be able to look at your hand and tell what partner has.

No one vul

1♣-Pass-1♡-Pass
2♣-Pass-Pass-Dbl
Pass-?

♠ K 2   Two hearts. Not a cue bid. You would prefer to bid
♡ J 10 7 6 3   one of partner's suits, but you haven't got one. There is
◊ K 5   a good chance however that partner has a 4-3-5-1 hand
♣ J 8 6 5   or 4-3-4-2 hand and hearts will be playable. Partner
                         knows your hearts will be a poorish five carder as with
better, you would have overcalled, and with less, you would have bid some other
suit.

If partner has something like

♠ Q 8 6 2
♡ K 3
◊ A 9 6 4 3
♣ 8 2

. . . then you get a bad result. But that would be unlucky all around.

5. Converting partner's reopening double for penalty.

1♣-Pass-1♠-Pass
2♣-Pass-Pass-Dbl
Pass-?

♠ A 6 5 4
♡ 4 2
◊ 9 6 3
♣ K J 8 3

Pass. Note that when the bidding goes

1♣-Pass-Pass-Dbl
2♣

. . . that the two club bidder shows a good suit plus good values. When the bidding goes as in the problem, the two club bid does not show a good hand, and on occasion, may have been made on a poor suit. Some hands do not offer convenient rebids, and opener may have had an awkward choice. Also, opener appears not to like spades, so responder's strength may not be of use to opener. It is far more likely that you will get a penalty on the given auction than if the bidding went

1♣-Pass-Pass-Dbl
2♣-?

. . . and you elected to try for a penalty. The two auctions are about two and one-half tricks apart to your side given the hand you hold.

1♣-Pass-1♠-Pass
2♣-Pass-2♠-Pass
Pass-Dbl-Pass-?

♠ Q 10 8 3
♡ J 6 5 4
◊ K 8 7
♣ 5 4

Pass. Partner could have bid two notrump if he had a shapely hand. He probably has good defense and a club stack

♠ 3 2
♡ A 8 7
◊ A J 5 4
♣ A 10 6 3

Partner is almost expecting you to sit for this double, although he is prepared to see you remove.

1♣-Pass-1♠-Pass
2♣-Pass-2♠-Pass
Pass-Dbl-Pass-?

♠ K 4 3 2
♡ J 8 7 5
◊ J 10 8 3
♣ 5

This one you aren't going to beat. Bid two notrump. Partner should get the idea that you don't have anything so will treat it as takeout. This way you don't have to guess which red suit to play it in. If you get doubled in two notrump you will redouble and trust partner to reconsider his pass. Admittedly, you will not have a hand this bad very often.

No one vul

LHO		RHO	YOU
1♡	Pass	1♠	Pass
2♣	Pass	2♠	Pass
Pass	Dbl	Pass	?

♠ A J 8 5
♡ 10 5
◇ Q 10 8
♣ 10 9 6 3

Another action double by partner. This time there is only one unbid suit, diamonds. Partner must have a very good hand with short spades. The spades you have are nice enough to pass for penalty. But in fact, partner was rather hoping they were even better. The hand he was looking for was

♠ Q 10 9 6 3
♡ 4 2
◇ A 6 3 2
♣ 8 3

His hand is a good 1-4-4-4 or a 2-4-3-4 with good defense but which didn't qualify for a one notrump overcall. His action is really committal. If he catches you with something like

♠ Q 8 4 3 2
♡ J 9 3
◇ 10 7
♣ K 5 4

. . . or even worse, you will have to pass and it will take a miracle for you to beat it. Partner probably has a stiff spade, so declarer will score a lot of trump tricks, notwithstanding that you have five of them. In your favor is that partner ought to have good defense against spades. He will have, or had better have, aces and kings, not queens and garbage.

For the sequence

1♡-Pass-1♠-Pass
2♣-Pass-2♠-Pass
Pass-Dbl

. . . partner should have

♠ 3		♠ 2
♡ A 10 6 2	or	♡ A K 7 5
◇ A K 6 3		◇ A K 10 5
♣ A 9 8 3		♣ Q 9 6 2

He should not have something like:

♠ 4		♠ 4
♡ K Q J 8 7	or	♡ K J 5 3
◇ K Q J 3		◇ Q J 8 7
♣ A 8 2		♣ K Q 9 3

A reopening double on this sequence will be left in quite often as partner will have the spade length over declarer. Dummy will seldom have more than one.

No one vul

1♡-Pass-1♠-Pass
1NT-Pass-2♣-Pass
Pass-3♣-Pass?

144

It doesn't matter what you have. This sequence won't happen. If it does, you will pass.

No one vul

1♥-Pass-1♠-Pass
1NT-Pass-2♣-Pass
Pass-Dbl-Pass-?

This sequence is a bit unusual. Partner probably has a good 1-4-4-4 that did not feel like doubling the one notrump rebid. He won't have a huge hand but he will have good defensive values. On this sequence, dummy will have two or even three spades, so it isn't as misfit a sequence as:

1♥-Pass-1♠-Pass
2♣-Pass-2♠-Pass
Pass-Dbl

However, partner is offering two suits for you to run to so it is not as dangerous an action as when there is only one unbid suit. Note that with a purely offensive hand, he could bid 2NT instead of double.

No one vul

1♣-Pass-1♠-Pass
2♣-Pass-2♠-Pass
Pass-Dbl-Pass-?

♠ K J 7 2
♥ A 3
◇ J 10 5 2
♣ J 8 4

When the opponents have bid as indicated, it is dangerous to reopen in a suit because the opponents can frequently turn their misfit into a defensive cross-ruff. But their sequence does afford you the chance to take advantage of their misfit. When you can reopen with a double, you may still end up playing the hand, but some of the time partner can pass for penalty. You can pass with this hand. Opener will not often have more than one spade and may have none. Contrast with a one notrump rebid which shows two or three. Note also that partner does not need as much when there are two live suits for you as when there is one.

No one vul

1♣-Pass-1♥-Pass
2♣-Pass-2♥-Pass
Pass-Dbl-Pass-?

♠ Q 10 8 7
♥ A 6 4 3 2
◇ J 10 5
♣ 3

You could pass but your hearts are much too poor. Declarer will be able to take five heart tricks plus some amount of side tricks. Since two spades should make, you should go for a plus and bid it.

No one vul

1♣-Pass-1♠-Pass
2♣-Pass-2♠-Pass
Pass-Dbl-Pass-?

♠ A 6 5 4 2
♥ Q 10 8 7
◇ J 10 7
♣ 3

More reasonable to pass on this auction because your alternative would be three hearts. I would still hesitate to pass but it would be a possibility. I would feel much better about this if I had some spade spots or if the opponents were vulnerable. Give partner:

♠ J
♡ A K 6 5
◇ K 8 6 4
♣ J 9 7 6

. . . and you have a play for three hearts and very little chance of beating two spades.

6. When the opponents end in one notrump.

Finally, there is the group of auctions where the opponents end in one notrump. When this is the case, you should be cautious out of regard for the fact that they have some values and the fact that they have no known fit. If they don't have a fit, there is no reason to think you have one. Frequently in fact, the only suits that your partnership has seven plus cards in are the suits the opponents have bid. Try untangling that.

There are very few hands on which you will reopen in a four card suit. This is because you won't often have reason to expect a fit. Actually, there are not many hands where you will reopen in a suit. There will be more cases when your side reopens with double, and that will frequently be for penalty. In the long run, you won't do much reopening after one notrump. Remember, they have shown values, and they haven't shown a fit. Both of these facts should be discouraging to your reopening plans. This plus the fact that you couldn't act earlier means you won't have a very good hand. When you don't have a good hand, you need some safety or expectation of finding a fit. That won't happen very often.

All of which means that when the opponents stop in one notrump, you will not often have to worry about what to do when partner reopens. If partner bids a suit, you will pass or run if it's obvious to do so. If partner doubles, you will judge that it is for penalty in which case you will pass most of the time. Or, you will judge the double to be for takeout, and you will either convert to penalty or you will bid something.

1♣-Pass-1♡-Pass
1NT-Pass-Pass-Dbl
Pass-?

This is primarily a penalty double showing heart strength with other values. You should usually pass although you might judge it to be for takeout.

1♡-Pass-1NT-Pass
Pass-Dbl-Pass-?

♠ Q 8 7 5   Another two-way double which is for penalty or
♡ Q J 5 4 2   takeout according to your holding in hearts. Your
◇ A 3   length says partner is making a takeout double. Since he
♣ J 2   is probably 4-1-4-4 he is not too strong or he would
               have doubled the round before. Bid two spades. Do not
try to beat one notrump. Partner is very lucky to find you with a four card suit. You could have another club and one less spade. That would be awkward.

No one vul

1♡-Pass-1NT-Pass
Pass-Dbl-Pass-?

♠ J 10 8 7 5   This is the converse of the previous hand. Partner is
♡ 3   making a penalty double and you should pass. He has a
◇ Q J 8   good hand with hearts behind the bidder. You should
♣ Q 6 4 2   pass and be happy to have the other suits more or less in

146

hand.

No one vul

1♠-Pass-1NT-Pass
Pass-Dbl-Pass-?

♠ K 10 8 7
♡ K 9 8 6 3
◊ K 8
♣ 9 3

This is not as clear cut. The one notrump bid tends to show good clubs, so this actually becomes a fit auction. Perhaps you should play that on this one sequence two clubs by partner is takeout and double is business. In the absence of a discussion, with this hand I would run to two hearts or would cue bid two clubs myself, asking partner to select a suit. One additional point which suggests that partner's double is for takeout is that some people play the one notrump bid shows extra values when it is in response to one club. You have too many high cards for partner's double to be for penalty, especially if one notrump shows a good hand.

If you had a singleton club, there would be a bit more ambiguity. The treatment of using two clubs as takeout would solve the problem.

When the bidding goes

1◊-Pass-1NT-Pass
Pass-Dbl

. . . you have similar considerations. Responder can hold enough diamonds that partner's double will be difficult to read. This is not always the case because responder won't always have good diamonds. Compare with the one notrump response to one club which does show good clubs.

It would be reasonable to play that two diamonds is for takeout in the reopening position, and double for penalty. That would clear up the ambiguity. Or perhaps play that two clubs is for takeout regardless of the suit opened.

I don't like using artificial conventions very much but here it might be okay. After all, when it goes

1◊-Pass-1NT-Pass
Pass-?

. . . you won't often want two clubs to be a natural bid because that suit is very dangerous.

To my mind, the best solution is to play that two clubs is for takeout and double is for penalty when the opponents have bid

1♠ or ◊-Pass-1NT

If they open with one heart or one spade, and the one notrump response is passed around to partner, both minors are dangerous, but it is possible to bid either in the natural sense. Also, since a double would not be ambiguous, the two way treatment will not suffer from confusion. Of course, if some wise guy responds one notrump to one spade when holding six spades, the final result could be amusing. But I wouldn't worry about that one.

CHAPTER TWELVE

Frequency of Reopening Actions

Each of the last few sections has been introduced with various warnings. I would like to put all this in perspective so you won't get the idea that they are all equally dangerous. For each of the following kinds of auctions, I'm going to present my ideas as to how often you will reopen with a suit, how often you will double, how often partner will continue to compete, what your expectations are, etc.

How Often Will You Reopen and
How Often Will You Compete Further After Various Sequences.

1. When one of a suit is passed out.

It would be impossible to break the possibilities down into percentages. So much can happen. It is fair to say that you will reopen about 75% of the time and that you end up buying the contract or doubling the opponents more than half of the time that you reopen. After a one bid is passed out, you will bid and make quite a few games. Enough that your bidding structure will cater to the possibility that game exists. This is why so much discussion has been devoted to the entire auction following a reopening bid.

2. When one of a suit has been raised and passed out.

According to the vulnerability and what the opponents' suit is, you will reopen around 75% of the time. Over half of this time you will compete if the opponents rebid. Because of the flexibility of the reopening double, you will compete more than after a somewhat rigid reopening in a suit. While you won't bid very many games, there will be a fair number of hands which are rightfully yours for a partscore.

3. When the opponents have an exchange ending in a guaranteed fit.

Because of the complexity of the various auctions, i.e., is there one unbid suit, two unbid suits, or three unbid suits as in the case of

1♣-Pass-1NT-Pass
2♣

. . . the frequency with which you will reopen varies.

If there are three suits available, you will reopen about 85% of the time and will compete further most of the time. It can easily be your hand.

If there are two suits available, that limits your options somewhat and you will reopen about 60% of the time. You will compete a little less than half of this time. Your expectations are usually to make a partscore or to get the opponents up where you can beat them.

If there is one suit available, you will reopen about 25% of the time. You will compete further less than half of this time. You can hope, as opposed to expect, to make a partscore and perhaps you can get them higher.

4. When the opponents have a semi-fit.

You will reopen about 25% of the time and will continue maybe one quarter of this. It's possible you can make something. A likely result will be one down. Because they don't have a good fit, they won't compete too far or too often, but they may double. When they do bid, you have a better chance of beating them than when they have a real fit.

5. When the opponents have no fit.

You will reopen about 30% of the time. 70% of these times will be via a take-out double which partner will frequently pass for penalty. Regardless of the method of reopening, you will compete further only rarely. If you don't have a situation where you can get a penalty, you won't make very many partscores. Small minuses are among your expectations.

6. When the opponents end in one notrump.

You won't disturb them too often. Maybe 30% of the time. Half of this will be with double which is usually for penalty. The other half is via a bid in a suit, and usually in a safe suit. You can hope to make some partscores in safe suits. You won't bid dangerous suits very often, and even when you think you have a good hand, you may be disappointed.

CHAPTER THIRTEEN

Reopening After a Weak Two Bid

When LHO opens with a weak two or three bid, you will have some problems and considerations quite different from those discussed earlier.

1. Opener has a well defined hand. Contrast with an opening one bidder who may have almost any shape and strength.

2. Because opener's strength is so well defined, responder may have passed knowing his side has as many as 23 or even 24 points. The responder to a one bid has no idea what opener has, so he has to keep the bidding open on cheese in order to find out. When one spade is passed out, you have no idea what opener has, but you have a good idea what responder has. Conversely, when two spades or three spades is passed out, you know what opener has, but responder's values are a mystery.

3. You have to reopen at a higher level. This takes away many of those special bids available to you after a one level bid.

4. Lastly, the opponent's high cards will not be concentrated in opener's hand. Rather, opener will have around nine points and his partner will have the rest.

Look how this affects you.

Let's say you have arrived in three notrump on the following hand and West leads the king of spades. What are your chances? Certainly it would help to know the auction, so I will provide you with two of them.

♠ 8 7
♡ J 7 4
◊ A 8 7 2
♣ A J 5 4

♠ Q 10 4
♡ A K Q
◊ Q J 10
♣ Q 10 9 6

On one auction, LHO opened with one spade which was passed around to you. You reopened with one notrump and partner made an aggressive raise. You continued to game.

On this sequence, your chances are excellent because opener rates to have both minor suit kings.

On the second sequence, LHO opened with two spades, passed to you. You reopened with two notrump and partner bid three. This time however, your chances are almost certainly nil, as opener will not have an extra king to go with his ace, king and probably jack of spades. Those minor suit finesses will lose.

What this means is that when you "find" partner with some high cards, they will not always be as useful after a preemptive opening by LHO as when LHO opened with a one bid.

A simpler example is the following.

LHO opens one spade and you have A Q 2 of clubs. Regardless of any other factors, your initial thought should be that the king of clubs is in opener's hand. You would discount that queen of clubs for the time being.

But if LHO opened with two or three spades, you would feel quite good about that queen of clubs.

Let's extend this a little. Let's say your clubs are A 3 2. LHO opens with one spade and you get a vision that your partner has the queen of clubs. This is good news if you end up playing the hand, that queen of clubs will be a likely winner. But if LHO opened with two or three spades and you could once again envision that queen of clubs in partner's hand, you wouldn't count on it to have much value.

Now in practice, you can't "see" which cards partner has, but you can make some educated guesses.

One last situation in this family. You have 8 7 2 of an unbid suit and you are wondering whether to bid or pass. If your LHO has opened with a one bid, you might feel that if partner has any strength in this unbid suit, it will be well placed for you. If partner has K J 3, it may produce a couple of winners. But if LHO has opened with a preempt, you should be wary of this 8 7 2 suit because now the missing strength will be in RHO's hand. If partner produces K J 3, you may have three losers instead of two winners.

Here are some of the more common situations.

No one vul

2 ◇ -Pass-Pass-?

♠ K 8 7 5   A reasonable minimum takeout double. In the section
♡ Q 6 5 4   on reopening after a one bid is passed out, I suggested
◇ 3   that with good shape, you could reopen on almost any-
♣ A 10 8 7   thing. If you will adopt a modicum of caution, you can
                         do so after a weak two bid as well. A rule of thumb is
                         this:

Take away a working queen from your hand. If you would double a passed out one bid of the same suit, then your hand is good enough to double a weak two bid. Here, if you did not have the heart queen, you would have a minimum double of one diamond.

Both vul

2 ♠ -Pass-Pass-?

♠ 8   Very close, but, not quite worth bidding. If you had
♡ K J 7 5   the ten of clubs or diamonds, it would just make it.
◇ A 9 6 5   Spades is always a hard suit to contend with, and this
♣ J 8 7 5   sequence is no different. Any suit partner chooses must
                         be at the three level. Add to this the fact that you are
                         vulnerable, and a pass is strongly suggested.

No one vul

2 ♡ -Pass-Pass-?

♠ Q 10 7   Another minimum. As your shape worsens, your val-
♡ A 2   ues increase. Note that you don't want to have three
◇ K J 8 7   cards in "the other major" if your hand is minimum.
♣ Q 9 7 6   There is an excellent chance that this suit will divide
                         poorly. After a weak two bid, the length and strength of
                         any given unbid suit may be on your right, sitting over
                         your partner. Three small will be a distinctly poor hold-
                         ing which would not be the case after an opening one
                         bid.

No one vul

2 ♡ -Pass-Pass-?

♠ J 8 7 6 5   Two spades. While this could be terribly wrong, you
♡ K 7   will lose a large number of partscore swings by passing.
◇ A 9 5   Note that there are no "safe" or "dangerous" suits here.
♣ K 8 4   Suits you can bid at the two level are safer only because

you are not at the three level.

Note also that the king of clubs is a distinctly good card. Opener is unlikely to have the ace. Compare with when opener bid one heart or perhaps one notrump. Now the club king would be a questionable card.

Do not reopen with double. That would run the risk of losing the spade suit and would expose your heart holding to immediate attack from RHO.

Both vul

2♠-Pass-Pass-?

♠ K 7
♡ A 6 5
◇ J 9 7 5 4
♣ K J 7

A good case could be made for passing. This hand is better than the previous hand, but the auction is different. If you bid your suit, it will be at the three level. If you double, partner will be declarer and the lead will be through your spade holding. Also double runs the risk of playing in a four-three fit rather than a five-four fit. This will happen if partner has four hearts and four diamonds and chooses to bid hearts.

If you are wondering about two notrump, then continue to the next hand.

No one vul

2♠-Pass-Pass-?

♠ 8 7
♡ K J 7
◇ A K J 7 5
♣ K Q 9

You could bid three diamonds, but with such a good hand, you run the risk of missing a game. An alternative bid exists, i.e. two notrump, and that would be a far better bid if your definition for it should include these approximate values.

What should two notrump show? There are two possible meanings. First is unusual for the minors. Second is a balanced hand of some point range with a stopper in the opponents' suit.

It is easy to reject the unusual notrump treatment. If you are missing the majors, then the opponents probably have a major suit fit, or partner has the majors and thus you have a misfit. Also, if two notrump is unusual, you will have a tough time describing useful balanced hands.

Consider also that you are far more likely to have a balanced hand. If you hold a minor-suited hand, someone else might have bid.

The next problem is for you to decide on a range for two notrump. Given that you are contracting for eight tricks, you should have a good hand. Experience suggests something in the range of a super 15 with tricks, up to a revolting 19.

Even with this range, you aren't safe, but it is a practical range that combines safety with optimism. If partner is broke, you are in trouble, but if he has a tad or two you will be okay, and if he has anything extra, he can continue. The important thing is to have a definition so that your partner will be able to make a reasonably accurate decision.

No one vul

2♡-Pass-Pass-?

♠ 3
♡ 8 2
◇ K Q 9 7 6
♣ A J 8 7 5

If you play two notrump as natural, you give up on hands like these or you try three diamonds. Here you run the risk of getting to the wrong suit, but you gain whenever you have a balanced 15 to 19. Come to think of it, having to pass with hands like this may not be so bad.

No one vul
Pass-Pass-2♡-Pass
Pass-?

♠ 3
♡ 8 2
♢ K Q 9 7 6
♣ A J 8 7 5

Having passed, you can't have the good balanced hand, so the meaning of two notrump reverts back to the unusual interpretation.

No one vul
2♠-Pass-Pass-?

♠ K Q 10
♡ Q J
♢ K Q J 7
♣ A J 7 3

Two notrump. Not much in the way of tricks. Just garbage points. Note that you do have a stopper.

No one vul
2♡-Pass-Pass-?

♠ K Q J 8 7 6
♡ 3
♢ A Q 9 7
♣ K 8

Three spades. Jumps are good hands with good six card or longer suits. You do not preempt after a preempt. You might double and then bid spades, but that would tend to show a five card suit.

No one vul
2♢-Pass-Pass-?

♠ K Q 8
♡ A K J 8 7
♢ 4 2
♣ A J 6

Double and correct to three hearts over two spades or three clubs. Raise two notrump to three.

Both vul
2♡-Pass-Pass-?

♠ A Q J 10 8 7
♡ 3
♢ A Q J
♣ A K 9

Double followed by four spades if partner, predictably, shows weakness. Three spades here would be an underbid as it could be passed by partner.

Both vul
2♡-Pass-Pass-?

♠ 4 2
♡ K 3
♢ A K Q J 8 7
♣ A J 5

Three notrump. This auction tends to show a solid suit plus a stopper plus another trick or so. It does not invite partner to bid a suit. If partner bids four spades, it is not because you implied them. You might even have a stiff spade.

No one vul
2♠-Pass-Pass-?

♠ A 6 5
♡ Q J 4
♢ A K 4
♣ A Q 10 7

You could bid three notrump, but it is better to double first and then bid three notrump. Partner will correct to a suit if his hand suggests he do so. He will expect you to have tolerance for all suits.

Note that if partner is truly broke, you won't make much of anything, but when you are faced with a preempt, you lose all kinds of bidding room. You have to hope partner has a few points and you act on that assumption. If you bid less than three notrump partner would have to do some very good guessing. For example, if you chose two notrump here, partner would not know if you had fifteen or twenty-one. It's too great a range. Preempts are hard to handle and they are going to fix you more times than you like. It is just part of the game.

No one vul

2♠-Pass-Pass-?

♠ 8 6 5
♡ A J 5
◇ A K Q 8
♣ A Q 9

Double. If partner bids three of a suit, you will cue bid three spades. The intent of this bid will be to look for three notrump. You can't come close to guaranteeing a game with this hand, but you can't just pass either. The preempt takes away so much room that you can not cater to the possibility that partner is broke. It is too impractical. Had opener bid one spade, you would have been able to double, cue bid, and then stop in three of a suit. You would have had room to find out if partner had the classic dud.

If the auction goes thusly,

2♠-Pass-Pass-Dbl
Pass-3♡-Pass-3♠
Pass-4♣-Pass-?

. . . you will bid four hearts and you should hate it. You would have preferred that partner bid three notrump. That would show a spade stopper. When partner bids four clubs instead, it doesn't promise a thing.

Incidently, when the bidding goes this way

2♠-Pass-Pass-Dbl
Pass-3♡-Pass-3♠
Pass-4♣-Pass-4♡
Pass-?

. . . partner should not feel that you have made a slam try. He should feel that you were looking for a game contract of some sort and you can easily hold the example hand already shown:

♠ 8 6 5
♡ A J 5
◇ A K Q 8
♣ A Q 9

However, if the bidding goes

2♠-Pass-Pass-Dbl
Pass-3♡-Pass-3♠
Pass-3NT-Pass-4♡
Pass-?

. . . partner will know that you are making a slam try. You obviously intended to play in hearts so the reason for the cue bid could not have been to look for the best game. It must have been a genuine control showing cue bid:

♠ 3
♡ A Q J 8
◇ A K J 9 7
♣ A Q 8

This hand is about right. Note that the cue bid does not guarantee the ace or a void.

154

No one vul

2♠-Pass-Pass-?

♠ 3
♡ A 2
◊ Q 10 8
♣ A K Q J 9 7 6

Very tough. Three clubs is an extreme underbid and four clubs gets you past three notrump. Your best alternative is to cue bid with the understanding that you are showing a hand like this one or a ~~good~~ hand not willing to double for fear that partner would pass. This hand should not double because

1. You do not want to hear partner pass.
2. It implies better hearts.

Both vul

2♡-Pass-Pass-?

♠ A K J 8
♡ — —
◊ A Q 8 7
♣ A J 6 5 4

Double. Do not cue bid. If partner can pass your double, he has a bunch of hearts which reduces the chance of your having a fit.

No one vul

2♠-Pass-Pass-?

♠ — —
♡ A K 9 8 7 2
◊ A 4
♣ A K 10 6 5

This is a miserable problem and I can't offer a clear solution.

It is still useful though to look at the possible answers and the problems of each.

1. Four hearts. This is likely to make, but will end the auction on many hands where you have an easy grand.

Opposite

♠ J 8 7 2
♡ 3
◊ Q 6
♣ J 9 8 4 3 2

You could even go down in four hearts with seven clubs cold.

2. Three spades. This could work, but will make it difficult for you to show your suits.

3. Double. This is the most flexible of all the possible calls and will leave you relatively well placed in comparison to other choices. For one thing, partner may pass. You won't care for this but it could be right.

Holding

♠ K 10 7 6 2
♡ 3
◊ K J 5 3
♣ J 8 4

. . . partner will pass and you will get some moderate penalty with slam being a questionable proposition. Note that partner is likely to have good spades as RHO did not raise. Many aggressive opponents will make a preemptive raise when holding three trumps. RHO's silence suggests that he does not have three or more spades, or it may mean that he has a good hand and does not object to your reopening. In either case, double will be your best action.

When partner does answer your double, he may bid one of your suits and the auction will be easy. And when he doesn't bid one of your suits, you will be no worse off than you were before you doubled.

155

Some questions for your partnership.

1.   2♦-Pass-Pass-Dbl
                            Pass-2NT-Pass-?

Would three hearts be forcing?
Would three clubs be forcing?
Without getting into theory, I would treat three hearts as forcing and three clubs as not.

2.   2♦-Pass-Pass-Dbl
                            Pass-2NT-Pass-3♦

Why didn't you bid three spades the first time?
Note that if you double and partner bids three diamonds, your hand is too good for three hearts.

The only good thing about this hand is that you are not going to run into it very soon. It's a good hand for the panel, and barring some odd conventional treatments I don't know about, no one will be enthusiastic about any choice.

CHAPTER FOURTEEN

Reopening After Three Bids

The higher the opponents preempt, the more difficult it is for you to judge the auction. I can offer a few guidelines, but they will be limited in scope. The best advice I can give you is to appreciate that the opponents' preempt is entitled to some good results. If you can accept this and can bring yourself to pass on those good hands which offer no safe bid, you will be ahead of the game. It seems to me that bad results are more often the result of bidding with good hands which were not suited to action. For example:

3♡-Pass-Pass-?

♠ 7 3
♡ Q 2
◊ K J 8 7 5
♣ A K Q 7

The person holding this hand couldn't stand passing and made a takeout double. Partner responded three spades and went down six. Four diamonds would have been down one. Three hearts would have been down two. I won't bother to give you partner's hand. His three spades was correct.

The point of this discussion is that there is no safe, or even relatively safe way to enter the auction with a hand such as this. More on this topic shortly.

Other than some matchpoint travesties, you will require either good shape, good suits, or good hands to reopen. And as you have already seen, not all good hands can act safely. Incidently, you won't be able to get away with much at matchpoints. When you're at the four level with inadequate values, even Mrs. Guggenheim can take a whack at you. The three or four level is no place to be on a prayer.

Here are your options after a three level preempt is passed around to you:
1. Double
2. Three of a suit
3. Four of a lower ranking suit
4. Four of a higher ranking suit
5. Three notrump
6. Pass

Note that I did not include a cue bid. The reason for this is that the goal of most cue bids is to try for three notrump. After a three level preempt, you either bid three notrump or you don't. No investigative cue bidding here. This means that a cue bid can only show some other sort of good hand, and I admit that in my entire experience, I can't remember wishing to cue bid after a three level preempt. There may be some possible reasons for a cue bid other than a good hand and I'll take a look at some of them in the example hands.

The takeout double after a preempt

When you are blessed with the perfect shape, 4-4-4-1 with the stiff in their suit, you can double on some rather light hands. You will be influenced by the vulnerability and by whether partner can respond at the three level or whether he must do so at the four level. Other hands with softer patterns will be influenced by this necessity and will require additional values to compensate for worsening distribution. Keep in mind that partner will try to respond in a major suit, so if you are weak in an unbid major, you will have to make allowances for that fact.

No one vul

3♡-Pass-Pass-?

♠ Q 10 8 7　　　　　　A minimum double. You are well prepared for the
♡ 3　　　　　　　　unbid major.
◇ A 9 8 7
♣ K J 4 2

Both vul

3♡-Pass-Pass-?

♠ Q 6 2　　　　　　　Marginal but acceptable to double at matchpoints.
♡ 3　　　　　　　　Probably not at IMPs. Note that you have only three
◇ A J 8 7　　　　　　spades. Partner will bid these in preference to another
♣ K J 9 5 4　　　　　suit because 1) They can be bid at the three level, which
　　　　　　　　　　is not true of clubs and diamonds, and 2) Partner would
like to have a decent club and diamond holding too, but sometimes you have to
take a chance. You imply clubs and diamonds, but you promise spades.

With this in mind, partner would bid three spades on

♠ K 9 7 5
♡ K 10 4
◇ 3
♣ Q 8 6 3 2

. . . and you would miss your ten card club fit. Remember this hand when you are
considering a takeout double with serious or even mildly imperfect distribution.

Note that those minor suit jacks are more valuable by far than when reopening
after a passed out one bid. Missing strength in these suits will seldom be with the
preemptor, so your finesses will win.

No one vul

3♠-Pass-Pass-?

♠ 8 3　　　　　　　Fairly nervous. Your bad hearts suggest a pass. I
♡ 9 4 2　　　　　　would do this but would hate it. Anyone who doubles
◇ K Q 8 7　　　　　will sometimes get good results, but watch out for the
♣ A Q J 5　　　　　bad ones. They will be huge. Don't try this one at IMPs.
　　　　　　　　　　Once again, the ugly spectre of ethics arises here. So
often the person holding this hand will have extra information. Partner took forever to pass or asked questions, or put his cards on the table and lit a cigarette.
Much easier to do the right thing now. Incidently, don't reopen with this hand if
vulnerable.

Both vul

3♠-Pass-Pass-?

♠ 8 3　　　　　　　This is the same hand as the previous one but with the
♡ K Q 8 7　　　　　suits rearranged and the vulnerability changed. Now it
◇ 9 4 2　　　　　　becomes a minimum matchpoint double because you
♣ A Q J 5　　　　　are prepared for the missing major. They may still dou-
　　　　　　　　　　ble you but at least the double won't be based on trump
　　　　　　　　　　tricks. Add the diamond queen and it would be worth
　　　　　　　　　　double at IMPs also.

No one vul

3♠-Pass-Pass-?

♠ — —
♡ 10 6 5 4
◇ K 8 7 6
♣ A 9 5 4 2

Dangerous to act because partner may convert double to penalty. Your heart length is adequate for a double, but partner will lead hearts in preference to another suit and declarer may get a couple of fast discards before you regain the lead. If you are going to double on hands like this when partner may pass for penalty, then you will once again want to look at your unbid major suits to see if you want partner to lead them.

No one vul

3♠-Pass-Pass-?

♠ 3
♡ K 8 7 6 5
◇ A Q J 8 3
♣ K 4

Double, intending to bid four diamonds if partner bids clubs. This auction is not to be construed as showing a huge hand but rather shows hearts and diamonds. You may not get to hearts every time they are right, but at least you don't get to hearts when they are wrong. If partner bids three notrump, you will have to make another decision, and that should be pass. You should feel that three notrump will make and not try to guess how many hearts partner has. Even if your hand were weaker, you should pass. See next hand.

No one vul

3♠-Pass-Pass-Dbl
Pass-3NT-Pass-?

♠ 3
♡ K 8 7 5 4
◇ K 8 6 3
♣ A 10 2

If you chose to double with this minimum hand, your only other option being to pass, you should sit for three notrump. It wasn't the bid you wanted to hear, but it didn't get doubled either. Pass.

No one vul

3♠-Pass-Pass-?

♠ 3
♡ K 2
◇ A 8 6 5 4
♣ K J 9 7 5

Pass. Double promises hearts and you haven't got them. Nor can you double and if partner bids hearts then convert to five clubs. Partner would interpret that as a huge hand with clubs and a heart tolerance. He will not interpret it as a weak five-five in the minors. Getting a bit ahead of myself here, three notrump by you would not be unusual for the minors. You haven't passed yet, so partner will interpret three notrump as natural. Not so serious. Competing with these hands is not such a hot idea. Lack of a systemic bid may be a blessing.

Reopening with three of a suit

This, and reopening doubles will comprise the bulk of your reopening actions. This is because the takeout double is flexible and therefore safer. On the other hand, when you bid a suit at the three level, it will be an economical action and will require fewer values than bidding at the four level. Four level actions require such good hands that they will be infrequent.

Any reopening bid is made with the expectation that partner will have a semi-useful seven count and when partner has that, he will make a minimal answer to a takeout double and will pass when you bid a suit. When you reopen, you should

159

act on the assumption that partner has this seven count and if that will suffice to make something, then you bid. Note that if you have enough to make game opposite this hypothetical seven count, you can't make a bid which he can drop. More on this in the following examples.

Both vul

3 ♡ -Pass-Pass-?

♠ Q J 7 6 5   Pass. Not even close. Poorish suit, wasted heart king.
♡ K 5 4
♢ A 8 7
♣ Q 2

No one vul

3 ♢ -Pass-Pass-?

♠ A 3   Three hearts. Opposite a moderate seven count
♡ 10 8 7 6 4 2   including a couple of hearts, this should be safe. If part-
♢ 3   ner has an additional king or more, he will consider bid-
♣ K J 9 7   ding on if his hand warrants it.

Vul vs. not

3 ♡ -Pass-Pass-?

♠ K J 8 7 3   This vulnerability is dangerous and your heart hold-
♡ 8 4   ing is poor. On the plus side, you have prime side cards
♢ A Q 6   and your spade spots are more than adequate. Do not
♣ A 7 3   underrate the 8-7 of spades. Bid three spades, but don't
           be too proud of it. Under no circumstances should you
           double.

Both vul

3 ♡ -Pass-Pass-?

♠ A K Q J 8   Pass. Even though you have five relatively sure
♡ 7 6   tricks, you have no potential to develop more. Note the
♢ 8 5 4   previous hand. On a bad day, it might take only four
♣ J 7 3   tricks. But given the auction, it rated to develop with
           luck into quite a few. This hand offers no such future.
Whatever cards partner produces will be of questionable value because RHO will rate to have the missing strength.

Look at these two hands side by side:

                ♠ K J 8 7 3
                ♡ 8 4
                ♢ A Q 6   *Your dummy*
                ♣ A 7 3   ♠ 10 9 4 2
                           ♡ Q 5
                           ♢ K J 3 2
                ♠ A K Q J 8   ♣ K 6 4
                ♡ 7 6
                ♢ 8 5 4
                ♣ J 7 3

It is true that the first hand has three more high card points than the second and on that count might be said to be a better hand than the second. But the second hand has sure tricks. In any event, the important point of this example is to show

how a reasonably random nine count varies in value opposite each of the two example hands. The first hand offers a good play for four spades. You will have to guess the trump suit, but as games go, this one is certainly up to par.

The second hand however, not only offers no play for game, it offers no play for three spades. Two spades will go down most of the time and even one spade will require minor miracles. On a bad day you could end up with your five trump tricks. When LHO has preempted, you have to give far more consideration to the "fillers" you have in the side suits, than when opener started with a one bid.

No one vul

3♣-Pass-Pass-?

♠ K 8 7 5 4 2   Too good to bid three spades. Here you can double
♡ A K   and then bid three spades. If partner jumps to four
◊ K Q 10   hearts or persists in hearts, you should pass and trust
♣ A 3   your high cards to see you through.

No one vul

3♡-Pass-Pass-?

♠ K 8 7 5 4 2   Same hand. This time you can't double because part-
♡ A K   ner will bid a minor and you will have to bid your
◊ K Q 10   spades at the four level. An immediate three spades is
♣ A 3   out as you are far too good for this. I would bid three
notrump and hope to be able to set up the spades or per-
haps find partner with a good minor suit. If you can't stand this answer, then you may as well jump to four spades or take the double route.

One reason you might bid four spades is that it more accurately reflects the strength of your hand. It will help you get to slam if slam exists. Far easier to bid slams after a jump to four spades than after an ill-defined three notrump.

The problem with bidding four spades is that your suit is poor. Partner may stick you in slam with a good hand but insufficient trumps.

Reopening with four of a lower ranking suit

This is a rather rare action. Bidding a suit at the four level requires good values and frequently, when you hold sufficient strength, you may decide to try three notrump instead. Except for the case where opener bid three spades and you are considering four hearts, your four level actions will be in a minor. This is sort of a never-never land. If you make it, you get 130. When you go down, it will have been in pursuit of a fairly nebulous reward. Only when partner can find a raise to five clubs or diamonds will you have achieved a significant return. Once in a while you will get to slam but that will be an uncommon result of your balancing.

If instead of bidding four clubs or four diamonds, you venture three notrump, you will be getting something worthwhile if you make it.

No one vul

3♣-Pass-Pass-?

♠ 3   Pass. You would be happy to reopen with this hand at
♡ 9 3 2   the three level, but at the four level it is just too tenuous.
◊ A Q 10 6 5 4   When you get past three notrump, one of your reason-
♣ K Q 7   able game contracts is no longer accesible. If you call
four diamonds, partner will put you in five far too often
for this hand to warrant that contract. Only if partner can find a miracle four heart bid would you really feel good about bidding four diamonds. Be concerned about those three little hearts.

Vul vs. vul

3♣-Pass-Pass-?

♠ K 3
♡ 4 2
♢ A Q J 7 5 4
♣ A 6 3

Three notrump. Typical of the hand which might reopen with four of a minor but which should decide to try for three notrump instead.

No one vul

3♡-Pass-Pass-?

♠ J 10 7
♡ A 3 2
♢ A K Q J 8 7
♣ 9

Same as above. Try three notrump.

Vul vs. vul

3♣-Pass-Pass-?

♠ 3 2
♡ K 2
♢ K Q J 8 7 6
♣ A Q 6

Four diamonds is right, although you might get away with three notrump.

Vul vs. not

3♠-Pass-Pass-?

♠ 3
♡ — —
♢ A Q J 8 6 3
♣ K Q 10 9 6 4

There is something to be said for playing four spades as unusual and four notrump as Blackwood. I would choose whichever was correct systemically. Barring either of those I would try only four diamonds. Partner probably has enough to raise or to bid four hearts, over which you will bid five clubs.

No one vul

3♠-Pass-Pass-?

♠ A 3
♡ Q J 8 6 5 4
♢ K 6 5 2
♣ 7

Four hearts. If partner has a few values you may make it, and partner won't raise to the five level as he might when your suit was a minor.

No one vul

3♠-Pass-Pass-?

♠ 8 3 2
♡ 7
♢ K Q 8 6 4 2
♣ K J 7

Pass. You can't get away with bad bids at the four level. Too easy for you to get doubled. And you still have to contend with partner. If you can make four diamonds, he will bid five. If you can't make four, you get doubled. No win.

No one vul

Pass-Pass-3♠-Pass
Pass-?

♠ 8 6
♡ 2
♢ A K J 10 7 6 2
♣ Q 5 4

Only if you are a passed hand may you bid with this hand. Most people would have opened this with one thing or another, but if it is not your style, then you could pass and then reopen. Partner should be able to draw the proper inferences from your chosen style to tell what sort of hand you might hold for this sequence.

Both vul

3♠-Pass-Pass-?

♠ A K
♡ K Q 10
◊ K 8 7 5 3 2
♣ A 3

This is the same as an earlier hand but with six diamonds instead of six spades. There it was suggested that a possible action was to jump to four spades over their preempt to show these approximate values. Granted, your suit was sub-marginal for the jump, but four spades was at least a tolerable solution (not my first choice). Here you haven't the ability to make distinctions. In the one case, you can overcall with three or four spades to show different values. But to bid this minor suit, your choices would be between four and five diamonds. I don't care what you say. This hand isn't worth five diamonds. Three notrump is the only choice here; there is no second choice.

Vul vs. not

3♡-Pass-Pass-?

♠ 8 2
♡ K 8
◊ K Q J 7 6
♣ K Q J 5

Good to give up. Much as I like the idea of three notrump, it will be necessary to find partner with at least two aces, and they will have to be the right ones besides. And even then, an inspired lead may set you a bunch. A spade lead through partner's spades followed by a heart shift and the opponents may make three notrump before you score a trick.

Reopening with four of a higher ranking suit

Whenever you have sufficient strength that game will be on opposite partner's random seven count, you should not make a bid that will permit your side to stop short of game. One solution will be a direct jump to game. Another solution will be to double and then bid your suit. In this later case, you may be able to express your values in such a way that partner will go to game with his seven count and pass with less. But some hands won't be suitably shaped to make this distinction and jumping to game will be your only answer.

3♡-Pass-Pass-?

♠ A Q J 10 7 6
♡ 3 2
◊ A Q
♣ A J 7

Four spades. If partner has nothing, this will go down, but you can't bid just three spades because partner will pass with a few working cards and you will miss a game. Doubling isn't so good here because you aren't really interested in anything but spades.

Both vul

3◊-Pass-Pass-?

♠ K Q 7
♡ A K Q 8 6
◊ 3
♣ A J 8 7

Double and bid four hearts over three spades or four clubs. Partner should expect you to have decent spades else you wouldn't have bothered doubling first.

Vul vs. not

3 ◊ -Pass-Pass-?

♠ 3
♡ A K J 10 7 6 3
◊ A Q 2
♣ A 8

Four hearts. Double followed by four hearts would imply some spades. Take the game and if you have missed a slam, unlucky. Be willing to be fixed. Perhaps everyone else went crazy with your hand and found partner with nothing. Fixes work both ways!

No one vul

3 ◊ -Pass-Pass-?

♠ K J 7 6 5 2
♡ A Q 2
◊ 3
♣ A Q 8

Double followed by three spades over three hearts and four spades over three notrump or four clubs. This auction will occasionally permit you to stay at three spades and it also keeps hearts open if partner has a stiff spade and good hearts.

No one vul

3 ♣ -Pass-Pass-?

♠ A K J 7 6
♡ Q 10 4
◊ A J 8 7
♣ 3

Double, followed by three spades if partner bids hearts or diamonds. You will pass three notrump.

Both vul

3 ◊ -Pass-Pass-?

♠ K 7 6 5 4
♡ A Q 2
◊ 3
♣ A K J 7

Tough. Too good for three spades and the suit is a bit shabby to double and then bid. I think I would double and raise either major to game. But I have no serious quarrel with doubling and then three spades. If partner responds to double with four clubs, you can't bid four spades with such freedom because partner won't be that sure of your club holding. He would expect you to hold some hearts for this sequence, but there is less emphasis on the minors. You could bid four spades, but there is a good chance that clubs is best. I would raise to five clubs.

No one vul

3 ◊ -Pass-Pass-?

♠ A Q J 8 6 4
♡ A K 8 7
◊ 3
♣ Q J

Double and then bid four hearts over three hearts, and four spades over anything else. As you can see, partner should not count on you to have a good club holding. See the previous hand.

Vul vs. not

3 ◊ -Pass-Pass-?

♠ 3
♡ A Q J 10 7
◊ A 6 4
♣ A Q 8 3

Another typical nightmare stemming from an opponent's preempt. Your shape excludes double, so you are left with three or four hearts or three notrump. I would eliminate three notrump. There is a reasonable chance for slam here and three notrump tends to end the auction. I would choose four hearts, definitely swayed by that ten of hearts. I appreciate that you may miss a club contract. But the only action which introduces clubs is double, and your spade holding precludes that.

Reopening with three notrump

Frequently, when you have a good hand with a stopper in their suit and no other convenient bid, you can choose three notrump as a least of evils bid. Partner will expect you to have something resembling an opening strong notrump, but because there are so many "unbiddable" hands, he should not rush to take out into a suit, nor should he make questionable slam tries without very sound values.

No one vul

3 ♡ -Pass-Pass-?

♠ K 7
♡ A Q 2
◇ A K J 8 7
♣ A Q 2

Three notrump. The practical bid. Stay fixed. Double may get partner to bid too many spades and it will be played from the wrong side. And if he bids four clubs or diamonds you will not be able to get back to three notrump. If partner bids four spades over three notrump, he will be doing so on his own. You have not promised spade support so your hand will be quite suitable.

No one vul

3 ♡ -Pass-Pass-?

♠ Q 8 7
♡ K J 3
◇ K J 8 7
♣ A Q 3

Very dicey matchpoint three notrump. At IMPs it would be too dangerous to contemplate.

Vul vs. not

3 ♣ -Pass-Pass-?

♠ A 2
♡ 9 7
◇ A Q J 8 7
♣ A 6 5 4

Far better to bid three notrump at IMPs with this than it was to bid three notrump on the previous hand at matchpoints. You have sure tricks and a good suit.

Vul vs. vul

3 ♡ -Pass-Pass-?

♠ A K Q 10 7 6
♡ Q J 2
◇ A 3
♣ Q 7

It looks obvious to bid some number of spades, but how many? Three is a big underbid and four may have too many losers. Too often, at a spade contract, heart ruffs on the go are a killer. I would try a slightly off-beat three notrump.

Vul vs. vul

3 ♡ -Pass-Pass-?

♠ 3
♡ 2
◇ Q J 10 8 7 6
♣ A Q 10 9 7

If you are not a passed hand, you have to either bid four diamonds, pass, or whatever it is that you use for unusual on this sequence. Note that by an unpassed hand, three notrump is not unusual. It is natural, catering to all the other hands discussed in this section. If three notrump were unusual, then you could handle this one, but what would you do on the other hands? Go back and try to find some alternatives. If you are a passed hand, then three notrump unusual would be fine.

No one vul

3 ◊ -Pass-Pass-?

♠ 4 2   Unlikely problem. Where are the highcards? Where
♡ 3   are the majors? Very likely, RHO has all of the above in
◊ K 8 7   a quantity insufficient for action. You can try three
♣ A K Q 8 7 6 5   notrump here, but its not as if you have a lock. You will
                            note on some of the other three notrump hands, you
were worried about one suit, but never about two suits. LHO will have a very
good chance of hitting his partner with either hearts or spades. They may be able
to run either or both majors and perhaps diamonds as well. Down nine!

This doesn't have to happen, but you are going to be a bit lucky to find partner
stopping both suits.

Another danger is partner! He might try to play in a major suit. After

3 ◊ -Pass-Pass-?

. . . partner, holding

♠ K J 10 7 3
♡ K J 2
◊ 3 2
♣ J 3 2

. . . would pass. He would not try four spades because it would be too unilateral.
If you didn't like spades, it would be hard or impossible to recover.

But if partner held

♠ Q J 10 8 7
♡ K J 8 6 2
◊ 4
♣ J 3

. . . he might try four diamonds, asking you to show your best major. Hopefully,
he would find you with four, but three would do. This would not be an unreasonable action because a three notrump reopener could be expected to have at least
one three card major suit holding.

This doesn't mean you shouldn't bid three notrump. It means you have to be
aware of the dangers. Your average number of tricks will be around nine, but that
number will be arrived at via a lot of overtricks and a lot of undertricks. And this
assumes you get to play it in three notrump. Be prepared to hear a sequence like
one of these.

No one vul

3 ◊ -Pass-Pass-3NT
Pass-4 ◊ -Pass-5 ♣
Pass-5 ◊ -Pass-6 ♣
Pass-Pass-Dbl-Pass
Pass-?

♠ 4 2   Six clubs isn't going to make. Did you notice the final
♡ 3   question mark? Maybe partner still has ideas of his
◊ K 8 7   own.
♣ A K Q 8 7 6 5

Or this one:

3◇-Pass-Pass-3NT
Pass-4◇-Pass-4NT
Pass-5◇-Pass-6♣
Pass-Pass-Pass-?

Do you think partner got the message that four notrump was natural? Is 5◇ answering aces, or is it still asking for a major? Don't laugh. I've seen it.

Passing after a preempt

I said earlier that some good hands just do not offer a realistic reopening action. If you can accept this and go quietly, you will be far better off than the person who couldn't resist bidding. Be willing to be fixed!

Here are a few hands in this family.

No one vul

3◇-Pass-Pass-?

♠ 3 2
♡ A Q J 3
◇ 8 6 3
♣ K Q J 7

Pass. Double is out. A matchpoint three hearts is possible, but not recommended. Partner will never credit you for less than a five card suit.

Vul vs. not

3♡-Pass-Pass-?

♠ Q 2
♡ A Q 8 7 6
◇ 4 2
♣ A K 8 7

Pass. This is a real hand. Everyone was serious.

No one vul

3♡-Pass-Pass-?

♠ K 10
♡ 8 6 3
◇ K Q 9 8
♣ A K 10 6

Typical of the hand that should pass. Weak in a major suit, and no stopper in theirs.

Not vul vs. vul

3◇-Pass-Pass-?

♠ J 7
♡ K Q J
◇ Q 5 4
♣ K Q J 9 7

Pass. A point count trap.

No one vul

3◇-Pass-Pass-?

♠ 8 7
♡ 8 6 4
◇ 10 3
♣ A K Q 10 8 7

Pass. Don't compete in a minor with poor hands.

Vul vs. not

3♠-Pass-Pass-?

♠ J 4 2
♡ 7 6 3
◇ K 7 2
♣ A K Q J

A good pass. Bad shape and poor holding in unbid major.

CHAPTER FIFTEEN

When Partner Reopens After a Preempt

When the opponents have started with a preempt, reopening sequences are going to be more cramped for space than after an opening one bid. The higher the preempt, the more difficult it is to overcome. No more nice scientific auctions with takeout doubles followed by cue bids and quantitative raises. No more dialogue. Instead, one, maybe two bids, and that's it.

For example:

1 ◊ -Pass-Pass-Dbl Pass-2 ◊ -Pass-2 ♡ Pass-3 ♡ -Pass-Pass Pass	A takeout double followed by a cue bid and a quantitative raise.
2 ◊ -Pass-Pass-Dbl Pass-3 ◊ -Pass-3 ♡ Pass-4 ♡	A takeout double followed by a cue bid and a guess.
3 ◊ -Pass-Pass-Dbl Pass-4 ◊ -Pass-4 ♡ Pass-Pass-Pass	A takeout double followed by a cue bid.
4 ◊ -Pass-Pass-Dbl Pass-4 ♡ -Pass-Pass Pass	A takeout double.

Because preemptive bidding does take up so much room, one rule has been developed to help differentiate reopening auctions after preempts from reopening auctions after one bids.

This rule has been alluded to before. It is this. When you reopen after a preempt, you are crediting partner with seven or so semi-working points. Plus, when you reopen in a suit, you are counting on finding partner with a holding slightly better than a medium doubleton.

The reason for this is that the preempt has taken away so much room that something had to give. It turns out that the thing least needed was a bid to show a hand of seven or so points.

When you open the bidding, that seven point hand can be shown by raising or bidding one notrump. But when partner reopens after a preempt, if you choose to bid with the seven point hands, the better hands become unmanageable. What has evolved is the realization that opposite most reopening bids, seven points isn't going anywhere anyway, so it usually passes instead.

The reason that partner assumes you have seven points rather than four or two or none is that if you waited for a good enough hand to make something opposite nothing, you would almost never reopen. Thus it becomes practical to assume that partner has this seven points and to bid accordingly.

With this in mind, let's see how you should respond to partner's reopening bids.

Partner Reopens After a Weak Two Bid

1. Partner doubles.

The most important thing here is to give partner some room. In the same way that you need good hands to take positive action when partner doubles a one bid, you need good hands to take positive action after a two bid. Likewise, two notrump by you should show some decent values. Sometimes, of course, you are stuck, but you should try not to bid two notrump with a bad hand. Look for an alternative.

Bidding after partner reopens is fairly easy because opener always passes (99%) so you won't be involved with free bids and such.

No one vul

2♠-Pass-Pass-Dbl
Pass-?

♠ Q 7 2
♡ K Q 8 7
♢ K 6 5
♣ J 9 4

Three hearts. According to the basic rules, partner is playing you for at least seven points. Your spade holding is questionable so you don't really have much more than a "minimum." Note that you don't even have an invitational bid available. Only a commital jump to four hearts. Remember this hand when you are thinking of reopening with double with a weak holding in the other major. This hand will not play too well if partner lays down 9 6 3 of hearts.

Vul vs. vul

2♢-Pass-Pass-Dbl
Pass-?

♠ K Q 6 4 2
♡ K 3
♢ 10 6 4
♣ K 9 8

Three spades is enough. This isn't even quite a maximum.

Vul vs. not

2♡-Pass-Pass-Dbl
Pass-?

♠ Q 3
♡ K 8 3
♢ 8 6 5
♣ Q 10 6 4 2

Three clubs. Two notrump should show more. This is not a good hand. It could be worse, but it is definitely not what partner was hoping for.

No one vul

2♠-Pass-Pass-Dbl
Pass-?

♠ Q 4 2
♡ J 7 3
♢ Q 9 5 2
♣ 10 7 3

This is the kind of bad hand you have to worry about. Bid three diamonds.

Both vul
2♠-Pass-Pass-Dbl
Pass-?

♠ K 10 5   Two notrump. About what the bid should show.
♡ Q 2   Slightly better than average.
◇ A 9 6 5
♣ Q 9 4 2

No one vul
2♡-Pass-Pass-Dbl
Pass-?

♠ 8 3   Three notrump. You need a good hand for this. This
♡ A Q   hand is about right. It will usually be in the super 13 to a
◇ K 10 8 7 5   so-so 16 that wasn't quite up to overcalling two
♣ A J 8 7   notrump.

Vul vs. not
2♠-Pass-Pass-Dbl
Pass-?

♠ Q J 3   Three notrump. About as much as you will have else
♡ K J   you would have acted earlier. Even so, you don't have
◇ K Q 6 3   any guarantees.
♣ K J 9 7   ♠ 4 2
                       ♡ A Q 10 5
                       ◇ A 7 2
                       ♣ Q 10 6 3

Opposite this, you will need three-three diamonds, assuming decent defense.

No one vul
2♠-Pass-Pass-Dbl
Pass-?

♠ Q 3   Three diamonds. This is a good hand, but there is no
♡ 10 8 5   suitable way to describe it short of a jump to four dia-
◇ A Q 10 8 7 6   monds or a cue bid. The problem with the cue bid is that
♣ K 3   partner will bid four hearts and now you will have to
                 bid five diamonds! This is especially bad when it goes
down and three notrumps turn out to be right.

If you think when you cue bid that partner ought to bid three notrump with a
spade stopper in lieu of showing a four card heart suit, then what do you want
him to do when your actual hand is

                       ♠ 4 2
                       ♡ Q 10 8 7
                       ◇ A K Q 3
                       ♣ Q 8 3

With this hand, you would like him to show four hearts in preference to showing a spade stopper.

No one vul

2 ◊ -Pass-Pass-Dbl
Pass-?

♠ K J 8 7
♡ Q J 8 7
♢ 4 2
♣ A J 8

Three diamonds. Forcing to three notrump or to four of a suit. If you cue bid and pass when partner bids three hearts or spades, you will have a disappointed and confused partner.

No one vul

2 ◊ -Pass-Pass-Dbl
Pass-?

♠ A 3
♡ Q 8 2
♢ 3 2
♣ A Q 7 6 4 2

Three diamonds. Somewhat hoping that partner can bid notrump. In practice, he won't. He'll bid a major. Now you'll have to bid four clubs and if three notrump is right, you've done the wrong thing. Four clubs incidently should be passable. If you had a hand good enough to force to the five level, you would have overcalled.

This hand came up in actual play. Partner's hand was

♠ K 10 4 2
♡ A 10 6 3
♢ K 7
♣ K 8 5

Three notrump was correct. In practice the auction was

2 ◊ -Pass-Pass-Dbl
Pass-3 ◊ -Pass-3 ♡
Pass-4 ♣ -Pass-Pass
Pass

Reopener discounted his king of diamonds and passed. As it was, four clubs was not cold.

No one vul

2 ◊ -Pass-Pass-Dbl
Pass-?

♠ Q 10 8 7
♡ K 2
♢ 8 6 5
♣ A K J 4

You could jump to three spades or you could cue bid. If partner bids spades, well and good, and it will be played from his side. A bonus: If partner bids three hearts, you will bid three spades. This should imply a four card holding, else you would have jumped earlier.

There is the question of whether this should be forcing. It sounds like it ought to be. But if you don't have a four-four fit, you may be quite high enough. Four-threes don't play well when they are dividing poorly.

If it sounds like I'm vacillating back and forth here, it's true. I haven't firm understandings on this sequence and I doubt that many others do either. To confirm this, I phoned a couple of my scientific friends and asked for their opinions on some of the hands in this section. I got a lot of words but in the final analysis, they couldn't tell me that their understandings were better than mine. Their understandings were different from mine, but they were equally vague.

The one thing I can say for sure here is that these problems have a low frequency of occurence. If you pick an understanding and stick to it, it will see you through most problems of this type.

No one vul

2 ◇ -Pass-Pass-Dbl
Pass-?

♠ Q 10 8 7 6 4　　　Four spades. An extra spade. Working values. A good
♡ A J 3　　　　　　playing hand with a long and probably weakish suit.
◇ 2　　　　　　　　Limited by the inability to bid over two diamonds.
♣ K 5 4

Both vul

2 ♠ -Pass-Pass-Dbl
Pass-?

♠ 3　　　　　　　　Four clubs. A good hand not interested in three
♡ K 7　　　　　　　notrump. Per force with good distribution. Note that
◇ K 10 8 7　　　　after two spades, you can't really start with the cue bid
♣ K J 10 7 4 3　　route as four hearts by partner will get you too high.
　　　　　　　　　　You have to pay off to the effectiveness of two spades.

2. The Lebensold convention.

There is a convention credited to but disclaimed by Mr. Lebensold which caters to many of the hands in this section. I don't use the convention, so my understanding of it is rather limited. But that doesn't mean it isn't a good one to use. Certainly, after working through the hands in this section, I can appreciate that it could be a lifesaver.

Here's how it works.

When partner doubles a weak two bid, Lebensold uses two notrump as an artificial bid which forces partner to respond three clubs. Responder either passes or bids his suit which is considered as a signoff. Thus after

2 ♡ -Pass-Pass-Dbl
Pass-?

These would be signoff auctions:

2 ♡ -Pass-Pass-Dbl　　　Weak hand with spades
Pass-2 ♠

2 ♡ -Pass-Pass-Dbl　　　Weak hand with clubs
Pass-2NT-Pass-3 ♣

2 ♡ -Pass-Pass-Dbl　　　Weak hand with diamonds.
Pass-2NT-Pass-3 ♣
Pass-3 ◇

This means that when partner doubles, any suit by you at the three level is forward going.

These sequences all show a hand with useful values.

2 ♡ -Pass-Pass-Dbl
Pass-3 ♣

2 ♡ -Pass-Pass-Dbl
Pass-3 ◇

2 ♡ -Pass-Pass-Dbl
Pass-3 ♠

Note that none of these bids is forcing. They show in the range of nine to 12. With stronger hands, you must either jump to game or cue bid.

Using this convention also gives you two ways to cue bid.

2 ♡ -Pass-Pass-Dbl
Pass-3 ♡

The immediate cue bid asks for a stopper with notrump interest. Probably you have a good minor suit.

2 ♡ -Pass-Pass-Dbl
Pass-2NT-Pass-3 ♣
Pass-3 ♡

The delayed cue bid is asking for the unbid major, or majors.

As with all conventions, it creates some problems. You give up the natural meaning of two notrump.

2 ♠ -Pass-Pass-Dbl
Pass-?

♠ K J 3
♡ K 7 6
◊ 5 4 3 2
♣ K J 3

Using Lebensold, you, can't bid two notrump natural any more because partner will convert it to three clubs. Is that what you want?

Also, if notrump is right from partner's side, he won't be able to play it if you start with an artificial two notrump.

♠ Q J 8 7	♠ K 10 6	2 ♡ -Pass-Pass-Dbl
♡ 8 3	♡ K 4	Pass-2NT-Pass-3 ♣
◊ K Q 5 4	◊ A 9 6 3	Pass-3 ♡ -Pass-?
♣ K Q 4	♣ A 10 5 2	

If partner chooses three notrump, his heart king will not likely be a stopper with North on lead.

I admit I've worked a bit at showing unflattering examples, but it would be unfair to say that the convention would solve everything. Hence both sides. I do feel that it doesn't come up so often that a casual partnership would need it. I know that I have not often wished to have it available, but I'm not much for conventions anyway, so I am biased.

Perhaps Mr. Lebensold (or if he doesn't want anything to do with it, someone else) can get the convention printed up in detail and have it made available in a pamphlet. It would be a useful contribution.

Note that this convention need not be restricted to reopening doubles. It can be used whether the double was in the immediate seat as well. The responses would be changed a bit in terms of values and some positional situations would have to be considered, but the gist would remain the same.

1. **Partner reopens with two of a suit.**

Your most common action will be to raise or to bid some number of notrump. Less common bids are to bid a new suit, non-forcing, or to cue bid. The cue bid is usually looking for notrump but may be a good balanced raise.

Whatever you choose, remember that partner is expecting you to have that seven or so points. Any bid by you except a change of suit shows more than this.

No one vul

2 ◊ -Pass-Pass-2 ♠
Pass-?

♠ Q 8 7
♡ A 9 7 3
◊ K 5 3
♣ 8 6 4

Pass. Partner will like your hand, but not enough to be higher than two spades. You might miss a miracle game, but it would be exceptional. Pass is in keeping with the theory that you should not trap partner.

I would rate this hand at about one queen less than a raise.

Both vul

2 ◊ -Pass-Pass-2 ♡
Pass-?

♠ K Q 3   Just three hearts. If partner passes, don't be surprised
♡ K J 8 7   if he goes down.
◊ 8 7
♣ Q 10 8 3

No one vul

2 ◊ -Pass-Pass-2 ♣
Pass-?

♠ J 10 6 4 2   Four spades. Hoping partner has more than a mini-
♡ A Q 3   mum. This may not be cold
◊ 4 3 2
♣ A J

Both vul

2 ◊ -Pass-Pass-2 ♡
Pass-?

♠ 10 7 3   Tough. Three clubs would be reasonable, but you
♡ K 5   have more than partner might expect. Three diamonds
◊ J 8   is a possibility, but if partner rebids three hearts you
♣ A K J 7 6 2   will have another decision. If partner rebids three
                           notrump, it will probably be adequate, but may not be a
bargain. I think I would choose three clubs. Note that if you do choose the cue
bid, partner will try not to rebid three hearts if he has a good hand but with no
diamond stopper.

                           ♠ A 8 2
                           ♡ A Q 10 8 5
                           ◊ 9 3
                           ♣ Q 10 4

As reopening two heart bids go, this is a good one and he would not wish to rebid
a weak sounding three hearts. He should choose three spades. Maybe I'm fanta-
sizing, but the auction would continue

                    2 ◊ -Pass-Pass-2 ♡
                    Pass-3 ◊ -Pass-3 ♠
                    Pass-4 ♣ -Pass-5 ♣
                    Pass-Pass-Pass

. . . or

                    2 ◊ -Pass-Pass-2 ♡
                    Pass-3 ◊ -Pass-3 ♠
                    Pass-4 ♣ -Pass-4 ◊
                    Pass-4 ♡ -Pass-Pass
                    Pass

On this last sequence, four diamonds would be a super scientific "pick your
game" bid. No one said this is an easy game.
    In practice, you will find that you have very few cue bidding sequences when
partner reopens at the two level. Partner's suit is always a major and the
ambiguity as to whether the cue bid shows a good raise or is looking for notrump
can not be untangled. Perhaps a cue bid should be defined as a good raise.

No one vul
2 ◊ -Pass-Pass-2 ♡
Pass-?

♠ A K J 7   An impossible hand. I can think of no satisfactory
♡ 3   sequence. All possibilities have serious traps.
◊ 9 7 5
♣ A Q 5 3 2

Both vul
2 ♡ -Pass-Pass-2 ♠
Pass-?

♠ J 2   Two notrump. An average hand.
♡ Q 10 4
◊ A 9 4 2
♣ A J 10 7

No one vul
2 ♡ -Pass-Pass-2 ♠
Pass-?

♠ Q 10   Three notrump. Double heart stop, spade fit, useful
♡ K J 7   side suit. The near equivalent of an opening one
◊ Q 8 6   notrump.
♣ A Q 10 6 4

No one vul
2 ♡ -Pass-Pass-2 ♠
Pass-?

♠ 8 2   No reason to disturb two spades. This is a good hand,
♡ J 3   but it would be excessive to look for game. The only
◊ A Q 6 2   sensible bid would be three clubs, and there is no reason
♣ A J 9 5 4   to think partner will bid over this. Good hands with
                  questionable futures should not get involved.

No one vul
2 ♡ -Pass-Pass-2 ♠
Pass-?

♠ 3   You know three clubs is better than two spades, but
♡ J 8 7 2   there is a good chance that partner will bid again expect-
◊ 3 2   ing a bit more. Pass and run to three clubs if two spades
♣ K Q J 9 7 3   gets doubled.

On those sequences where partner reopens at the two level, you pass, and LHO
raises the weak two bidder, or even bids a new suit, you don't want to be too
active about competing. Your first thought should be, "Can we beat them?" and if
you think you can, then pass, or perhaps double. Only if you decide they can
make their bid should you continue. This means that with scattered queens and
jacks and with poor shape, you should be passing since these are defensively oriented values.

No one vul
2 ◊ -Pass-Pass-2 ♠
Pass-Pass-3 ◊ -Pass
Pass-?

♠ Q J 7
♡ A J 10 4 2
◊ 8 7 3
♣ 9 2

This was not worth a raise the first time, but is good enough to compete with now. Three spades. Your three little diamonds look better now than before because the auction both suggests partner is short in diamonds and implies no wasted high cards there.

Both vul
2 ◊ -Pass-Pass-2 ♠
Pass-Pass-3 ◊ -Pass
Pass-?

♠ Q 6 2
♡ K J 8 3
◊ Q 9 7
♣ K 6 4

I would pass although a matchpoint hungry double could work. I would have to be pretty desperate to try that. The important thing is not to bid three spades. Bad shape, no aces, soft cards.

No one vul
2 ◊ -Pass-Pass-2 ♠
Pass-Pass-3 ◊ -Pass
Pass-?

♠ A 2
♡ J 10 9 3
◊ Q 10 8 7
♣ K 5 2

Double. You have good diamonds plus some defense. Incidently, lead the heart jack. Partner's two spades did not promise that much in spades.

No one vul
2 ◊ -Pass-Pass-2 ♠
Pass-Pass-3 ◊ -Pass
Pass-?

♠ J 2
♡ K Q J 9 8 7
◊ 8 4
♣ Q 3 2

Three hearts. You need a good suit for this and consequently will not have much on the side or you would have bid earlier. You would not do this with

♠ J 2
♡ K J 6 5 4 2
◊ Q 3
♣ Q 9 5

This is about the only sequence where partner reopens with a suit and you pass and then back in later. All other sequences would force you to act at the four level. There are very few hands which can make so delicate a decision.

4. **Partner reopens with three of a lower ranking suit.**

This will usually be in a minor. You will seldom raise and will either pass, bid three notrump, or make a cue bid which this time will clearly be a try for three notrump, probably confirming a mild or better fit. Seldom will you bid a new suit. Because partner needs a better hand for three level bids than for two level bids, you will have a better idea of your side's potential.

No one vul

2♡-Pass-Pass-3◇
Pass-?

♠ J 7
♡ K 8 2
◇ A 6 5
♣ K J 9 7 5

Three notrump. About average. Unexceptional hand. Do not cue bid three hearts. True, three notrump might be better from partner's side, but he may not be able to bid it.

Both vul

2♡-Pass-Pass-3♣
Pass-?

♠ A Q 6 5
♡ 8 7
◇ K Q 5 4 2
♣ 9 7

Pass is not unreasonable. You have no club fit so partner will need an exceptionally good suit to bring home three notrump. Your diamond suit may run, but if partner has the ace, plus a heart stopper, he won't have too many fast tricks in clubs.

Vul vs. not

2♡-Pass-Pass-3♣
Pass-?

♠ A 10 6 5
♡ 8 7
◇ K Q 5 4
♣ Q 9 7

Still a pass, but certainly closer to a cue bid than the previous hand. You have club help for partner. If partner can't bid three notrump, you won't mind getting to four clubs.

No one vul

2♡-Pass-Pass-3♣
Pass-?

♠ A 8 7
♡ 9 6 3
◇ A J 7
♣ K 9 6 4

Finally. A classic cue bid. If partner can bid three notrump, you'll make. Note that those aces are fast tricks. It's not as though you have kings and queens and must concede the lead numerous times before coming to nine tricks.

One problem with the cue bid is that it is not clear whether you have a whole stopper, a partial stopper, or no stopper. It seems to me that with a full stop, you just bid three notrump, other things being equal, but you still can't differentiate between a half stopper and no stopper. There is just no room.

I do play that the cue bid asks for a full stopper, and this is not always successful. It might be feasible to use the bid of some unbid suit to ask for a full stopper and use the cue bid to show a half stopper, but that is inefficient because it gives up the natural meaning of the bid.

2♡-Pass-Pass-3◇
Pass-?

♠ A 8 2
♡ 8 6 2
◇ A J 7
♣ K Q 8 2

You could use three spades to deny a half stopper and use three hearts to show a whole stopper, but whenever you want to show a spade suit, you are in trouble. Best not to bother with this treatment. I suggest using the cue bid to ask for a full stopper and to give up on those hands where you each have a half stopper.

No one vul
2♠-Pass-Pass-3♡
Pass-?

♠ 8 7 5　　　　　　　　Bid four hearts. This sequence is special because it is
♡ K J 5　　　　　　　the only time you would go to the four level with a so-so
◇ A 6 5 4　　　　　　hand. This is because four hearts pays off a game bonus
♣ Q 10 2　　　　　　which four of a minor suit does not. If partner had bid
　　　　　　　　　　　three clubs or diamonds, you should pass as five of a
　　　　　　　　　　　minor would be well against the odds, even if partner
　　　　　　　　　　　accepted an invitation.

Both vul
2♠-Pass-Pass-3♣
Pass-?

♠ 8　　　　　　　　　A rare hand which would raise a minor rather than
♡ A 8 6 5 2　　　　　look for three notrump. Bid four clubs. Partner should
◇ K 3 2　　　　　　　work out that you have good shape. Note that partner
♣ Q 10 8 7　　　　　probably has fair length in spades, or they would have
　　　　　　　　　　　been raised so he does not rate to have much in hearts.

Vul vs. not
2♡-Pass-Pass-3◇
Pass-Pass-3♡-Pass
Pass-?

♠ 8 6 5　　　　　　　An infrequent example of a hand which passed part-
♡ 10 5 4　　　　　　ner's reopening three level bid and which bid later. The
◇ K Q 5 4　　　　　criteria are simple. Nothing wasted. The three small
♣ K Q 9　　　　　　hearts have become much better than two small would
　　　　　　　　　　　have been. Partner hopefully is both short in hearts and
has no wasted heart honors. Very similar to the example hand earlier which
passed partner's reopening two spades and later competed to three spades. This
hand is more unusual because your subsequent action was at the four level.

5. Partner jumps to the three level.

This is a very rare action. It is also easy to handle. Partner shows a good suit
and a good hand with strong game interest. The main problem for you is one of
definition and if you define it as I have described, you will continue to game with
anything resembling one and one-half tricks and a couple of trumps.

No one vul
2◇-Pass-Pass-3♠
Pass-?

♠ J 3　　　　　　　　A solid raise to four spades. Note that all of these
♡ A Q 6 5 4　　　　jumps will be a major suit. Note also that if you are
◇ 8 6 5 2　　　　　interested in three notrump, you will just have to bid it.
♣ 10 3　　　　　　　The cue bid is not available.

Both vul

2 ♡ -Pass-Pass-3 ♣
Pass-?

♠ 3
♡ Q 10 8 7
◇ K 9 6 4
♣ K J 6 3

Three notrump. Even with a misfit, you need only a moderate hand to bid three notrump.

No one vul

2 ◇ -Pass-Pass-3 ♠
Pass-?

♠ J 10 6 3
♡ A 2
◇ A Q 3
♣ J 10 8 6

Four diamonds. This sequence can lead to a few slams and this cue bid is a start in that direction.

Both vul

2 ◇ -Pass-Pass-3 ♡
Pass-?

♠ K Q J 9 6 5
♡ 10
◇ 6 5 4
♣ Q 10 5

Three spades. Forcing. You will pass four hearts or three notrump.

Vul vs. not

2 ♡ -Pass-Pass-3 ♠
Pass-?

♠ 8 3
♡ Q 10
◇ Q J 6 3
♣ Q 9 5 4 2

Pass. Game may be on, but it would require a perfect fit.

6. **Partner reopens with two notrump.**

This is either natural with the approximate values of an opening notrump, or it is unusual if partner has passed originally.

When it is strong, there will be some question of what your bids mean. If you bid a new suit, is it forcing? If you bid three clubs, is it asking for the majors? What does a cue bid mean?

The first of these questions is the most difficult.

♠ J 10 8 7 5 4   ♠ Q J 10 6 5
♡ 3   ♡ 4 2
◇ J 9 7   ◇ K J 7
♣ 10 6 4   ♣ K 5 4

After

2 ♡ -Pass-Pass-2NT
Pass-?

With the first hand you would like to bid three spades and have partner pass it while on the second hand, you would like to bid three spades forcing. I am going to offer a systemic solution to this which will also answer the other questions as well. But barring a systemic treatment, I suggest you play all new suits as forcing. Your game bidding will be accurate at sacrifice of some part scores.

7. The Wolff Signoff

This convention was invented I believe by Robert Wolff of the US Aces and was adapted by Robert Goldman, also of the US Aces, to the following treatment. This convention can be used equally well when partner has overcalled two notrump as when he has reopened with two notrump.

Here are the mechanics.

2♠-Pass-Pass-2NT
Pass-?

Three clubs is an artificial call forcing partner to bid three diamonds. He has no alternatives. This initiates weak signoff sequences. Three diamonds and three hearts are natural and forcing. Three spades is a game force guaranteeing four hearts and implies a stiff spade.

When the auction proceeds

2♠-Pass-Pass-2NT
Pass-3♣-Pass-3◊
Pass-?

Responder passes with a weak hand and a diamond suit. Responder bids three hearts or four clubs with a weak hand and the suit bid. Responder bids three spades which is still a game force with four hearts, but implies a balanced hand. Responder bids three notrump to show a good hand with clubs.

Here are a few hands to illustrate the convention.

YOU

2♠	Pass	Pass	2NT
Pass	3♠	Pass	3NT
Pass	Pass	Pass	

♠ 3
♡ K J 8 6
◊ A 10 9 3 2
♣ Q J 5

Three spades is game forcing, and shows four hearts plus a stiff spade. Partner with Q 6 2 of spades may elect to change his mind about notrump. Note if he had

♠ K Q 10 8
♡ 9 7 5 3
◊ K J
♣ A K 10 6

. . . he could choose to ignore the four-four heart fit.

YOU

2♠	Pass	Pass	2NT
Pass	3♡	Pass	4♡
Pass	Pass	Pass	

♠ 3 2
♡ A J 9 7 5
◊ K J 8 7
♣ 5 4

Three hearts is game forcing.

YOU

2♠	Pass	Pass	2NT
Pass	3◇	Pass	3♠
Pass	3NT	Pass	Pass
Pass			

♠ 8
♡ K J 7
◇ A 10 9 6 5 4 2
♣ J 3

Three diamonds is game forcing, but because it is a minor suit, you require a better hand than for three hearts. Usually, your hand will be distributional, else you would just bid three notrump.

YOU

2♡	Pass	Pass	2NT
Pass	3♣	Pass	3◇
Pass	3♠	Pass	Pass
Pass			

♠ 10 8 6 5 4 2
♡ 5 2
◇ Q 10 6 4
♣ 7

This is the signoff sequence. Partner will never act over three spades except on rare inspired hands. Hard to imagine.

YOU

2♡	Pass	Pass	2NT
Pass	3♣	Pass	3◇
Pass	3NT	Pass	Pass
Pass			

♠ K 7 6
♡ 8
◇ K 9 7
♣ K J 9 8 7 6

This shows a forward going hand with clubs. Clubs is the only suit you can't bid naturally after partner's two notrump so you have to manufacture this sequence. Because you are looking for a minor suit game, you need shape.

YOU

2♠	Pass	Pass	2NT
Pass	3♣	Pass	3◇
Pass	3♠	Pass	4♡
Pass	Pass	Pass	

♠ J 9
♡ Q 8 6 5
◇ A K 9 3
♣ 10 6 4

This auction shows a balanced hand with four hearts. Partner can choose.

YOU

2♠	Pass	Pass	2NT
Pass	3♠	Pass	4♣
Pass	5♣	Pass	Pass
Pass			

♠ 3
♡ A 7 6 5
◇ Q 9 4 2
♣ K 8 7 5

Unusual. Partner must have a weak spade stopper plus a good five card suit. He might have one of these hands:

	♠ Q 4 2			♠ 10 6 5 2
	♡ K 3	or even		♡ Q J
	◊ K J 10			◊ A K
	♣ A Q J 6 3			♣ A J 10 9 4

You might not care for this two notrump bid on the second of these hands, but there is no easy bid to make. I would not object to the choice.

YOU

2♡	Pass	Pass	2NT
Pass	3♣	Pass	3◊
Pass	3♡	Pass	3♠
Pass	4♠	Pass	Pass
Pass			

♠ Q 8 6 2
♡ K
◊ Q 8 7 3
♣ A 9 8 4

I would not treat this hand as distributional. The stiff king of hearts is probably worth something. It is usually an error to treat a stiff honor as any other singleton on this sequence.

Partner Reopens After a Three Bid

If your options were few when partner reopened after a weak two bid, you will feel positively cramped when he reopens after a three bid.

Except in response to a takeout double, there will be no cue bids, short of the occasional slam try, and there is exactly one invitational sequence. You can introduce a new suit now and then, but generally speaking, you will either bid a game or you will pass.

Remembering the seven point rule, here are some hands.

1. Partner doubles.

No one vul
3♡-Pass-Pass-Dbl
Pass-?

♠ Q 10 6 3
♡ J 9 6 4
◊ 8 2
♣ K 10 5

Three spades. Be happy with what you have, but feel that it is not up to the seven point standard partner is expecting.

Vul vs. not
3◊-Pass-Pass-Dbl
Pass-?

♠ K 7 6
♡ Q J 4 2
◊ 3 2
♣ A 9 6 5

Four diamonds. Just strong enough. Partner with four-four in the majors will bid hearts first.

Not vs. vul
3♡-Pass-Pass-Dbl
Pass-?

♠ 10 8 7 5 4
♡ K 10 5
◊ A 2
♣ 8 6 5

Three spades. If you had the jack of hearts you could pass for penalty. But only at matchpoints. Here you have a good place to play, i.e. spades.

No one vul
3♡-Pass-Pass-Dbl
Pass-?

♠ 8 6 2
♡ K J 5
◊ 8 3 2
♣ K J 8 3

Pass. Not because you hope to beat them but because partner's double does not strongly guarantee clubs. Your chances of beating three hearts are at least as good as making four clubs. Three notrump would be too optimistic.

Both vul
3♠-Pass-Pass-Dbl
Pass-?

♠ J 7 5
♡ K 6 5 4
◊ 2
♣ A 10 6 4 2

Four hearts. This hand is good enough that you can hope to make something. Hence four hearts. Hope partner has four of them. Remember some of those marginal reopening actions where the determining factor was how good your holding was in the unbid major?

Vul vs. not
3♠-Pass-Pass-Dbl
Pass-?

♠ J 7 5
♡ 10 8 6 5
◊ 3
♣ Q J 10 9 5

A case could be made for passing, but with a good club suit, I would take that route. Four clubs. Bid your best suit with bad hands such as this. It is harder for the opponents to double you.

No one vul
3♡-Pass-Pass-Dbl
Pass-?

♠ Q 10 6 3
♡ 4 2
◊ K Q 6 5
♣ A 6 3

A confident four spades. Certainly at IMPs. You won't make this all the time, but you have too much for a simple three spades.

No one vul
3♡-Pass-Pass-Dbl
Pass-?

♠ J 3
♡ Q 10 7
◊ K 8
♣ K 10 6 5 4 2

Three notrump. With worse clubs, you would not try this.

Vul vs. not
3♣-Pass-Pass-Dbl
Pass-?

♠ Q 9 4 2
♡ 8 6 5
◊ Q 9 6 3
♣ J 2

Pass, IMPs or pairs. If you choose four diamonds, your partner will raise you with good hands, getting you too high, and you will get doubled when partner has normal values.

Vul vs. not
3 ♡ -Pass-Pass-Dbl
Pass-?

♠ K 3　　　　　　　　　Five clubs. You have much more than the seven
♡ 8 7 5 2　　　　　　　points partner will play you for. Plus, what you have is
◇ 3　　　　　　　　　　all working overtime.
♣ A Q J 9 6 4

Not vul vs. vul
3 ♡ -Pass-Pass-Dbl
Pass-?

♠ K Q 3　　　　　　　　Four clubs. Even though you have a good hand, you
♡ 8 7　　　　　　　　　have losers all over, plus an atrocious heart holding. I
◇ Q J 3　　　　　　　　started to write down that you could pass at match-
♣ K 10 6 5 4　　　　　points and decided against it. When it doesn't work, it
　　　　　　　　　　　　creates a severe strain on the partnership. Very unnec-
　　　　　　　　　　　　essary.

2. Partner bids a suit at the three level.

No one vul
3 ♡ -Pass-Pass-3 ♠
Pass-?

♠ 3 2　　　　　　　　　Pass. Not much more than your seven.
♡ K 8 7
◇ A 10 6 5 4
♣ Q 9 3

Vul vs. not
3 ◇ -Pass-Pass-3 ♡
Pass-?

♠ Q 10 6 3 2　　　　　Four hearts. Just barely enough. Don't err by bidding
♡ K 9 5　　　　　　　　three spades.
◇ 4 2
♣ A J 9

Both vul
3 ♡ -Pass-Pass-3 ♠
Pass-?

♠ 8　　　　　　　　　　Three notrump. This requires a decent hand. You are
♡ Q J 3　　　　　　　　not bidding because you have a stiff spade. You are bid-
◇ A 10 6 4 3　　　　　ding because you have a good hand.
♣ K Q 10 7

Vul vs. not
3 ♡ -Pass-Pass-3 ♠
Pass-?

♠ 3　　　　　　　　　　Pass. If this gets doubled, you can consider redoub-
♡ K 2　　　　　　　　　ling for rescue.
◇ J 10 8 7 6
♣ A 10 9 5 4

No one vul
3 ◊ -Pass-Pass-3 ♡
Pass-?

♠ K J 9 7 6 2
♡ J 2
◊ A 9 6
♣ 10 2

This is unclear. Three spades or pass would easily work out. I think that three spades should be non-forcing if you choose it, but it could get your side too high. I would choose three spades on this hand but would pass if holding one less diamond and one more club. I anticipate that the third diamond can be ruffed in partner's hand, so it looks a little like a winner.

Vul vs. not
3 ♣ -Pass-Pass-3 ◊
Pass-?

♠ A J 6 2
♡ K J 2
◊ K 10 8 5
♣ 4 2

Four diamonds. It would be nice to try for three notrump, but you can't do it. You could try three spades, but partner might pass it. What's left is a raise or a cue bid. I prefer the raise because the cue bid will create further problems. Will partner think that you are making a slam try? This auction incidently is the one invitational sequence that exists after a preempt.

No one vul
3 ♡ -Pass-Pass-3 ♠
Pass-?

♠ K 2
♡ 8 3
◊ A J 4
♣ Q 10 6 5 4 2

Pass. Four clubs would show a good suit. In this case, you have no objection to spades so there is no reason to introduce a nebulous suit.

No one vul
3 ♡ -Pass-Pass-3 ♠
Pass-?

♠ Q 10
♡ 4 2
◊ A J 8
♣ A J 8 6 5 4

Four spades. Four clubs could be passed.

3. Partner bids three notrump.

The thing to remember here is that partner is expecting you to have seven points, and frequently he is hoping for more. He is under the gun and may have been forced to take a serious chance. Don't hang him for it.

Vul vs. not
3 ♡ -Pass-Pass-3NT
Pass-?

♠ Q J 3
♡ J 2
◊ A Q 8 6
♣ K 9 7 4

Pass. You can credit partner with about 17 points. He may have less. He may have lots more. If he has 22, then you miss a slam. If he has 16, you may be high enough. Take your occasional fix and go quietly on these hands.

No one vul

3♡-Pass-Pass-3NT
Pass-?

♠ Q J 8 6 4
♡ 3
◇ K 6 5
♣ Q 9 4 2

Do not bid four spades! Partner has not promised spades and may even have a singleton. Unlikely perhaps, but a small doubleton would be no surprise.

Vul vs. not

3♡-Pass-Pass-3NT
Pass-?

♠ K 3
♡ 4 2
◇ A 8 6
♣ K 10 9 6 5 4

Don't bother trying for a club slam. It's too hard to bid accurately on this sequence. Whenever you have an unclear road to a questionable slam, pass.

Vul vs. not

3♡-Pass-Pass-3NT
Pass-?

♠ Q 2
♡ 3
◇ J 8 7 6 5 4 2
♣ 10 6 5

Pass. Four diamonds would be forcing. Run when you get doubled.

4. Partner bids four of a lower ranking suit.

Rare. Partner has a good hand and chose not to bid three notrump. He usually has good shape for this or an extra good hand which couldn't double and which lacked a stopper in their suit.

No one vul

3♣-Pass-Pass-4♣
Pass-?

♠ K 8 7
♡ Q J 6 4
◇ K 2
♣ J 9 8 7

Pass. Too bad. You are past your most likely game. This happens. Partner had to guess and he guessed wrong this time. Your values are too slow to raise.

Vul vs. not

3♡-Pass-Pass-4♣
Pass-?

♠ A 6 2
♡ 4 2
◇ K 9 8 6
♣ Q 6 4 2

Five clubs. Those two little hearts are especially bad because partner did not bid three notrump. He is likely to have two fast heart losers also.

No one vul

3◇-Pass-Pass-4♣
Pass-?

♠ K Q 8 7 6 4
♡ J 2
◇ 10 6 5
♣ Q 2

A guess. Four spades or pass. I go with pass.

Both vul

3♡-Pass-Pass-4♣
Pass-?

♠ K 2
♡ K J 2
◇ K 10 8 6
♣ K 9 6 4

If you were to choose four notrump, would it be natural or Blackwood?

Vul vs. not

3◇-Pass-Pass-4♣
Pass-?

♠ 8 6 5 4 2
♡ A 2
◇ A 10 7
♣ K J 3

It is possible that a slam exists. Try four diamonds.

5. Partner jumps to game.

You will usually pass this unless you care to make a slam try. Partner is showing a good hand which expects to make a game opposite your seven. If you have
it or less, then pass. With more and useful values you may act. The definition
here is what's important.

Vul vs. not

3♣-Pass-Pass-4♣

♠ K 3
♡ A J 6 5
◇ K Q 8 6 2
♣ 4 2

Five hearts should be a cue bid here. Another possibility is to bid five spades, asking for club control. But that
runs the risk that partner would go to slam off two aces
if he had something like this

♠ A Q J 10 6 5 4
♡ K Q 9
◇ J
♣ K 10

This hand might not even make five spades.

No one vul

3♣-Pass-Pass-4♡
Pass-?

♠ Q 8 7
♡ K Q 6
◇ J 8 6
♣ K J 8 2

Pass. All garbage except for the good trump holding.

Vul vs. not

3♣-Pass-Pass-4♡
Pass-?

♠ Q 10 8 7 6 5 2
♡ 3
◇ A 5 4
♣ J 2

Pass. No reason to run. Your hearts may be better
than partner's spades.

Bidding Again When You Have Reopened After a Preempt

Some of the time, you will have quite a good hand when you reopen and you will wish to bid again. The question here is how good a hand do you need to take a second bid.

In practice, the only time you need worry about this is when you double and partner makes a simple response. When you reopen in a suit, the auction is usually over by the time it gets back to you.

No one vul

3 ◊ -Pass-Pass-Dbl
Pass-3 ♡ -Pass-?

♠ A J 9 7　　　　　　　Raise to four hearts. You are playing partner to have
♡ K Q J 6　　　　　　seven points and there is no way to find out otherwise.
◊ 3 2　　　　　　　　Raise to game and hope he has them.
♣ A Q 8

Vul vs. not

3 ◊ -Pass-Pass-Dbl
Pass-3 ♡ -Pass-?

♠ A Q 10 8 6　　　　　Three spades. This sequence is one which almost by
♡ K J 7　　　　　　　accident allows partner to tell you whether he has seven
◊ 3 2　　　　　　　　or two.
♣ A K 6

Both vul

3 ◊ -Pass-Pass-Dbl
Pass-4 ♣ -Pass-?

♠ A Q 8 7　　　　　　Five spades. Asking about partner's diamond hold-
♡ A K J 8　　　　　　ing. Partner has a hand of 11 or 12 points with a good
◊ 3 2　　　　　　　　spade suit, but may or may not have two losing
♣ A J 8　　　　　　　diamonds.

No one vul

3 ◊ -Pass-Pass-Dbl
Pass-3 ♣ -Pass-?

♠ K Q J 3　　　　　　Pass. The seven point rule makes this easy as long as
♡ K Q 5 3　　　　　　you trust partner to bid his values. Discount the dia-
◊ Q 2　　　　　　　　mond queen.
♣ K 6 5

Vul vs. not

3 ♣ -Pass-Pass-Dbl
Pass-3 ♠ -Pass-?

♠ K J 8 7　　　　　　Four clubs. This is a slam try with good spade sup-
♡ A K J 10 8　　　　　port. Partner will count on you for something like this.
◊ K Q 9　　　　　　　If he has a good hand within his seven points, he will
♣ A　　　　　　　　cooperate with your slam try. With

♠ Q 10 6 4 2　　　　　He will bid four diamonds.
♡ 9 3
◊ A 6 2
♣ 9 5 4

♠ A Q 9 6 4
♡ 9 6 2
◇ 4 3
♣ 10 9 5

He will jump to five spades, showing a good suit.

♠ 9 6 4 2
♡ Q 4 2
◇ J 8 3
♣ K J 7

He will sign off with four spades. Even this could go down. Better he should have the ten of spades instead of the club king.

CHAPTER SIXTEEN

Quiz

The following quiz is divided into two parts.
1. Problems of the reopener
2. Problems of reopener's partner

To get the most out of these hands, I suggest you get a card and cover the bids attributed to your hand. Do this for each round of the auction to its completion.

Some of the time, there will be a bid and a number in parentheses behind the bid actually chosen.

e.g. 3 ◊ (Pass = 80 DBL = 40)

This means that three diamonds is the best call, but that pass and double are alternatives.

Reopener's Problems

No one vul

♠ K 8 7
♡ A 6 5 4
◊ 4 2
♣ Q 10 9 8

1 ◊	Pass	Pass	Dbl
Pass	2 ◊	Pass	2 ♡
Pass	3 ♡	Pass	Pass
Pass			

No one vul

♠ Q 10 8 7
♡ A J 5 4
◊ K J 9 7
♣ 8

—	—	—	Pass
1 ♣	Pass	Pass	Dbl
Pass	1 ♠	2 ♣	2 ♠
Pass	3 ◊	Pass	4 ♠
Pass	Pass	Pass	

As a passed hand, you can't have more. Partner knows you couldn't open and he still has game interest.

Not vul vs. vul

♠ K Q 10 7
♡ 8 6 5 4
◊ A J 3
♣ 8 2

1 ♠	Pass	Pass	Dbl
Pass	1 ♠	Pass	Pass
2 ♣	Pass	Pass	2 ♠
Pass	Pass	Pass	

With good trumps, you can offer a second push. Partner rated to have nine or ten points but was unable to take further action. He probably has poor spades.

No one vul

♠ A 8 7 5
♡ K Q 10 7
◊ 3
♣ A 9 6 5

1 ◊	Pass	Pass	Dbl
2 ◊	Pass	Pass	Dbl
Pass	2 ♡	Pass	Pass
Pass			

Your second double confirms sound values and is clearly for takeout.

Both Vul

♠ A K 8 7
♡ Q 6 5 4
◊ K 3
♣ J 10 5

1 ◊	Pass	Pass	Dbl
Pass	2 ♠	Pass	Pass
Pass			

Partner's jump shows 11 or 12 points with a poor suit. Aside from your good spade support, your values are soft. Pass.

No one vul

♠ K J 8 6
♡ A Q 9 6
◊ 8 2
♣ K 8 7

1◊	Pass	Pass	Dbl
Pass	2◊	Pass	3◊
Pass	3♡	Pass	4♡
Pass	Pass	Pass	

You could bid two hearts at your second turn instead of three diamonds. The important thing is to appreciate that as reopening doubles go, this is a good one and is worth a cue bid.

Vul vs. not

♠ K 4 2
♡ 4 2
◊ K 10 7
♣ A K Q 8 5

1♡	Pass	Pass	Dbl
Pass	1♠	Pass	2♣
Pass	2♠	Pass	Pass
Pass			

Both vul

♠ 3 2
♡ A 8 6
◊ K Q 4
♣ A K J 7 5

1♠	Pass	Pass	Dbl
Pass	2♡	Pass	3♣
Pass	3◊	Pass	3♡
Pass	Pass	Pass	

Your auction is quite strong. No need to do more than three hearts at your second turn. There is a suggestion that you have a semi-balanced hand as you might have jumped to three clubs at your first opportunity.

Not vul vs. vul

♠ Q J
♡ K J 2
◊ 10 8 7 5 3
♣ K J 9

| 1♠ | Pass | Pass | Pass |

One notrump would show more and two diamonds a better suit. With suspect values and distribution, you should pass at IMPs and likely matchpoints as well. Wasted values such as the Q J of spades should strongly influence you on close hands.

No one vul

♠ Q 10 3
♡ K Q 5 4
◊ J 2
♣ A J 8 3

1◊	Pass	Pass	Dbl
2◊	2♠	Pass	Pass
3◊	3♡	4◊	Pass
Pass	Pass		

Don't hang partner. His strength is limited by the two spade bid. Three hearts was just an effort to get them a bit higher. Pass.

Both vul

♠ K 10 7
♡ A 4
◊ Q 10 9 7
♣ A 10 8 7

1♠	Pass	Pass	1NT
Pass	2NT	Pass	Pass
Pass			

Your range is 12 to 16. This hand is under average. Pass.

Both vul

♠ K 10 3
♡ A 4
◊ Q 10 9 7
♣ A 10 8 7

1♣	Pass	Pass	1NT
Pass	2NT	Pass	3NT
Pass	Pass	Pass	

After one club, the range for one notrump is 12 to 14. This hand is good enough to continue. Compare the previous hand.

No one vul

♠ Q J 3
♡ K 5
◇ A Q 6 5
♣ K 4 2

1♠	Pass	Pass	1NT
Pass	3♡	Pass	3NT
Pass	Pass	Pass	

The only question is whether three hearts is forcing. I suppose it should be, in which case you must bid three notrump.

Both vul

♠ A K 3
♡ Q 10 5
◇ Q 4
♣ K 8 7 6 4

1♡	Pass	Pass	1NT
Pass	2♣	Pass	Pass
Pass			

The only reason this hand is included is to offer the question of whether two clubs should be Stayman. I did not include this discussion earlier because it did not occur to me at that time to do so. In retrospect, I have never wished to have Stayman available which explains the oversight. I suggest you don't worry about it and play everything as natural except a cue bid.

Both vul

♠ 8 3
♡ A Q 10
◇ K Q J 7 3
♣ A 10 5

1♠	Pass	Pass	Dbl
Pass	2♠	Pass	3NT
Pass	Pass	Pass	

You are far too good to bid one notrump or one diamond at your first turn. Two diamonds would have been a thoughtful choice but it would have been a bit of a mis-description. This is an unusual situation where you can double with a weak holding in a major suit. You have to have a good hand for this. Partner is not likely to get carried away with spades, but it could happen.

No one vul

♠ Q 10 8
♡ K Q 5 4
◇ Q 8 3
♣ K 10 7

—	—	—	Pass
1♣	Pass	Pass	Dbl
Pass	2♣	Pass	2NT
Pass	3NT	Pass	Pass
Pass			

Partner has made an invitational bid opposite a passed hand. Two notrump shows a maximum pass. If you were not a passed hand, you would pass two spades.

No one vul

♠ K 4 2
♡ Q 10 7 5 4
◇ A 6 5 3
♣ 9

1♣	Pass	Pass	1♡
Pass	3♡	Pass	4♡
Pass	Pass	Pass	

Everything is working. Not even close to passing. Partner has four trumps and good distribution else he would have started with a cue bid.

Both vul

♠ K J 10 7
♡ 3 2
◇ A 5
♣ 8 7 5 4 2

1♡	Pass	Pass	1♠
Pass	2♡	Pass	2♠
Pass	Pass	Pass	

Three clubs would show a better hand. Two spades does not promise a five card suit. It does deny extra strength.

No one vul

♠ Q J 8 7
♡ K 8 3
◇ A Q 6 3
♣ 10 7

1♡	Pass	Pass	1♠
Pass	2♡	Pass	2NT
Pass	3NT	Pass	Pass
Pass			

With good values, you can show them with two notrump.

No one vul

♠ Q 10 8 7 5
♡ J 2
◇ A 10 9 5 4
♣ 7

1♣	Pass	Pass	1♠
2♣	Pass	Pass	2◇
Pass	Pass	3♣	Pass
Pass	Dbl	Pass	Pass
Pass			

You have all of your bids. When you bid two diamonds, you were merely 'rebidding' your partner's values.

Both vul

♠ 10 8 7 5 3
♡ A 5 4
◇ A Q J
♣ 9 2

—	—	—	Pass
1♣	Pass	Pass	Dbl
Pass	1♡	Pass	1♠
Pass	2NT	Pass	3NT
Pass	Pass	Pass	

Having passed, you have a maximum and can accept the invitation.

No one vul

♠ Q J 10 7 5
♡ K Q 5
◇ A 8
♣ Q 6 2

1♣	Pass	Pass	1♠
Pass	1NT	Pass	2NT
Pass	3NT	Pass	Pass
Pass			

No one vul

♠ A Q 2
♡ 8 7 5 4 2
◇ K 7
♣ 8 6 4

1♣	Pass	Pass	1♡
1♠	2♡	2♠	Pass
Pass	Pass		

Both vul

♠ A Q 10 8
♡ A 6 4 3
◇ Q 9 8
♣ 3 2

1♡	Pass	Pass	1♠
Pass	2♡	Pass	2NT
Pass	3♣	Pass	4♣
Pass	Pass	Pass	

Note that when partner cue bids, it becomes a game force if you have the strength required to bid two notrump.

No one vul

♠ 8 2
♡ J 10 8 7 5
◇ K J 9 6
♣ K 3

| 1◇ | Pass | Pass | Pass |

(1 ♡ = 7 0)
Where are the spades? This plus the fact that one diamond could be your best spot suggests pass.

Both vul

♠ A 8 7 5 4 2
♡ A 10 7
◇ 3
♣ K J 5

1◇	Pass	Pass	1♠
2◇	Pass	Pass	Dbl
Pass	2♡	Pass	Pass
Pass			

Vul vs. not

♠ Q 8 2
♡ 3
◇ K Q 9 7 5 3
♣ Q 8 5

| 1♠ | Pass | Pass | Pass |

(2 ◇ = 4 0)
No defense against hearts and soft defense against spades.

Both vul

♠ A J 8 7
♡ 5 3
◇ 9 3
♣ A K 10 8 7

1♡	Pass	Pass	2♣
2♡	Pass	Pass	2♠
Pass	3♣	Pass	Pass
Pass			

Both vul

♠ A J 8 7   1♡ Pass Pass 2♣
♡ 9 6 5   2◊ Pass Pass Dbl
◊ 3   Pass 2♠ Pass Pass
♣ A K 10 8 7   Pass

No one vul

♠ Q J 8 7 5 4   1♣ Pass Pass 2♠
♡ A Q 8   Pass 3♠ Pass Pass
◊ A 7   Pass
♣ Q 2

Not vul vs. vul

♠ 8 2   1♡ Pass Pass Pass
♡ 7 3
◊ K Q J 10 8 7 4
♣ 9 7

No one vul

♠ — —   1♠ Pass Pass 3◊
♡ J 8 7   Pass 3NT Pass Pass
◊ A K Q 10 7 5 3   Pass
♣ Q J 4

Both vul

♠ K Q J 8 7 6   1♡ Pass Pass 2♡
♡ 3   Pass 3♣ Pass 3♠
◊ A K J 9 6   Pass 3NT Pass 4◊
♣ A   Pass 4♠ Pass Pass
   Pass

Both vul

♠ K J 7   1♠ Pass Pass 2NT
♡ A K J 9 6   Pass 3NT Pass Pass
◊ K 2   Pass
♣ A J 5

No one vul

♠ 8 7   1♠ Pass Pass Dbl
♡ A J 3   Pass 2♡ Pass 2♠
◊ K Q 9   Pass 3◊ Pass 3♡
♣ A K Q 10 7   Pass Pass Pass

No one vul

♠ A J 7   1♣ Pass Pass Dbl   One notrump after one club
♡ K J 8 5   Pass 1◊ Pass 1NT   shows 12 to 14. This sequence
◊ A 5   Pass Pass Pass   shows around 15 to 18.
♣ K 10 9 7

Both vul

♠ A Q 3   1◊ Pass Pass 2♣
♡ J 2   Pass 3♣ Pass 3♠   (3 ◊ = 8 0)
◊ 8 6 5   Pass 4♣ Pass Pass
♣ A K J 7 4   Pass

Both vul

♠ Q J 10 7 6 4
♡ 4 2
◇ 8 3
♣ A 9 7

1NT Pass Pass 2♣
Pass Pass Pass

Both vul

♠ 4
♡ A K Q
◇ 8 7 6
♣ K 10 8 7 5 4

1NT Pass Pass 2♣
Pass 2♦ Pass Pass
Pass

If two clubs is natural, you can bid it. If it is conventional, you must pass.

Vul vs. not

♠ Q J
♡ K Q 10
◇ K 8 7 6 4
♣ Q J 4

1NT Pass Pass Pass

No one vul

♠ 8 7 6 4 3
♡ A 8 6 5 3
◇ K 8
♣ 2

1NT Pass Pass 2♣
Pass 3♡ Pass Pass
Pass

If two clubs is natural you have to make a very good guess. What is your system?

No one vul

♠ 7 3
♡ K J 7 5
◇ A 10 7 5
♣ 8 7 5

— — 1♣ Pass
2♣ Pass Pass 2♡
3♣ 3♡ Pass Pass
Pass

Both vul

♠ J 10 8 6
♡ A 10 6 4
◇ 3
♣ Q 9 6 3

— — 1◇ Pass
2◇ Pass Pass Dbl
Pass 2♡ 3◇ Pass
Pass Pass

No one vul

♠ 10 9 7
♡ A Q 8
◇ 6 5 3 2
♣ A 10 3

— — 1◇ Pass
2◇ Pass Pass Dbl
Pass 2♠ Pass Pass
Pass

Both vul

♠ J 10 8 7 5
♡ 3
◇ Q J 10 6 4
♣ A 3

— — 1♣ Pass
2♣ Pass Pass 2♠
3♣ Pass Pass 3◇
Pass Pass Pass

Not vul vs. vul

♠ J 10 9 5
♡ 3 2
◇ A 4
♣ K J 9 7 6

— — 1◇ Pass
2◇ Pass Pass 2♠
Pass Pass Pass

Spades are a 'safer' suit than clubs.

Both vul

♠ 8 6 5
♡ 3
♢ A J 9 7
♣ A 10 7 5 4

	—	—	1♠	Pass
2♣	Pass	Pass	2NT
3♡	Dbl	3♠	Pass
Pass	Pass

At matchpoints, you could double three spades. Partner ought not to double three hearts with no defense against spades.

No one vul

♠ Q 8
♡ K J 6
♢ Q 5
♣ K Q 9 7 6 4

| | — | — | 1♢ | Pass |
| 2♢ | Pass | Pass | Pass |

Bad shape. Poor cards. Wasted diamond queen, plus clubs is a dangerous suit.

No one vul

♠ Q 10 3
♡ 9 7 4
♢ A 8 7 5
♣ K Q 3

	—	—	1♡	Pass
2♡	Pass	Pass	Dbl
Pass	3♣	Pass	Pass
Pass

No one vul

♠ 8 3
♡ 8 6 5
♢ A Q 6 5
♣ K Q 5 4

	—	—	1♠	Pass
2♠	Pass	Pass	2NT
Pass	3♢	Pass.	Pass
Pass

Double would get partner to bid hearts on many hands where a minor suit would be better. If you had some high cards in hearts, then double would be ok. As with many reopening actions, you are really just hoping to get them one trick higher.

Both vul

♠ 8 3
♡ A 6 5
♢ Q J 8 7 5
♣ K J 4

| | — | — | 1♠ | Pass |
| 2♠ | Pass | Pass | Pass |

(Dbl = 50)
(3♢ = 50)
All suits are dangerous. Pass at IMPs for sure.

No one vul

♠ Q 4
♡ 4 2
♢ A 4 3
♣ K J 9 7 6 3

	—	—	1♠	Pass
2♠	Pass	Pass	3♣
3♠	Pass	Pass	Pass

(Pass = 100)
Pass at IMPs.

No one vul

♠ 7 6 3
♡ 2
♢ A 4 3
♣ K J 9 7 6 3

	—	—	1♠	Pass
2♠	Pass	Pass	3♣
Pass	Pass	Pass

This hand is worth a lot more than the previous hand.

No one vul

♠ 3 2
♡ A 10 8 6
♢ K Q 9 6
♣ 10 6 4

1♣	Pass	1♠	Pass
2♠	Pass	Pass	Dbl
Pass	3♢	3♠	Pass
Pass	Pass

No one vul

♠ J 8 7 6 5 4
♥ A 6
◊ K 10 8 2
♣ 7

1♣	Pass	1♥	Pass
2♥	Pass	Pass	2♠
Pass	Pass	3♣	3◊
Pass	3♠	Pass	Pass
Pass			

Both vul

♠ — —
♥ J 9 8 6 4
◊ K Q 10 6 4
♣ 8 6 3

1♣	Pass	1♠	Pass
2♠	Pass	Pass	2NT
Pass	3◊	3♠	Pass
Pass	Dbl	Pass	Pass
Pass			

Two notrump and double both force partner to bid at the three level. Two notrump was chosen because you didn't want partner to pass if you doubled instead. Don't yank partners' penalty double. He knows you have a weak hand else you would have reopened with double.

No one vul

♠ Q J 8 5
♥ 10 6 5
◊ K 7
♣ A 6 4 2

1♣	Pass	1♥	Pass
2♥	Pass	Pass	2♠
Pass	Pass	Pass	

No one vul

♠ K J 8 7 3
♥ 8 6 5
◊ A 6 4
♣ 9 2

1♣	Pass	1♥	Pass
2♥	Pass	Pass	2♠
3♣	3♥	Pass	4♠
Pass	Pass	Pass	

Unusual, but partner's three heart bid is a clear game try. You don't have to worry about what he may or may not have. You have a good reopening hand with a fifth trump and an ace, as opposed to a four card suit with some questionable kings and queens.

No one vul

♠ Q J 3
♥ 10 7 5
◊ A Q 9 6 4
♣ 8 5

1♣	Pass	1♥	Pass
2♥	Pass	Pass	Dbl
Pass	2♠	Pass	Pass
Pass			

Not vul vs. vul

♠ K J 8 2
♥ A 7 5 3
◊ 9 3
♣ J 8 3

—	—	1♣	Pass
1♥	Pass	1NT	Pass
2♣	Pass	Pass	2♠
3♣	3♠	Pass	Pass
Pass			

Note that three spades is strictly competitive. If partner wanted to make a game try, he would bid three hearts.

Both vul

♠ A 6 3
♥ Q 10 6 4 3
◊ 10 8 6
♣ J 2

—	—	1♣	Pass
1◊	Pass	1NT	Pass
2♣	Pass	Pass	2♥
Pass	3♥	Pass	Pass
Pass			

When partner's bid is not competitive, it reverts to invitational. Pass, but with another working queen or perhaps the major suit jacks, you should go on.

No one vul

♠ 8 3	—	—	1♡	Pass
♡ J 9 7	1♠	Pass	1NT	Pass
◊ A Q 6 2	2♡	Pass	Pass	Dbl
♣ K Q 10 8	Pass	3♣	Pass	Pass
	Pass			

Partner should play you for a decent hand as with a poor one, you would have bid two notrump instead. Remember, if two notrump forces partner to a higher level in one of your suits than double, then you can't make this strength distinction.

No one vul

♠ K 7 6	—	—	1♡	Pass
♡ 3 2	1NT	Pass	Pass	Pass
◊ K 4 3				
♣ K Q 9 6 3				

Both vul

♠ Q 9 7 5 3	1♠	Pass	1◊	Pass
♡ A 2	1NT	Pass	Pass	2♠
◊ 10 7 4	Pass	Pass	Pass	
♣ K 10 9				

No one vul

♠ Q 9 8 6 5	—	—	1♡	Pass
♡ K 8	1NT	Pass	Pass	2♠
◊ K 2	3♣	3♡	Pass	3♠
♣ 7 5 4 2	Pass	Pass	Pass	

This is an actual hand. Partner held

♠ K J 7
♡ A 10 7 6 4 2
◊ A 6 5 2
♣ — —

Note the amount of room that responder allowed his partner.

Both vul

♠ 8 7 5	1♡	Pass	1♠	Pass
♡ Q 10 6	1NT	Pass	Pass	Pass
◊ K J 9 7 5 4				
♣ A				

So much wrong with this hand. Dangerous suit and immensely dangerous major suit holdings.

Both vul

♠ K Q 7	—	—	1♡	Pass
♡ K Q 10 7	1NT	Pass	Pass	Dbl
◊ 10 5	Pass	Pass	Pass	
♣ K Q 10 5				

This is the 'penalty or takeout' double. Partner looks at his hand and determines which it is. His length in hearts will tell him.

No one vul

♠ 5	—	—	1♠	Pass
♡ Q J 10 4	1NT	Pass	Pass	Dbl
◊ Q J 7 3	Pass	Pass	Pass	
♣ K 8 6 4				

The reciprocal of the 'two way double.'

No one vul

♠ K 7 5	—	—	1♡	Pass
♡ Q 2	1♠	Pass	2◊	Pass
◊ 9 7	2♡	Pass	Pass	Pass
♣ K Q 8 7 6 4				

Both vul

♠ A Q 3
♡ K 6 4
♢ J 8 7 6 3
♣ K 5

1♢	Pass	1♡	Pass
1♠	Pass	Pass	1NT
Pass	2NT	Pass	Pass
Pass			

Both vul

♠ J 7 6 5 4
♡ A 3
♢ 8 7 5
♣ A Q 2

1♢	Pass	1NT	Pass
2♢	Pass	Pass	2♣
3♢	Pass	Pass	Pass

No one vul

♠ 8 6 3
♡ A Q 10 7 5
♢ 5
♣ A J 6 3

1♢	Pass	1♡	Pass
2♢	Pass	Pass	2♡
Pass	Pass	Pass	

Both vul

♠ K 3
♡ A Q 10 5 4 2
♢ 3
♣ K 10 6 5

1♢	Pass	1♡	Pass
1NT	Pass	Pass	Pass

No one vul

♠ K 8 6 5 3 2
♡ K J 4
♢ 5
♣ A 5 4

1♢	Pass	1♠	Pass
2♢	Pass	Pass	Pass

No spade spots.

No one vul

♠ Q 10 8 7 5
♡ 3 2
♢ K 10 9 7 5
♣ 7

1♣	Pass	1♡	Pass
2♣	Pass	Pass	Dbl
Pass	2♢	Pass	Pass
3♣	Dbl	Pass	3♢
Pass	Pass	Pass	

With far better offense than you might have had and far less defense, you should yank this, although unenthusiastically. You did not have two notrump available as a reopening bid because it would arbitrarily have forced your side to the three level which your takeout double did not do. Partner wasn't able to draw any inferences about your hand. Pass could be right.

No one vul

♠ A Q 7 5 2
♡ 10 8 6 3
♢ Q 7 4
♣ 8

—	—	1♢	Pass
1♡	Pass	2♣	Pass
2♡	Pass	Pass	Pass

You won't reopen often after this auction. You have no guarantee of a fit and both opponents can have something in reserve.

No one vul

♠ 3
♡ K 2
♢ A 10 9 7 6 5
♣ Q 5 4 2

—	—	1♡	Pass
1♠	Pass	2♣	Pass
2♠	Pass	Pass	Pass

Two diamonds on the first or second round might have been reasonable, but three now would be too much.

Both vul

♠ A 6 4 2	—	—	1 ◇	Pass
♡ 8	1 ♡	Pass	2 ♣	Pass
◇ A Q 10 5 3	2 ♡	Pass	Pass	Dbl
♣ A Q 5	Pass	Pass	Pass	

A rare action. Shows support for the one unbid suit plus a very good hand with shortness in the doubled suit. Partner frequently passes for penalty on this sequence.

Vul vs. not

♠ K 5 4	Pass	Pass	1 ◇	Pass
♡ K 9 6	1 ♡	Pass	Pass	1NT
◇ A Q 10 6 4	2 ♡	Pass	Pass	Pass
♣ Q 3				

No one vul

♠ 10 8 6 5	1 ♣	Pass	Pass	Dbl
♡ A K 7	Pass	1 ♠	Pass	2 ♣
◇ A 10 9 6 4	Pass	Pass	Pass	
♣ 3				

Both vul

♠ Q J 8 7	1 ♣	Pass	Pass	Dbl
♡ A J 4	Pass	1 ♠	2 ♣	2 ♠
◇ A 10 6 5	Pass	Pass	Pass	
♣ 8 2				

No one vul

♠ A K 9 8 6 5	1 ♡	Pass	Pass	1 ♠
♡ 3	2 ♡	Pass	Pass	2 ♠
◇ J 10 7	Pass	Pass	Pass	
♣ 8 6 4				

No one vul

♠ Q J 3 2	1 ♡	Pass	Pass	2 ♣
♡ 3	2 ◇	Pass	Pass	2 ♠
◇ 8 7	Pass	2NT	Pass	3 ♣
♣ A Q J 6 5 4	Pass	Pass	Pass	

No one vul

♠ A 6 2	1 ♣	Pass	Pass	Dbl
♡ K J 8 7	2 ♣	2 ♡	3 ♣	3 ♡
◇ K 6 5 4 2	Pass	Pass	Pass	
♣ 7				

Both vul

♠ Q J 8 7	1 ♡	Pass	Pass	Dbl
♡ Q 2	2 ♡	2 ♠	Pass	Pass
◇ K Q 7 6	3 ♣	Pass	3 ♡	Pass
♣ A 9 6	Pass	Pass		

Both vul

♠ A 8 6 4	1 ♡	Pass	Pass	Dbl
♡ A 2	2 ♡	3 ♣	Pass	Pass
◇ J 10 7 6	Pass			
♣ K Q 3				

No one vul

♠ A Q 6
♡ 8 6
◇ K Q 10 9
♣ A K J 5

1♡	Pass	Pass	Dbl
Pass	1♠	Pass	2♡
Pass	3♠	Pass	4♠
Pass	Pass	Pass	

Partner did not jump the first time. He probably has five spades plus six or more points.

No one vul

♠ K Q 5
♡ A Q 6 4
◇ 10 5
♣ A 10 9 5

1◇	Pass	Pass	Dbl
Pass	1NT	Pass	2NT
Pass	Pass	Pass	

Both vul

♠ K J 8 7
♡ A K 6 4
◇ 3
♣ A 9 6 3

1◇	Pass	Pass	Dbl
2♣	Pass	2◇	Dbl
Pass	2♠	Pass	Pass
3◇	Pass	Pass	Pass

No one vul

♠ Q 10 6 5
♡ K Q J 3
◇ A K 10 7
♣ 3

1♣	Pass	Pass	Dbl
3♣	Pass	Pass	Dbl
Pass	4♣	Pass	4♡
Pass	Pass	Pass	

Both vul

♠ A K Q
♡ A 2
◇ Q 8 7 6
♣ K J 5 4

1♡	Pass	Pass	Dbl
2♡	Pass	Pass	Pass

(Dbl = 70)

Both vul

♠ K J 4
♡ A Q J 6 2
◇ A 8 7
♣ 3 2

1♠	Pass	Pass	1♡
Pass	2♡	Pass	4♡
Pass	Pass	Pass	

Both vul

♠ K J 4
♡ A Q J 6 2
◇ A 8 7
♣ 3 2

1♣	Pass	Pass	1♡
2♣	2♡	Pass	3♡
Pass	Pass	Pass	

No one vul

♠ 8 3
♡ A 3
◇ A 5
♣ K 10 8 7 6 5 4

1♠	Pass	Pass	2♣
2♠	3♣	Pass	3♠
Pass	3NT	Pass	Pass
Pass			

Hope partner has the ace of clubs!

No one vul

♠ A 2
♡ Q 10 9 6 5 4
◇ 3 2
♣ A Q 2

1◇	Pass	Pass	1♡
Pass	2NT	Pass	3♡
Pass	4♡	Pass	Pass
Pass			

Three hearts with the understanding that it is forcing. If it is not forcing jump to four hearts.

Both vul

♠ Q J 8 7 6	1♣	Pass	Pass 1♠
♡ Q 3 2	Pass	2♣	Pass 2◊
◊ A K 8	Pass	2♠	Pass 3♠
♣ 8 7	Pass	4♠	

No one vul

♠ J 7	1♣ Pass Pass 1◊	Possibly going down one. Part-ner should have a squarish 12 or 13 with no club stopper which is not quite worth a takeout double. Partner does not have a heart suit. Perhaps he has
♡ A 2	Pass 2♣ Pass 3◊	
◊ A Q 10 9 8 7	Pass 3♡ Pass 4◊	
♣ 8 6 5	Pass Pass .Pass	

♠ A 10 7
♡ K Q 5 2
◊ K 10 7
♣ J 5 4

If clubs are four-three, you will have missed three notrump.

Not vs. vul

♠ A K 8 5 4 2	1♣	Pass Pass 1♠
♡ 10 6 3	2♣	Dbl Pass Pass
◊ 8 2	Pass	
♣ 7 2		

No one vul

♠ J 10 8 7 5	1◊	Pass Pass 1♠
♡ A Q 5 4 2	2♣	Dbl Pass 2♡
◊ 4	Pass	2♠ Pass Pass
♣ 9 7	Pass	

Both vul

♠ J 10 7 3	1♡	Pass Pass 2◊
♡ — —	2♡	Dbl Pass 2♠
◊ A Q 9 8 6 4	Pass	2NT Pass 3♣ (Pass or 3◊ =100)
♣ Q 8 2	Pass	3◊ Pass Pass
	Pass	

No one vul

♠ 3	1♠	Pass Pass 2♡
♡ A K 8 7 5	2♠	Pass Pass Dbl
◊ K 5 4	Pass	3♣ Pass Pass
♣ Q 7 6 2	Pass	

No one vul

♠ K 5	1♣	Pass Pass 1♡
♡ A J 8 7 5	1♠	Pass Pass 1NT
◊ 10 5 4	Pass	Pass Pass
♣ A J 8		

Both vul

♠ 3	1♠	Pass Pass 2♡
♡ K J 8 7 5	Pass	Pass 2♠ Dbl
◊ A J 9 4	Pass	3♣ Pass Pass
♣ K 10 8	Pass	

No one vul

♠ K 10 7 2
♥ 3
◇ K Q 10 9 7
♣ A 5 4

```
1♣   Pass Pass 1◇
Pass Pass 1♥   1♠
2♥   Pass Pass Dbl
Pass 2♠   Pass Pass
Pass
```

Problems of Partner of the Reopener

Both vul

♠ J 7 6 4 2
♥ A Q 3
◇ K 8 6
♣ Q 5

```
—    —    1◇   Pass
Pass Dbl  Pass 2♣
Pass 3♣   Pass 4♣
Pass Pass Pass
```

No one vul

♠ J 8 7 5
♥ Q 3
◇ K Q 6 4
♣ K 10 5

```
—    —    1♣   Pass
Pass Dbl  Pass 1NT
Pass Pass Pass
```

Both vul

♠ Q J 3 2
♥ A J 6 5
◇ K Q 4
♣ 8 2

```
—    —    1◇   Pass
Pass Dbl  Pass 2◇
Pass 2♥   Pass 3♥
Pass Pass Pass
```

If partner has a good 12 plus, he should go on to game.

Both vul

♠ A Q 2
♥ 8 6 5 4
◇ K Q J
♣ K 8 7

```
—    —    1♥   Pass
Pass Dbl  Pass 2♥
Pass 2♠   Pass 3♠
Pass 4♠   Pass Pass
Pass
```

Very difficult. Three hearts instead of three spades, looking for three notrump, might have been better. As it is, four spades could be your best spot. You have extra values which should help you through. I repeat. A tough hand.

No one vul

♠ J 10 8 7
♥ Q 5 4
◇ Q 5 4
♣ J 6 2

```
—    —    1♠   Pass
Pass Dbl  Pass 1NT
Pass 3NT  Pass Pass
Pass
```

Partner expects more. You should try to avoid one notrump with less than seven or eight points. Here you had no alternative.

Both vul

♠ Q J 7 6 5
♥ K 2
◇ Q 10 9 6
♣ A 3

```
—    Pass 1♠   Pass
Pass Dbl  Pass Pass
Pass
```

Even with this hand you shouldn't expect too much. Partner can have a very shapely minimum.

Vul vs. not

♠ K J 6 2
♥ Q 9 6 4 2
♦ K 7 6
♣ 8

		1♥	Pass
Pass	Dbl	Pass	2♠
Pass	Pass	Pass	

With clear offensive potential, it is better to try for game than to pass for penalties. You want better hearts to compensate for the possible game in spades.

No one vul

♠ K Q J 7
♥ 8 7 5
♦ 4
♣ J 6 5 4 2

		1♦	Pass
Pass	Dbl	1♥	1♠
2♦	Pass	Pass	2♠
Pass	Pass		

No one vul

♠ 10 8 2
♥ Q 10 7 6
♦ 3
♣ A 9 8 7 5

		1♠	Pass
Pass	Dbl	Pass	2♥
2♠	Pass	Pass	3♣
Pass			

Partner should not return to hearts without four of them. With a five card suit, you would tend to rebid them in preference to mentioning clubs.

Not vul vs. vul

♠ Q 10 6 4 2
♥ 8 7 3
♦ 2
♣ A J 7 6

		1♣	Pass
Pass	Dbl	2♣	2♠
Pass	3♣	Pass	4♠
Pass	Pass	Pass	

No one vul

♠ K 3
♥ K 9 7 6
♦ 10 6 4 2
♣ 8 6 3

		1♦	Pass
Pass	Dbl	2♣	2♥
3♣	Pass	Pass	Pass

No one vul

♠ K J 7 4 3
♥ Q J 5
♦ 3 2
♣ 9 6 5

		1♦	Pass
Pass	Dbl	3♦	3♠
Pass	Pass	Pass	

Just enough to bid.

Both vul

♠ 10 8 7 5
♥ K 5 4 2
♦ K Q
♣ K 7 6 5

		1♥	Pass
Pass	Dbl	2♥	2♠
Pass	Pass	Pass	

Vul vs. not

♠ K 3 2
♥ Q 9 8 6 4
♦ K Q
♣ J 8 7

		1♦	Pass
Pass	Dbl	2♣	2♥
3♣	Pass	Pass	Pass

Having shown some values, it is not necessary to rebid them. To bid again would require better shape with less wasted in their suits.

Both vul

♠ Q J 3
♥ K Q 8 7
♦ Q 6 2
♣ K 9 5

Pass	Pass	1♦	Pass
Pass	Dbl	Pass	1♥
Pass	Pass	Pass	

Opposite a passed hand, there is no need to get excited.

Vul vs. not

♠ J 2
♡ Q J 8 7 5
◊ K 4 2
♣ A 10 6

		1◊	Pass
Pass	Dbl	1NT	2♡
Pass	Pass	Pass	

Best to play it rather than try to defend against one notrump doubled.

No one vul

♠ K Q 7
♡ 4 2
◊ A 9 6 5
♣ 10 7 4 2

		1◊	Pass
Pass	1♠	Pass	2♠
Pass	3♠	Pass	4♠
Pass	Pass	Pass	

Vul vs. not

♠ Q J 3
♡ 8 7 5
◊ K 9 6 5
♣ J 10 5

		1♡	Pass
Pass	1♠	Pass	Pass
2♡	Pass	Pass	2♠
Pass	Pass	3♡	Pass
Pass	Pass		

Vul vs. not

♠ Q J 3
♡ 8 7 5
◊ K 9 6 5
♣ J 10 5

		1♡	Pass
Pass	1♠	2♡	2♠
3♡	3♠	Pass	Pass
Pass			

A free raise actually shows less than if opener passed and you raised. See previous hand.

No one vul

♠ 10 8 7 5
♡ 4 2
◊ A J 3
♣ K J 8 7

		1♠	Pass
Pass	2♠	Pass	3♠
Pass	Pass	Pass	

Don't err by passing hands like these. Among other things, you may still have a game, or perhaps LHO was about to bid two hearts.

No one vul

♠ Q J 8 7
♡ Q 8 6
◊ K Q 5
♣ Q J 3

		1♡	Pass
Pass	2◊	2♡	2NT
Pass	Pass	Pass	

In spite of thirteen points, even two notrump could go down due to a lack of fast tricks. Perhaps it would have been better to bid three diamonds.

No one vul

♠ 8
♡ K J 8 7
◊ Q J 5 4
♣ A 8 6 2

		1◊	Pass
Pass	1♡	Pass	3♡
Pass	4♡	Pass	Pass
Pass			

Both vul

♠ Q J 3
♡ K Q 7 3
◊ J 8 7
♣ K 5 4

		1◊	Pass
Pass	1♡	Pass	2◊
Pass	2♡	Pass	Pass

No one vul

♠ A K 8
♥ 7
♦ J 8 7 6 5
♣ Q J 4 2

—	—	1♥	Pass
Pass	1♠	Pass	2♥
Pass	3♣	Pass	3♦
Pass	4♦	Pass	Pass
Pass			

Both vul

♠ 8 2
♥ K J 7
♦ K J 8 6
♣ K J 4 2

—	—	1♣	Pass
Pass	1♥	Pass	2♣
Pass	2♦	Pass	2♥
Pass	3♥	Pass	4♥
Pass	Pass	Pass	

No one vul

♠ A J
♥ 8 7 5
♦ 8 7 5
♣ A K J 5 4

—	Pass	1♥	Pass
Pass	1♠	Pass	2♥
Pass	2♠	Pass	Pass
Pass			

Tough. Two clubs would be too much of an underbid.

No one vul

♠ 8 3
♥ 7 6 5
♦ K 6 5
♣ A K 6 4 2

—	—	1♥	Pass
Pass	1♠	Pass	Pass
Pass			

Not vs. vul

♠ 3
♥ J 6 5
♦ A 4 2
♣ K J 10 7 6 4

—	Pass	1♥	Pass
Pass	1♠	Pass	2♣
Pass	2♦	Pass	Pass

No one vul

♠ K Q 2
♥ Q 6 4
♦ Q J 3 2
♣ Q 8 7

—	—	1♥	Pass
Pass	1♠	2♥	2♠
Pass	Pass	3♥	Pass
Pass	Pass		

No one vul

♠ K Q 10
♥ 8 6 5
♦ A J 8 6 5
♣ Q 2

—	Pass	1♥	Pass
Pass	2♣	2♥	3♣
Pass	Pass	Pass	

(2♣ = 100)

Two spades, if treated as on page 93 would be a useful approach.

Both vul

♠ Q 3 2
♥ 5 4 2
♦ A K 6 3
♣ K 10 5

—	—	1♥	Pass
Pass	1♠	2♣	2♥
Pass	2♠	Pass	Pass
Pass			

No one vul

♠ K Q 4 3
♥ 10 6 5
♦ A J 4
♣ K 8 7

—	—	1♥	Pass
Pass	1♠	2♣	2♥
Pass	2♠	Pass	3♠
Pass	Pass	Pass	

Barely enough to raise after a signoff from partner.

Both vul

♠ 10 6 5 4 2
♡ A 6 5
◊ 8
♣ K J 7 5

Pass	Pass	1♣	Pass
Pass	2◊	2♠	Pass
Pass	Pass		

Both vul

♠ K 8 7 6
♡ K 5 4
◊ K 8 7 5
♣ Q 2

Pass	Pass	1♡	Pass
Pass	2♣	2♡	Pass
Pass	Pass		

No one vul

♠ Q 10 7 5
♡ K 4
◊ K 9 7 6 5
♣ Q 2

1♠	Pass	2♠	Pass
Pass	Dbl	Pass	3◊
3♠	Pass	Pass	Pass

Don't double.

Both vul

♠ J 9 8 7
♡ Q J 10 7
◊ A Q 3
♣ 8 2

1♡	Pass	2♡	Pass
Pass	Dbl	Pass	2♠
Pass	Pass	3♡	Dbl
Pass	Pass	Pass	

Even this may not be success-ful. At IMPs, pass could be right.

No one vul

♠ K J 5 4
♡ 10 8 7
◊ Q J 3
♣ K Q 4

1◊	Pass	2◊	Pass
Pass	2♡	3◊	Pass
Pass	Pass		

Both vul

♠ J 8
♡ A Q 10 8 7
◊ Q 4 2
♣ 9 7 6

—	—	1♣	Pass
1♡	Pass	2♣	Pass
Pass	2♠	Pass	Pass
Pass			

No one vul

♠ Q 7 6 4
♡ Q 9 6 3
◊ K 4 2
♣ 7 3

1♣	Pass	1♠	Pass
2♣	Pass	2♠	Pass
Pass	Dbl	Pass	3♡
Pass	Pass	Pass	

This is not a good hand. Bid three hearts without looking concerned. Partner has a semi-bal-anced hand with some defense since he choose double rather than two notrump. Even so, you should not convert this to pen-alty. Your spade spots are too poor.

No one vul

♠ 3 2
♡ Q 8 6 4 2
◊ J 8 7
♣ Q 10 5

1♠	Pass	1NT	Pass
Pass	Dbl	Pass	Pass
Pass			

Partner's double is either take-out or penalty. Your spade length says partner has spades so this time the double is for business.

No one vul

♠ 8 6 2
♡ Q 6 3
◇ K Q J 9 8 5
♣ 4

1◇	Pass	2◇	Pass
Pass	3♣	Pass	3◇
Pass	Pass	Pass	

Not vul vs. vul

♠ 10 8 7 6 5 4
♡ 3 2
◇ A J
♣ K 4 2

1♡	Pass	2♡	Pass
Pass	Dbl	Pass	2♠
Pass	Pass	3♡	3♠
Pass	Pass	Pass	

Seldom do you take a second bid on this sequence.

Vul vs. vul

♠ A 8 6 5 2
♡ K 6 5
◇ J 2
♣ Q 9 8

1◇	Pass	1♡	Pass
1NT	Pass	2◇	Pass
Pass	Dbl	Pass	2♠
Pass	Pass	3◇	Pass
Pass	Pass		

No one vul

♠ A 6 2
♡ 3
◇ J 10 7 4 2
♣ K 7 6 3

1♡	Pass	1♠	Pass
2◇	Pass	2♡	Pass
Pass	Dbl	Pass	Pass
Pass			

There is no way this can be for takeout.

Both vul

♠ Q 9 6 3
♡ Q J 4
◇ Q 9 8 7
♣ 8 3

1♣	Pass	1NT	Pass
Pass	Dbl	Pass	2♣
Pass	Pass	Pass	

This depends on whether you play the two way double after a minor suit and a one notrump response. See page 147

50 HIGHLY-RECOMMENDED TITLES

CALL TOLL FREE 1-800-274-2221
IN THE U.S. & CANADA TO ORDER ANY OF
THEM OR TO REQUEST OUR
FULL-COLOR 64 PAGE CATALOG OF
ALL BRIDGE BOOKS IN PRINT,
SUPPLIES AND GIFTS.

FOR BEGINNERS
#0300 Future Champions' Bridge Series 9.95
#2130 Kantar-Introduction to Declarer's Play 10.00
#2135 Kantar-Introduction to Defender's Play 10.00
#0101 Stewart-Baron-The Bridge Book 1 .... 9.95
#1121 Silverman-Elementary Bridge
      Five Card Major Student Text 4.95
#0660 Penick-Beginning Bridge Complete 9.95
#0661 Penick-Beginning Bridge Quizzes 6.95
#3230 Lampert-Fun Way to Serious Bridge 10.00

FOR ADVANCED PLAYERS
#2250 Reese-Master Play 5.95
#1420 Klinger-Modern Losing Trick Count 16.95
#2240 Love-Bridge Squeezes Complete 7.95
#0103 Stewart-Baron-The Bridge Book 3 .... 9.95
#0740 Woolsey-Matchpoints 14.95
#0741 Woolsey-Partnership Defense 12.95
#1702 Bergen-Competitive Auctions 9.95

BIDDING — 2 OVER 1 GAME FORCE
#4750 Bruno & Hardy-Two-Over-One Game Force:
      An Introduction 9.95
#1750 Hardy-Two-Over-One Game Force 14.95
#1790 Lawrence-Workbook on the Two Over One System 12.95
#4525 Lawrence-Bidding Quizzes Book 1 .... 13.95

Prices subject to change without notice.

DEFENSE
#0520 Blackwood-Complete Book of Opening Leads 17.95
#3030 Ewen-Opening Leads 18.95
#0104 Stewart-Baron-The Bridge Book 4 .... 7.95
#0631 Lawrence-Dynamic Defense 11.95
#1200 Woolsey-Modern Defensive Signalling 4.95

FOR INTERMEDIATE PLAYERS
#3015 Root-Commonsense Bidding 15.00
#0630 Lawrence-Card Combinations 12.95
#0102 Stewart-Baron-The Bridge Book 2 .... 9.95
#1122 Silverman-Intermediate Bridge Five
       Card Major Student Text 4.95
#0575 Lampert-The Fun Way to Advanced Bridge 11.95
#0633 Lawrence-How to Read Your Opponents' Cards 11.95
#3672 Truscott-Bid Better, Play Better 12.95
#1765 Lawrence-Judgment at Bridge 9.95

PLAY OF THE HAND
#2150 Kantar-Test your Bridge Play, Vol. 1 .... 10.00
#3675 Watson-Watson's Classic Book on
       the Play of the Hand 15.00
#1932 Mollo-Gardener-Card Play Technique 21.95
#3009 Root-How to Play a Bridge Hand 15.00
#1124 Silverman-Play of the Hand as
       Declarer and Defender 4.95
#2175 Truscott-Winning Declarer Play 10.00
#3803 Sydnor-Bridge Made Easy Book 3 .... 8.00

CONVENTIONS
#2115 Kantar-Bridge Conventions.. 10.00
#0610 Kearse-Bridge Conventions Complete 29.95
#3011 Root-Pavlicek-Modern Bridge Conventions 15.00
#0240 Championship Bridge Series (All 36) 25.95

DUPLICATE STRATEGY
#1600 Klinger-50 Winning Duplicate Tips 14.95
#2260 Sheinwold-Duplicate Bridge.. 4.95

FOR ALL PLAYERS
#3889 Darvas & de V. Hart-Right Through The Pack 14.95
#0790 Simon: Why You Lose at Bridge 11.95

DEVYN PRESS INC.

3600 Chamberlain Lane, Suite 230, Louisville, KY 40241

1-800-274-2221

CALL TOLL FREE IN THE U.S. & CANADA
TO ORDER OR TO REQUEST OUR 64 PAGE
FULL COLOR CATALOG OF BRIDGE BOOKS,
SUPPLIES AND GIFTS.

Andersen THE LEBENSOHL CONVENTION COMPLETE .... $ 8.95
Baron THE BRIDGE PLAYER'S DICTIONARY $19.95
Bergen BETTER BIDDING WITH BERGEN,
    Vol. I, Uncontested Auctions $11.95
Bergen BETTER BIDDING WITH BERGEN,
    Vol. II, Competitive Auctions $11.95
Blackwood COMPLETE BOOK OF OPENING LEADS $17.95
Blackwood-Hanson PLAY FUNDAMENTALS .... $ 8.95
Boeder THINKING ABOUT IMPS $12.95
Bruno-Hardy 2 OVER 1 GAME FORCE: AN INTRODUCTION $11.95
Darvas & De V. Hart RIGHT THROUGH THE PACK $14.95
DeSerpa THE MEXICAN CONTRACT .... $ 5.95
Feldheim FIVE CARD MAJOR BIDDING IN
    CONTRACT BRIDGE $12.95
Flannery THE FLANNERY 2 DIAMOND OPENING .... $ 7.95
Goldman WINNERS AND LOSERS AT THE
    BRIDGE TABLE .... $ 3.95
Grant BRIDGE BASICS 1: AN INTRODUCTION $11.95
    BRIDGE BASICS 2: COMPETITIVE BIDDING $11.95
    BRIDGE AT A GLANCE .... $ 9.95
    IMPROVING YOUR JUDGMENT: DOUBLES $11.95
Groner DUPLICATE BRIDGE DIRECTION $14.95
Hardy
    COMPETITIVE BIDDING WITH 2-SUITED HANDS .... $ 9.95
    TWO-OVER-ONE GAME FORCE $16.95
    TWO-OVER-ONE GAME FORCE QUIZ BOOK $11.95
Harris BRIDGE DIRECTOR'S COMPANION (4th Edition) $24.95
Kay COMPLETE BOOK OF DUPLICATE BRIDGE $16.95
Kelsey THE TRICKY GAME $11.95
Lampert THE FUN WAY TO ADVANCED BRIDGE $14.95
Lawrence
    CARD COMBINATIONS $12.95
    COMPLETE BOOK ON BALANCING $11.95
    COMPLETE BOOK ON OVERCALLS $11.95
    DYNAMIC DEFENSE $11.95
    HAND EVALUATION $11.95
    HOW TO READ YOUR OPPONENTS' CARDS $12.95

Lawrence
  JUDGMENT AT BRIDGE $11.95
  PARTNERSHIP UNDERSTANDINGS ....$ 5.95
  PLAY BRIDGE WITH MIKE LAWRENCE $11.95
  PLAY SWISS TEAMS WITH MIKE LAWRENCE ....$ 9.95
  WORKBOOK ON THE TWO OVER ONE SYSTEM $12.95

Lipkin INVITATION TO ANNIHILATION ....$ 8.95
Michaels & Cohen 4-3-2-1 MANUAL ....$ 4.95
Penick BEGINNING BRIDGE COMPLETE ....$ 9.95
Penick BEGINNING BRIDGE QUIZZES ....$ 6.95
Robinson WASHINGTON STANDARD $24.95
Rosenkranz
  BRIDGE: THE BIDDER'S GAME $12.95
  TIPS FOR TOPS ....$ 9.95
  MORE TIPS FOR TOPS ....$ 9.95
  TRUMP LEADS ....$ 7.95
  OUR MAN GODFREY $10.95
Rosenkranz & Alder BID TO WIN, PLAY FOR PLEASURE ....$ 9.95
Rosenkranz & Truscott BIDDING ON TARGET $10.95
Silverman
  ELEMENTARY BRIDGE FIVE CARD MAJOR STUDENT TEXT ....$ 4.95
  INTERMEDIATE BRIDGE FIVE CARD MAJOR STUDENT TEXT ......$ 4.95
  ADVANCED & DUPLICATE BRIDGE STUDENT TEXT ....$ 4.95
  PLAY OF THE HAND AS DECLARER
    & DEFENDER STUDENT TEXT ....$ 4.95
Simon
  CUT FOR PARTNERS ....$ 9.95
  WHY YOU LOSE AT BRIDGE $11.95
Truscott BID BETTER, PLAY BETTER $12.95
Woolsey
  MATCHPOINTS $14.95
  MODERN DEFENSIVE SIGNALLING ....$ 5.95
  PARTNERSHIP DEFENSE $14.95
World Bridge Federation APPEALS COMMITTEE DECISIONS
  from the 1994 NEC WORLD CHAMPIONSHIPS ....$ 9.95